ACCESS TO JUSTICE FOR THE CHINESE CONSUMER

This book offers a socio-legal exploration of localised consumer complaint processing and dispute resolution in the People's Republic of China – now the second largest consumer market in the world – and the experiences of both ordinary and 'professional' consumers.

Drawing on detailed analysis of an impressive body of empirical data, this book highlights local Chinese understandings and practice styles of 'mediation', and identifies in popular consciousness a continuing sense of reliance on the government for securing consumer rights in China. These are not only important features of consumer dispute processing in themselves, but also help to explain why no ombudsman system has emerged.

This innovative book looks at the nature of China's distinctive dispute resolution and complaints system, issues within that system, and the experiences of consumers within it. The book illustrates the access to justice processes locally available to aggrieved consumers and provides a unique contribution to comparative consumer law studies in Asia and elsewhere.

Volume 11 in the series Civil Justice Systems

Civil Justice Systems

Series General Editor: Christopher Hodges, Director, Swiss Re/CMS Research Programme, Centre for Socio-Legal Studies, University of Oxford

This series covers new theoretical and empirical research on the mechanisms for resolution of civil disputes, including courts, tribunals, arbitration, compensation schemes, ombudsmen, codes of practice, complaint mechanisms, mediation and various forms of Alternative Dispute Resolution. It examines frameworks for dispute resolution that comprise combinations of the above mechanisms, and the parameters and conditions for selecting certain types of techniques and procedures rather than others. It also evaluates individual techniques, against parameters such as cost, duration, accessibility, and delivery of desired outcomes, and illuminates how legal rights and obligations are operated in practice.

Volume 1: *The Costs and Funding of Civil Litigation: A Comparative Perspective*
edited by Christopher Hodges, Stefan Vogenauer and Magdalena Tulibacka

Volume 2: *Consumer ADR in Europe*
Christopher Hodges, Iris Benöhr and Naomi Creutzfeldt-Banda

Volume 3: *Law and Corporate Behaviour: Integrating Theories of Regulation, Enforcement, Compliance and Ethics*
Christopher Hodges

Volume 4: *A Comparative Examination of Multi-Party Actions*
Joanne Blennerhassett

Volume 5: *Redress Schemes for Personal Injuries*
Sonia Macleod and Christopher Hodges

Volume 6: *Ethical Business Practice and Regulation: A Behavioural and Values-Based Approach to Compliance and Enforcement*
Christopher Hodges and Ruth Steinholtz

Volume 7: *Delivering Collective Redress: New Technologies*
Christopher Hodges and Stefaan Voet

Volume 8: *Pharmaceutical and Medical Device Safety: A Study in Public and Private Regulation*
Sonia Macleod and Sweta Chakraborty

Volume 9: *Delivering Dispute Resolution: A Holistic Review of Models in England and Wales*
Christopher Hodges

Volume 10: *Regulatory Delivery*
Graham Russell and Christopher Hodges

Volume 11: *Access to Justice for the Chinese Consumer*
Ling Zhou

Access to Justice for the Chinese Consumer

Handling Consumer Disputes in Contemporary China

Ling Zhou

BECK · HART · NOMOS

HART PUBLISHING

Bloomsbury Publishing Plc

Kemp House, Chawley Park, Cumnor Hill, Oxford, OX2 9PH, UK

1385 Broadway, New York, NY 10018, USA

HART PUBLISHING, the Hart/Stag logo, BLOOMSBURY and the Diana logo are trademarks of Bloomsbury Publishing Plc

First published in Great Britain 2020

A catalogue record for this book is available from the British Library.

Library of Congress Cataloging-in-Publication data

Names: Zhou, Ling, 1987- author.

Title: Access to justice for the Chinese consumer : handling consumer disputes in contemporary China / Ling Zhou.

Description: Oxford, UK : Hart Publishing, an imprint of Bloomsbury Publishing, 2020. | Series: Civil justice systems ; volume 11 | Based on author's thesis (doctoral - University of Oxford, 2018). | Includes bibliographical references and index.

Identifiers: LCCN 2019053721 (print) | LCCN 2019053722 (ebook) | ISBN 9781509931057 (hardcover) | ISBN 9781509931071 (Epub)

Subjects: LCSH: Consumer protection—Law and legislation—China. | Dispute resolution (Law)—China.

Classification: LCC KNQ3276 .Z48 2020 (print) | LCC KNQ3276 (ebook) | DDC 343.5107/1—dc23

LC record available at https://lccn.loc.gov/2019053721

LC ebook record available at https://lccn.loc.gov/2019053722

ISBN: HB: 978-1-50993-105-7
HB: 978-3-406-75339-8 (CH Beck)
HB: 978-3-8487-6345-0 (Nomos)
ePDF: 978-1-50993-106-4
ePub: 978-1-50993-107-1

Typeset by Compuscript Ltd, Shannon
Printed and bound in Great Britain by TJ International Ltd, Padstow, Cornwall

PREFACE

This book explores the nature and significance of consumer dispute processes in China. It examines issues of consumers' access to justice, with particular reference to both consumer experience and the roles that the state, legal professionals and other social actors play in the consumer dispute processes. It focuses on one local area (Shenzhen, China) and uses an in-depth ethnographic approach to offer a realistic picture of consumer dispute resolution in China's socialist market economy. The principal question addressed is: how are consumer disputes resolved in this part of China today?

The book analyses consumer dispute resolution practices in terms of various channels, including the handling of cases in the Consumer Council, the regulator's reporting system, the courts, the media and online platforms. It determines that mediation or *tiaojie* in Chinese (by whatever provider) continues to be the dominant type of consumer dispute process. However, the style of mediation used – this often differs from the approach to mediation in the common law world – is conducted by staff in public bodies and is a didactic process used largely to contain the impact of the dispute. The study also explores 'professional' consumers, who may well see themselves as ordinary consumers or mere citizens, but who develop expertise through repeat assertion of consumer rights in various consumer dispute processes. These professionals are regarded in this study as a modest form of 'consumer citizen' in China, and their activities do encourage reforms, despite sometimes hostile official attitudes.

The book contributes to our understanding of consumer protection and legal developments in China, and through its analysis of the China case offers contributions to the more general literature on dispute resolution, consumers' access to justice, and consumer protection.

ACKNOWLEDGEMENTS

This study could not be possible without the thoughtful guidance, continuous encouragement, and strong support of my doctoral supervisor at the University of Oxford, Professor Fernanda Pirie, to whom I owe a great deal and extend my grateful thanks.

I also express my gratitude to other teachers and colleagues, including in particular Professor Christopher Hodges, for their kind advice on various aspects of this research project. I thank the Centre for Socio-Legal Studies (Law Faculty), St. Peter's College, and University of Oxford for providing a stimulating and supportive environment for my research work.

Thanks are also due to my many friends and acquaintances in the consumer world of Shenzhen, whose support and advice during my fieldwork was invaluable. Last but not least, I am grateful to my mother and my family for their steadfast care for me in this endeavour.

TABLE OF CONTENTS

TABLE OF ABBREVIATIONS

ADR	Alternative Dispute Resolution
CDR	Consumer ADR
CCA	China Consumers' Association
CCP	Chinese Communist Party
CPD	Consumer Protection Department
MSA	Market Supervision Administration
NGO	Non-Governmental Organizations
PRC	People's Republic of China
RMB	Renminbi (Chinese currency)
SAIC	State Administration of Industry and Commerce
SEZ	Special Economic Zone
SZCC	Shenzhen Consumer Council

TABLE OF LEGISLATION

People's Republic of China

European Union

United Nations International Covenants

1

Introduction

I. Introduction

This book is addressed mainly to readers interested in one or more of the following fields: consumer protection, dispute resolution, the Chinese legal system, and more generally, comparative legal studies. For students of consumer protection, this book offers an ethnographic exploration of the local organisation of consumer complaint processing and dispute resolution in a selected area of the People's Republic of China ('PRC', or 'China'), and how consumers – both ordinary and 'professional' – experience the local system. The China case is neglected in the general and comparative consumer protection discourses, which hitherto have been based almost exclusively on the situation in Western societies. It is hoped that the book will also provide insights for those who are interested in the relationship between culture and dispute resolution through its examination of local Chinese understandings and practice styles of 'mediation', as well as identifying a continuing sense of reliance on the government for securing consumer rights and the associated failure as yet of an ombuds-type system to emerge in China, both generally and for the handling of consumer complaints. For analysts of the Chinese legal system, the book offers, inter alia, a new account of a much neglected dimension of the system namely, consumer issues. The field of Chinese studies continues to be dominated by concerns with economic reform, economic growth and production, and the book brings together and analyses an area of social life which is highly significant but also one given only limited attention by many Western researchers: the consumer dimension of Chinese society. Indeed, China specialists will find that the study of consumers throws light on more general social and political processes in the People's Republic. Shopping malls, online shopping, and so on increasingly have significance on the lives of Chinese citizens. It is also hoped that in exploring these issues, the present study of consumer dispute resolution in the PRC will interest many readers in the wider fields of comparative legal studies and regulatory studies.[1]

In the course of the post-Mao reforms, the 'consumer' has emerged in China as a distinct social category, and one worthy of legal protection. As Croll has emphasised, China's

[1] As Hodges suggests, 'Regulatory theory has developed significantly in the past 40 years, largely as a result of empirical analysis by socio-legal scholars of what regulators actually do "on the ground, out there", rather than on the basis of theoretical assumptions about "how law works"'. C Hodges, 'The Consumer as Regulator' in D Leczykiewicz and S Weatherill (eds), *The Images of the Consumer in EU Law: Legislation, Free Movement and Competition Law* (Oxford, Hart Publishing, 2016) 252.

transition into a 'socialist market economy' (*shehui zhuyi shichang jingji*)[2] has altered the lifestyle of people in terms of their working, purchasing, consumption, education and so on. As a result, the socio-economic and political classification of the general public as 'comrades' in every aspect of life, has gradually given way to the perception of the public as 'consumers'.[3] This status has increased in importance as business is planned less by the state but, rather, run by entrepreneurs in a more competitive market. By 1992, China's transformation had generated a perceived need for economic law making, where law is called for to regulate commercial transactions and market competition. The regulatory framework for what was now a socialist market economy included (and still includes) not only the Law on the Protection of Consumer Rights and Interests (hereinafter, Consumer Protection Law) 1993, last revised 2013 but also a Company Law 1993, last revised 2018, a Law for Countering Unfair Competition 1993, last revised 2019, a Product Quality Law 1993, last revised 2018, an Advertising Law 1994, last revised 2018, a Law on Negotiable Instruments 1995, last revised 2004 and so on.

A complicating issue in the development of consumer protection is that the state has, despite its support of the growth of market forces, continued to be closely involved in the ownership and management of the economy. Although concerned to promote economic efficiency and growth through allowing a greater role for market forces, the state has largely retained a monopolistic control over China's most profitable industries – telecommunications, transportation, banking and insurance, both in order to retain its power, and because the state is not altogether convinced of the value of market forces. In the resulting unequal market conditions, China's private sector struggles to assert itself.[4] There has been an imperfect embrace of market forces.

In recent years, some sensational cases have arisen where consumers' rights have been infringed and consumers' health has been put in danger. Victims' attempts to secure compensation have been made difficult by problems in the justice system. One important reason for such difficulties has been the misconduct of a number of large businesses. Subsequently many scholars within China and other countries have called for better regulation of the market, improvements in the conduct of producers and sellers, and higher industrial – especially product quality – standards. Several new laws have been introduced and older legislation revised in order to tackle these issues. Developments include the Anti-Monopoly Law 2007, Food Safety Law 2009, Tort Liability Law 2009, and revisions to the Consumer Protection Law in 2013 and to the Food Safety Law in 2015.

[2] The notion of a 'socialist market economy' is discussed in ch 2. Briefly stated, China has allowed some areas of the economy to be more market-orientated than under the old state planned economy, but retained certain features such as state ownership that, for example, have made it difficult for the World Trade Organisation and the United States to accept that China should be accorded 'market economy' status. See eg US Congressional Research Service, 'China's Status as a Nonmarket Economy (NME)' (CRS In Focus, 10 January 2019) by WM Morrison, at fas.org/sgp/crs/row/IF10385.pdf. Also see X Gong and C Cortese, 'A Socialist Market Economy with Chinese Characteristics: The Accounting Annual Report of China Mobile' (2017) 41 *Accounting Forum* 206.

[3] E Croll, *Desires and Destinies: Consumption and the Spirit of Confucianism* (SOAS, University of London 1997) 2; E Croll, *China's New Consumers: Social Developments and Domestic Demand* (Abingdon and New York, Routledge, 2006) 16–19.

[4] N Lardy, 'Markets over Mao: The Rise of Private Business in China' (2014) *Critical Issues Confronting China Seminar Series*, 8 October 2014, at https://fairbank.fas.harvard.edu/wp-content/uploads/2018/09/2014-15_CICC_Summaries.pdf. We might note that employees in the state sector generally benefit from higher wages and greater welfare support than their counterparts in the private sector.

It is against such a backdrop that the book asks, how are consumer disputes resolved in China today, and in particular, in what ways do Chinese consumers pursue their grievances and secure resolution to their disputes? We need not only to consider the ways the consumer is protected in law, but also the manner in which consumers are able to bring complaints and resolve their disputes with sellers and others. To date, however, there is only limited research on China's consumer dispute resolution systems, including extra-judicial processes. In particular, there is no empirical research on consumer dispute resolution practices and the role that various actors, including judges, lawyers, consumer disputants, businesses and the regulator play in the consumer dispute resolution systems. Many law firms working within China offer short news items from time to time on some of the key developments and issues in consumer law and procedures, but no major academic research project has been carried out on consumer issues in the past few years. Even if we focus on the existing English-language studies that do exist, we find that these are for the most part nearly a decade old.[5] My interest is in how dispute resolution practices in China impact on and serve the interests of aggrieved consumers. This is an important question in its own right, given China's recent emergence as the second largest consumer market in the world, but in answering it we are also likely to be able to throw new light on the significance of legal development, more generally in post-Mao China.

The book focuses on one local area (Shenzhen, China), and explores the day-to-day handling of consumer disputes, rather than trying to offer a broad coverage of the national law and macro-level analysis of consumer protection in China. A locally-focussed study is needed because law on the books in China diverges significantly in many areas of social life from actual legal practices. To address the central research question identified above, this book has employed qualitative research methods – in particular, participant observation in key local agencies. I spent over one full year continuously in the field, and during this fieldwork conducted participant observation and in-depth interviews through internships in a number of important local organisations. During my time in these organisations, I was able to collect a large amount of data on such matters as the 'insiders' perspectives' on consumer issues and had the chance to experience directly a number of key events. I was able to observe consumer disputes closely and to obtain detailed accounts of individual experiences.[6] On the basis of such qualitative data, this book attempts to depict a realistic and contextualised picture of consumer disputes and their resolution in China today.

II. The Market, State and Consumer Law

The growing importance of consumption and consumer markets in China raises the question of choice of appropriate legal framework for markets, and the role and limits of

[5] It is perhaps surprising that so little attention has been given to consumer issues in English-language social science analysis of China given that, as Croll has emphasised, since the early 2000s China has pursued a development strategy which has not only 'attached a new importance to increasing individual well-being and promoting social development alongside maintaining economic growth but also placed domestic demand at the heart of China's political agenda to counter its undue dependence on the vagaries of global demand' – see Croll, *China's New Consumers* 2. See also below my observations in the section 'Studies of Consumer Protection in China'.

[6] Some disputes were handled by myself, as I was sometimes asked during my fieldwork to substitute for the Consumer Council staff on leave.

consumer law and policy in addressing consumers' needs. Let us explore briefly the various rationales offered by scholars for protecting consumers in a market economy (to which China now aspires).

Academic discourse on consumer policy and law in market economies has centred on the nature and extent of the government's role in the market. A libertarian model of the role of markets and government, within which economic freedom is the most important value, holds that the government is encouraged to play a modest role, primarily coping with situations where the market system fails.[7] Milton Friedman, for example, viewed market competition as the best consumer policy. He did not favour extensive consumer regulation.[8] Friedman argued that so long as effective freedom of exchange in the market is maintained, the central feature of the market – competition – will protect consumers from unfair dealing and coercion by sellers. The existence of other, alternative, sellers who the consumer can deal with will protect the consumer from malpractice.[9] In Friedman's view, the state should do no more than enforce the 'rules of the game', which is to maintain a competitive market. It is not the role of the state to intervene so as to shape individual and community lifestyles, including consumption behaviour.[10]

On the other hand, for example, John Rawls argues that market outcomes depend on arbitrary factors such as 'natural' talent and ability and fail to protect the least-advantaged groups in society in the long run. Thus, the government has a duty to rectify market failures and to redistribute income.[11] Another important critique of Friedman's position is found in the work of the economist, Galbraith, who points to the fact that in certain sectors of the modern consumer economy, large corporations have gained excessive power over the market by means of advertising, marketing, packaging, and so on. As a result, the idea of the market responding to individual choices and the notion of the market as a mechanism fulfilling consumer's needs is unrealistic. Individuals' preferences for particular products and their consumption desires, more generally, may be created through the marketing activities of large firms rather than rational decision-making by the individual.[12]

To a large extent, Friedman's analysis of the market is infused with the beliefs of consumer sovereignty – that 'consumers are … sovereign economic actors, with stable preferences that have been formulated rationally and autonomously, and who have the potential to exercise power in the economic system by their purchasing choices'.[13] In this model of consumer sovereignty, consumer regulations mainly aim to ensure that producers and sellers respond to consumers' preferences. Therefore, the role of consumer protection in this model lies in creating an environment in which consumers can make choices effectively, and directing market production to meet the demand of consumers so that the competitive market will achieve an efficient allocation of resources.[14] However, the arguments of scholars such as

[7] I Ramsay, *Consumer Law and Policy: Text and Materials on Regulating Consumer Markets*, 2nd edn (Oxford, Hart Publishing, 2007) 32.

[8] M Friedman, *Capitalism and Freedom* (Chicago, University of Chicago Press, 1962).

[9] ibid at 14.

[10] ibid at 15.

[11] J Rawls, *A Theory of Justice* (Cambridge, MA, Belknap Press of Harvard University Press, 1971).

[12] J Galbraith, *The Affluent Society* (London, Penguin Books, 1999).

[13] C Scott and J Black, *Cranston's Consumers and the Law*, 3rd edn (Cambridge, Cambridge University Press, 2000) 1.

[14] ibid.

Rawls and Galbraith against this free-market perspective show us that consumer wants and needs are to a significant extent 'socially created', largely because of the dominant power that large producers can exercise over the market. Influenced by the marketing strategies and techniques of large corporations, consumers may be persuaded to buy things that are neither urgent nor necessary.[15] Furthermore, consumer desires may not be solely created by influential producers. Rather, the desire to consume may derive from a social value system where individuals are evaluated in large part by what they consume.[16] In the classic study of 'conspicuous consumption', Thorsten Veblen has shown how the value system of a consumption culture works, with individuals purchasing and using luxury goods in order to display their social status and economic power, rather than for the intrinsic value or worth to them of such goods.[17] The idea that markets are simply a mechanism responding to individual demands is thus an unrealistic characterisation. Consumer wants and needs do not exist in a vacuum, but, rather, are socially created. As Rawls argues, 'an economic system is not only an institutional device for satisfying existing wants and needs, but a way of creating and fashioning wants in the future'.[18]

This debate on the function of the market has inspired a rethinking of the role of the state in relation to the market, and the ways in which the government regulates activities concerning consumers. Expanding the government's role to include policies that 'manage the subject of consumption – the consumer – through education, expert advice and knowledge', is seen by many as necessary.[19] This means that a government would step in to correct the imbalances in bargaining power between consumers and producers by offering consumers direct protection, rather than relying on market competition alone to safeguard them.[20]

Ramsay has identified two crucial potential market failures that justify governmental intervention in the market. The first is 'information failure', where consumers suffer from a lack of information about the costs and benefits of a product and are therefore unable to make rational decisions.[21] In particular, with the rapid development of science and technology over the past few decades, consumers bear increasing risks when making purchases, as it has become more difficult for them to obtain sufficient knowledge and proper information in order to make 'rational' decisions, unless the producer chooses to offer such information, or is compelled to do so.[22] The other is the failure of the traditional private law system – a counterpart of the market system – in securing performance in a mass consumption economy. As Ramsay suggests, in such an economy the impact of harm on any one individual may be relatively small, but the impact may be large for consumers as a whole. However, the private law system of individual enforcement of rights is often expensive for the

[15] Galbraith, The Affluent Society, 124–125.

[16] ibid at 126.

[17] T Veblen, *The Theory of the Leisure Class: An Economic Study in the Evolution of Institutions* (Oxford, Oxford University Press, 2009).

[18] J Rawls, *A Theory of Justice* (Cambridge, MA, Belknap Press of Harvard University Press, 1971) 259.

[19] I Ramsay, *Consumer Law and Policy*, 3rd edn (Oxford, Hart Publishing, 2012) 8.

[20] eg, the law may modify the preferences of certain groups, such as the insane and infants, on the ground that they are unable to make competent, rational decisions as consumers. ibid at 61.

[21] I Ramsay, *Rationales for Intervention in the Consumer Marketplace* (London, Office of Fair Trading, 1984) 15–24.

[22] The information failure is also stressed by Rawls, with particular reference to the influence of technological development on consumers' access to market information. See J Rawls, *A Theory of Justice* (Cambridge, MA, Belknap Press of Harvard University Press, 1971) ch 8.

plaintiff, and this cost may exceed the expected remedies that consumers can obtain for their claims. The growth of public regulation of consumer protection is regarded as one of the responses to the failure of the private remedy scheme, and also raises the issue of how best to strike a balance between public and private enforcement.[23] The access to justice movement, which has evolved from the late 1960s onwards, is another approach to addressing this failure, where new legal processes and institutions such as class actions, small claims courts, legal aid and mediatory intervention have been proposed, to tackle the issues of expensive transaction costs, as well as the difficulties of representing diffuse interests in large-scale tort cases, and in order to provide more flexible approaches for consumer dispute resolution.

III. Consumers and Access to Justice

A. Dispute Resolution Studies

It is observed in much of the consumer law literature that the value of consumer claims is usually small compared to the high costs encountered by plaintiffs when seeking private law remedies. However, consumer interests are diffuse and diverse, and it is rather difficult for aggrieved consumers to seek redress as a group.[24] Trebilcock has pointed out three main reasons for this difficulty.[25] First, consumer interests are diffuse over an enormous range of products and services, and nearly everyone in society is a consumer.[26] The products or services that individuals purchase usually are small value, so consumers may not consider the interest involved worth time and effort when infringed.[27] Since consumer interests are widely shared, there may be difficulty in agreeing on what the infringed consumer interest should consist of before acting collectively as a group.[28] Secondly, consumer interests are often diverse. For example, consumers with low incomes and other vulnerable groups (such as people with little access to basic financial services) may want to make demands in law that differ from those put forward by more affluent consumers.[29] Thirdly, the representation of consumer interests also faces the 'free rider' problem. As also suggested by Olson, 'rational' members of society may rely upon already existing large lobbying organisations that work in their interests, without contributing the money, time and expertise to the organisation that existing members have sacrificed.[30] Rational and self-interested individuals tend not to act in unison in order to achieve the collective goals or common interests of the group, unless the number of individuals in the group is quite small, or effective measures are taken to make sure that individuals act in the common interest.[31]

[23] I Ramsay, *Rationales for Intervention in the Consumer Marketplace* (London, Office of Fair Trading, 1984) 21.
[24] See eg M Trebilcock, 'Winners and Losers in the Modern Regulatory System: Must the Consumer Always Lose?' (1975) 13 *Osgoode Hall Law Journal* 620.
[25] ibid.
[26] ibid.
[27] ibid at 621.
[28] C Scott and J Black, *Cranston's Consumers and the Law*, 3rd edn (Cambridge, Cambridge University Press, 2000) 13.
[29] See details in Scott and Black's discussion on vulnerable consumers at 8–11.
[30] M Olson, *The Logic of Collective Action: Public Goods and the Theory of Groups* (Cambridge, MA, Harvard University Press 1971) 12.
[31] ibid at 13–14.

The problems encountered by consumers in their search for redress have been widely discussed in the access to justice literature, particularly in respect of the representation of diffuse and fragmented interests, and the creation of efficient and cost-friendly dispute resolution schemes. As Cappelletti suggests, 'the new social, collective, diffuse rights and interests can be protected only by new social, collective, "diffuse" remedies and procedures'.[32] Cappelletti and Garth consider the legal mechanisms of class actions and public interest actions to be the main forces for gaining justice for people with diffuse interests, such as consumers.[33] They also suggest that a broad variety of institutions and devices are emerging, such as reforms of general litigation procedure, the development of alternative and informal procedures (such as alternative dispute resolution) and specialised tribunals concerning public interest.[34]

These issues also arise in the case of China. As China moves towards a more market-orientated economy so important questions arise: How does China cope with the diffuse consumer interests that are emerging as a result of its economic development? What are the mechanisms available to Chinese consumers to use to resolve their disputes and secure consumer justice? How do these mechanisms work in practice?

Much literature shows that China emphasises 'informal' mechanisms (particularly mediation) for resolving civil disputes, where parties are assisted through a didactic process leading to a compromise outcome, rather than seeing their case adjudicated according to the application established legal rules and principles.[35] It seems that Mao's 'theory of contradictions' continues to affect dispute resolution in the post-1976 context, so that mediation and other democratic methods (education, criticism and persuasion) are encouraged as a means of addressing conflicts (civil disputes) among 'the people', while the law (criminal law, with its heavy punishments) is applied to disputes between 'the people' and criminals ('the enemy').[36] The prevalence of mediation also reflects a continuing Confucian-derived emphasis on settlement and informal justice, the importance of 'yielding', and an 'anti-litigation' culture.[37] In this book, I explore the practical use of mediation, as well as other dispute processes, on consumer cases in China, and try to identify the features of Chinese mediation and how mediators go about handling consumer disputes (including their approach to and styles of mediation).

Mediation, like other forms of alternative dispute resolution (ADR), tends to be more efficient and cost-friendly than court procedures, and indeed is favoured by many jurisdictions for civil justice reform purposes. However, Nader's criticism of mediation also reminds us of the fact that while mediation may be promoted in the name of 'harmony', it can also sometimes be rather coercive, and that the 'harmony ideology' that justifies reliance

[32] M Cappelletti, 'Vindicating the Public Interest through the Courts: A Comparativist's Contribution' (1975–1976) 25 *Buffalo Law Review* 643 at 647.

[33] M Cappelletti and B Garth (eds), *Access to Justice: A World Survey* (Alphenaan den Rijn, Sijthoff and Noordhoff, 1978) 35–48.

[34] ibid at 66–84.

[35] H Fu and R Cullen, 'From Mediatory to Adjudicatory Justice: The Limits of Civil Justice Reform in China' in M Woo and M Gallagher (eds), *Chinese Justice: Civil Dispute Resolution in Contemporary China* (Cambridge, Cambridge University Press, 2011) 28.

[36] M Palmer, 'Mediation in China' in DS Clark (ed), *Encyclopedia of Law and Society: American and Global Perspectives* (New York, Sage Publications, 2007) 1010.

[37] ibid.

on mediation may well have 'rights suppressing' functions.[38] China's official embrace of a 'socialist harmonious society' more than a decade ago is clearly relevant in this respect. On the other hand, in contemporary China, there seems to be bottom-up pressure for legal reform and the expansion of access to courts, particularly since China's official adoption of the principle of the 'rule of law' (*yifa zhiguo*) in the 1999 amendments to its 1982 Constitution, and also the changes to the Preamble in the 2018 revised Constitution. The introduction of new processes (including public interest litigation) in the revised Civil Procedure Law 2012 for dealing with consumer complaints is perhaps one such response to bottom up pressures for legal reform.[39] This kind of change is important not only because infringement of consumers' interests may cause serious social problems, such as those that have happened in the food industry, but also because ADR type processes may suppress – rather than highlight – problems, legal consciousness, and reform initiatives. So, this book also considers if an emphasis on mediation and other informal processes does actually limit the ability of the aggrieved consumer to secure justice in China today.

B. Studies of Consumers' Access to Justice

Within comparative legal studies, and the literature on Chinese legal development, there have been surprisingly few advances in our understanding of consumer disputes over the past two decades or so (and indeed, more generally). The general literature on access to justice, especially in relation to consumer issues, often does not take into account East Asian experiences. Instead, the emphasis tends to be on the issues found in mature market economies with relatively democratic systems of governance, where ideas of consumer protection are already well developed. In China, by contrast, it is only since the 1980s that even the concept of a 'consumer', let alone the idea of 'consumer protection', has emerged. One important general study in the consumer field is the collection of essays by Rickett and Telfer entitled *International Perspectives on Consumers' Access to Justice*. Essays in this book examine consumers' access to justice in different areas, such as contract and tort, services, bankruptcy, civil procedures, and conflict of laws. The focus in the papers in this volume is placed on North America and Europe.[40] But what is the Chinese experience? How do consumers access justice in China's more socialist and authoritarian context?

Ramsay has published widely on consumers' access to justice, and deals with both international dimensions and domestic aspects of consumer protection in the United Kingdom. His recent study – looking at issues such as whether individualised redress procedures provide an effective solution for low-income and disadvantaged groups, such as consumers, tensions between neo-liberal and social market approaches, consumer protection and consumer choice, and so on – does not involve analysis of China. The work of Ramsay has

[38] L Nader, 'Controlling Process of the Rule of Law: Hierarchy and Pacification in the Movement to Re-Form Dispute Ideology' (1993) 9 *Ohio State Journal on Dispute Resolution* 1.

[39] Art 55 of the Civil Procedure Law (2012) provides that 'relevant organs and organizations prescribed by law may initiate lawsuit at competent courts against conduct jeopardizing the public interests, such as causing environment pollution or damaging the interests of a large number of consumers'.

[40] C Rickett and T Telfer (eds), *International Perspectives on Consumers' Access to Justice* (Cambridge, Cambridge University Press, 2003).

been very significant in the development of literature on consumer protection, and some aspects of his analysis of consumer justice are relevant to this book.[41] In his examination of consumer issues, he suggests that the consumer complaint, as a negotiation channel, is a potentially important problem-solving mechanism for consumers, and that intermediaries often play a key role in the provision of consumers' access to justice.[42] As Ramsay sees the situation, the intermediaries, which might include actors such as lawyers, social workers, debt counselors and consumer advisors, 'may influence the type of remedy that is obtained by a consumer, and they may also be important political actors in any proposed reforms of consumer rights'.[43] In particular, he highlights the role of the lawyers as intermediaries, and their role in mediating between business and consumers, and sometimes even their influence on consumers' choices. Ramsay also, more generally, emphasises the importance of socio-legal research in consumer law, and the lack of empirical data on how consumer policies work in practice. These works encourage us to consider both the issue of consumer complaints and who (if any) are the 'intermediaries' in consumer dispute resolution in China, and what roles they play in the dispute processes.

Hodges' impressive body of work similarly offers an important focus on procedural aspects of consumer protection, and indeed takes the emphasis much further, but the regional focus is again on the United Kingdom and Europe.[44] Part of his work has been focused on examining the 'CDR' (consumer ADR) schemes that help to resolve cross-border consumer disputes in the EU, while other work has considered the emergence and value of extra-judicial schemes for protecting consumers' collective interests. Hodges is concerned with the issue of the high cost and low efficiency of some of the more formalised ADR processes and court procedures for handling consumer disputes – in some contexts such as the United Kingdom (UK), ADR processes have been criticised for failing to achieve their potential. They too easily can become costly and very formal, and 'CDR' schemes – such as the consumer ombudsman – seem to offer better solutions for the aggrieved consumers.

Hodges' analysis is echoed in some ways in the approach taken in China, where the use of mediation as a cheap and efficient way of resolving consumer disputes is important. Disputes over consumer matters are often only small in value, and it is rare for individual

[41] See eg, I Ramsay, *Consumer Law and Policy*, 3rd edn (Oxford, Hart Publishing, 2012); G Howells, I Ramsay and T Wilhelmsson, 'Consumer Law in its International Dimension' in G Howells et al (eds), *Handbook of Research on International Consumer Law* (Cheltenham, Edward Elgar Publishing, 2010) 18; I Ramsay, 'Consumer Redress and Access to Justice' in C Rickett and T Telfer (eds), *International Perspectives on Consumers' Access to Justice* (Cambridge, Cambridge University Press, 2003) 17–45.

[42] I Ramsay, 'Consumer Redress and Access to Justice' in C Rickett and T Telfer (eds), *International Perspectives on Consumers' Access to Justice* (Cambridge, Cambridge University Press, 2003) 17–45.

[43] ibid at 34.

[44] See eg C Hodges, 'The Consumer as Regulator' in D Leczykiewicz and S Weatherill (eds), *The Images of the Consumer in EU Law: Legislation, Free Movement and Competition Law* (Oxford, Hart Publishing, 2016); C Hodges, 'Unlocking Justice and Markets: The Promise of Consumer ADR' in J Zekoll, M Bälz and I Amelung (eds), *Dispute Resolution: Alternatives to Formalization – Formalization of Alternatives*? (Leiden, Brill, 2014); C Hodges, 'Consumer ADR and Appeals' in A Uzelac and CH van Rhee (eds), *Nobody's Perfect. Essays on Appeals and Other Methods of Recourse against Judicial Decisions in Civil Matters* (Cambridge, Intersentia, 2014); C Hodges, 'Consumer Redress: Ideology and Empiricism' in K Purnhagen and P Rott (eds), *Varieties of European Economic Law and Regulation: Liber Amicorum for Hans Micklitz* (New York, Springer, 2014); C Hodges and A Stadler (eds), *Resolving Mass Disputes. ADR and Settlement of Mass Claims* (Cheltenham, Edward Elgar Publishing, 2013); C Hodges, 'New Modes of Redress for Consumers and Competition Law' (2012) 11/12 *Revista de Concorrência e Regulação* 227; C Hodges, 'Consumer ADR in Europe' (2012) 15 *Zeitschrift für Konfliktmanagement* 195; C Hodges, I Benöhr and N Creutzfeldt-Banda, *Consumer ADR in Europe* (Oxford, Hart Publishing, 2012).

consumers to attempt to enforce legal rights through private litigation. Often the best approach resolving consumer disputes, Hodges also suggests, is cooperation between the CDR agency such as an ombuds and the regulator. Where the consumer ombuds works well with the regulator – for example, by supplying information about consumer enquiries and complaints – the regulator thus well-informed, and with sanctioning powers, can regulate traders better and enhance compliance with and enforcement of consumer rights.[45] Although the Chinese context might be thought to be fertile ground for such ideas, it does in fact throw up some distinctively different issues and problems. Key aspects of the Chinese context include the fact that extra-judicial settlement of disputes is a preference which has been deeply entrenched in social practice and the law in various ways, the judicial system (including the courts) is firmly in the hands of the party-state,[46] the government administers the country in a spirit of paternalist authoritarianism, and the newly-emerging market economy still bears the imprint of the old system of socialist planning. All these factors affect the actual functioning of consumer dispute resolution in China and in these circumstances, we need to ask if the nature of consumer dispute resolution in China differs in important ways from systems found elsewhere in the world, and query whether they limit the possibility of establishing an independent ombuds for consumers which might function to promote consumer welfare in the manner that Hodges encourages.

Also, as we have suggested, if consumer justice is to be meaningful, then in China (as elsewhere) consumers not only need substantive rights, but also to be able to realise their rights and secure justice through courts and other dispute resolution forums.[47] So, an important issue to be addressed in this book is how do consumers actually access consumer justice. Considering the issues of enforcement of law in China, as well as the divergence between law in the books and social practice, this book has chosen to offer a detailed study of the situation on the ground in one Chinese city, namely Shenzhen. I have used an in-depth ethnographic approach, rather than providing a broad overview of the consumer dispute resolution mechanisms in which it is assumed that law and local practice do not diverge significantly across the whole country.

[45] C Hodges, 'The Consumer as Regulator' in D Leczykiewicz and S Weatherill (eds), *The Images of the Consumer in EU Law: Legislation, Free Movement and Competition Law* (Oxford, Hart Publishing 2016) 256.

[46] Although in constitutional theory China is a multi-party political system, in reality it is a one 'party-state' in which the Chinese Communist Party (CCP) exercises a great deal of control over the political and legal systems. Much of this control is expressed and justified through the idea of Deng Xiaoping that China should pursue development through adherence to 'four fundamental principles': the socialist road, the people's democratic dictatorship, the CCP's leadership, and the primacy of Marxism-Leninism–Mao Zedong Thought. These principles were placed in the preamble to the 1982 Constitution, and although subject to some amendment since, remain crucially important today. See eg AHY Chen, 'Through Pathways of Western Liberal Constitutional Development in Asia: A Comparative Study of Five Major Nations' (2010) 8 *International Journal of Constitutional Law* 849.

[47] As Leila Choukroune has emphasised, the United Nations Committee on Economic, Cultural and Social Rights has explicitly argued that one of the main problems of human rights in China is that second generation rights (that is, those primarily of an economic and social nature, found in the Covenant on Economic, Cultural and Social Rights, of which China is a state-party) cannot be realised in practice because of the lack of effective procedural rights of the sort offered in the International Covenant on Civil and Political Rights (which China has signed but not yet acceded to). See L Choukroune, 'Justiciability of Economic, Social and Cultural Rights: The UN Committee on Economic, Social and Cultural Rights: Review of China's First Periodic Report on the Implementation of the International Covenant on Economic, Social and Cultural Rights' (2005) 19 *Columbia Journal of Asian Legal Studies* 30. The present work has clear relevance for this issue.

C. Studies of Consumer Protection in China

Studies of consumer protection law in post-Mao China have been published by, for example, Gao and King, Overby, Hooper, Williams, and Palmer.[48] However, there has been no major analysis of this area for more than a decade, and even though the Consumer Protection Law was amended in several important ways in 2013, consumer protection has not become a major academic topic in Chinese legal studies. Most of the English literature that can be found is concerned with food safety issues in China (since the Food Safety Law was published in 2009), or substantive consumer law issues, such as deceptive advertising and definition of the consumer, and newly emerging issues such as financial consumer rights and e-commerce.[49]

Similarly, in the Chinese language literature, although some research has been published, on the situation of the Chinese consumer in the 1980s and 1990s, this work mainly focuses on consumer law-making and concepts in consumer protection law.[50] Within China the introduction of a Consumer Protection Law in 1993 also increased interest in the topic for a while, but except for the period leading up to the recent revision of the Consumer Protection Law in 2013, it has not been in any sense a 'hot topic' within Chinese legal studies. Moreover, as we have just suggested, most of the literature focuses on the substantive law of consumer protection and mainly provides doctrinal analysis.[51] Scholars suggest,

[48] See T Gao, 'Chinese Consumer Protection Philosophy' (1992) 14 *Journal of Consumer Policy* 337; B Hooper, 'Consumer Voices: Asserting Rights in Post-Mao China' (2000) 16 *China Information* 92; B Hooper, 'The Consumer Citizen in Contemporary China' (2005) *Working Paper in Contemporary Asian Studies No.12*, Centre for East and South-East Asian Studies, Lund University; DB King and T Gao, *Consumer Protection in China: Translations, Developments, and Recommendations* (Littleton, Fred B. Rothman & Co, 1991); AB Overby, 'Consumer Protection in China after Accession to the WTO' (2005–2006) 33 *Syracuse Journal of International Law and Commerce* 347; M Palmer, 'The Emergence of Consumer Rights: Consumer Protection Law in the People's Republic of China,' in S Thompson, K Latham and J Klein (eds), *Consuming China: Approaches to Cultural Change in Contemporary China* (Abingdon and New York, Routledge, 2006); M Williams, 'Foreign Business and Consumer Rights: A Survey of Consumer Protection Law in China' (2000) 18 *UCLA Pacific Basin Law Journal* 252.

[49] See eg D Prévost, 'Food Safety in China: Implications of Accession to the WTO' (2012) 89 *China Perspectives* 39. L Jérôme and JJ Sun (eds), *Building Food Safety Governance in China* (2018), Project financed by the Partnership Instrument of the European Union, at eeas.europa.eu/sites/eeas/files/building_food_safety_governance_in_china_0.pdf; D Yang, 'Consumer Protection and Reform of China's Financial Law' (2014) 44 *Hong Kong Law Journal* 303; K Thomas, 'Analysing the Notion of "Consumer" in China's Consumer Protection Law' (2018) 6 *The Chinese Journal of Comparative Law* 294.

[50] See eg MY Li and ZC Wang, 'Tan Weihu Xiaofeizhe Quanyi' [A Discussion on the Protection of Consumer Quanyi] (1987) 3 *Beijing Shangxueyuan Xuebao [Journal of Beijing Business School]* 47. H Hai, 'Zhiding Xiaofeizhe Baohufa de Biyaoxing he Lifa Yuanze' [The Necessity of Establishing the Consumer Protection Law and the Legislative Basis] (1986) 02 *Faxue [Law Science]* 35. It might be pointed out here that although a national-level Consumer Protection Law was introduced in 1993, preliminary steps were taken towards the creation of this Law by the introduction of local regulations on consumer protection in various parts of China in the 1980s.

[51] See eg JY Wang, *Xiaofeizhe de Falü Baohu Wenti [The Problems on Consumers' Legal Protection]* (Beijing, Law Press China, 1990); HQ Yu, 'Cong Xiaofeizhe Quanyi Beisunhai de Xianzhuang Tan Xiaofeizhe Quanyi Baohu Wenti' [A Discussion on the Protection of Consumer Rights and Interests from the Perspective of the Current Situations of Consumer Rights and Interests Infringement] (1994) 4 *Guizhou Shangxueyuan Xuebao [Journal of Guizhou University of Commerce]* 33. CL Li and MY Xu, *Xiaofeizhe Baohu Fa [The Law on Consumer Protection]* (Beijing, Law Press China, 1997); HX Liang, 'Zhongguo Xiaofeizhe Zhengce he Xiaofeizhe Lifa' ['China's Consumer Policy and Consumer Legislation'] (2000) 5 Faxue [*Law Science*] 20; YS Li, 'Shilun Woguo Xiaofeizhe Suopeiquan de Xianzhuang he Wanshan' [On Current Situations and Perfection of Consumers' Right to Claim in China] (2012) 28 *Sichuan Jiaoyu Xueyuan Xuebao [Journal of Sichuan College of Education]* 45. CM Tian, 'Wo Guo

for example, that there are ways to better define the concept of the consumer in the law; to expand the scope of consumer rights under the Consumer Protection Law; to improve punitive damages articles in the Consumer Protection Law; to improve the rules of evidence (particularly the burden of proof) in favour of consumer plaintiffs; and to promote the establishment of detailed rules on bringing public interest litigation for aggrieved consumers, and so on.

Over the past decade or so, there have been rapid social changes in Chinese society. Urban areas, in particular, are now major centres of consumption as well as production. Shopping malls, for example, have become important locations for consumer spending and social life in the bigger cities. It is not clear, however, that English-language analysis of China's changing society has given nearly enough attention to this change. What is clear is that consumer issues and access to justice are of increasing concern, particularly after a series of food safety problems in 2006 and subsequently, such as the tainted milk powder scandal, use of 'gutter oil' (recycled cooking oil considered by experts to be carcinogenic) in restaurants, the 'lean meat powder' scandal, and so on.[52] More importantly, very little work has been carried out on the current, unfolding, situation of consumer dispute resolution, looking at what actually happens on the ground. The realities of access to consumer justice in the PRC have yet to be explored in any kind of depth. The practices of consumer grievance and redress and the manner in which local consumer complaint and redress schemes are used in everyday life remains unexamined.

This book aims to fill the gaps in this area, by providing an in-depth empirical analysis of actual processes of consumer disputes and dispute resolution in the local arena. It offers the first extended empirical analysis of consumer access to justice based on participant observation research. In particular, it examines consumer dispute resolution through consumers' own experiences, especially those of aggrieved consumers.

For China, the term 'alternative dispute resolution' (ADR) is not necessarily an appropriate characterisation of the extra-judicial processes of consumer dispute resolution. This is because such extra-judicial processes are actually mainstream. Even in the courts, in most civil cases the process of mediation is central, rather than alternative.[53] Moreover, important processes for consumer dispute resolution are provided by public bodies. Most of the literature on the Chinese mediation has focused on judicial mediation and the people's mediation at the neighbourhood level, and very little research and analysis has been carried

Xiaofeizhe Quanyi Baohu Xianzhuang jiqi Wanshan' [Our Country's Consumer Rights and Interests Protection Present Situation and Its Consummation' (2008) 24 *Gansu Lianhe Daxue Xuebao (Shehui Kexue Ban)* [*Journal of Gansu Lianhe University (Social Science Edition)*] 44; TQ Sun, 'Jinrong Xiaofeizhe Baohu: Xingwei Jingji Xue de Lilun Jiexi yu Zhengce Jianyi' [Financial Consumer Protection: Theoretical Analysis and Policy Implications Based on Behavioral Economics] (2014) 28 *Jinrong Jianguan Yanjiu* [*Financial Regulation Research*] 32. An important topic that is generating significant discussion in recent years in the Chinese-language discourse is about the need to establish laws for protecting consumers using financial services.

[52] See news on tainted milk powder, 'Timeline: China Milk Scandal' (*BBC News*, 25 January 2010) news.bbc.co.uk/1/hi/7720404.stm; news on gutter oil, Reuters Staff, 'China to Ramp up Crack-Down on "Gutter Oil"' (*Reuters*, 24 April 2017) uk.reuters.com/article/us-china-food-security/china-to-ramp-up-crack-down-on-gutter-oil-idUKKBN17Q18O; news on lean meat powder, A Olesen, '"Lean Meat Powder Banned in China"' (*Washington Times*, 27 January 2011) washingtontimes.com/news/2011/jan/27/lean-meat-powder-banned-in-china/.

[53] Much literature has addressed the mediatory feature of the Chinese civil justice system. See eg MYK Woo and ME Gallagher (eds), *Chinese Justice: Civil Dispute Resolution in Contemporary China* (Cambridge, University of Cambridge Press, 2011).

out on administrative body mediation.[54] This book attempts to fill this lacunae by providing in-depth analysis of mediation practices in the Consumer Council in Shenzhen, a public body that offers mediation services for aggrieved consumers.

D. Studies of the Consumer Citizen

In the academic literature on consumer protection, the concept of 'consumer-citizen' has been extensively discussed in recent times, and such discussion provides one approach to understand better the protection of consumers.[55] This combined concept of 'consumer' and 'citizen', which addresses the interplay between consumer interests (citizen's economic goals) and citizens' social and political rights, seems also to be emerging in the Chinese context. Briefly stated, I suggest that from this point of view, the individual who was once seen most clearly as a 'comrade', has become transformed into a 'consumer' in the socialist market economy, and is now slowly also assuming the role of 'consumer citizen'. In this book, I draw on the concept of the 'consumer-citizen' in exploring 'consumer activism' in the Chinese context, and alongside it the various strategies that Chinese consumers use to gain access to justice.

Against the model of a free-market economy in which consumers are rational actors with a single set of preferences, it has been argued that in fact consumers have multiple preferences, reflecting the different roles they play in different situations.[56] Some scholars, therefore, have combined the concept of 'consumer' with 'citizen', by referring to people who express different preferences when they play different roles as 'consumer' and as 'citizen'.[57] The role of consumer often refers to individuals' activities in the market, where they possess interests and desires in the economy; while the role of citizen is largely located in a political setting, where individuals voice their opinions, values and beliefs concerning the public good of the whole society.[58]

[54] On recent insights into Chinese judicial mediation see eg V Waye and P Xiong, 'The Relationship between Mediation and Judicial Proceedings in China' (2011) 6 *Asian Journal of Comparative Law* 1; KH Ng and X He, 'Internal Contradictions of Judicial Mediation in China' (2014) 39.2 *Law and Social Inquiry* 285. On people's mediation see eg Y Wu, 'People's Mediation Enters the 21st Century' (2015) 10 *Journal of Comparative Law* 25. On administrative mediation by governmental bodies see YH Zhao, 'Mediation of Environmental Disputes' (2015) 10 *Journal of Comparative Law* 237, and my own essay in the same issue, 'Consumer Council Dispute Resolution: A Case Study' (2015) 10 *Journal of Comparative Law* 254.

[55] Many scholars have discussed the concept of 'consumer-citizen'. See eg D Lewinsohn-Zamir, 'Consumer Preferences, Citizen Preferences and the Provision of Public Goods' (1998–99) 108 *Yale Law Journal* 378; S Livingstone and P Lunt, 'Representing Citizens and Consumers in Media and Communications Regulation' (2007) 611 *The Politics of Consumption* 56; I Benöhr and Hans-W Micklitz, 'Consumer Protection and Human Rights' in G Howells et al (eds), *Handbook of Research on International Consumer Law* (Cheltenham, Edward Elgar Publishing, 2010) 19.

[56] H Margolis, 'A New Model of Rational Choice' (1981) 91 *Ethics* 265.

[57] See E Anderson, *Value in Ethics and Economics* (Cambridge, MA, Harvard University Press, 1993) 144; CR Sunstein, 'Social Norms and Social Roles' (1996) 96 *Columbia Law Review* 903, 923–25; D Lewinsohn-Zamir, 'Consumer Preferences, Citizen Preferences and the Provision of Public Goods' (1998–99) 108 *Yale Law Journal* 377; S Livingstone and P Lunt, 'Representing Citizens and Consumers in Media and Communications Regulation' (2007) 611 *The Politics of Consumption* 51.

[58] D Lewinsohn-Zamir, 'Consumer Preferences, Citizen Preferences and the Provision of Public Goods' (1998–99) 108 *Yale Law Journal* 378.

Understanding consumers in the context of the rhetoric of 'citizen' or 'citizenship' draws our attention to a particular aspect of consumer law and policy making, namely, how should state policy and law address the requirement of citizenship on issues when citizens act as consumers. Livingstone and Lunt suggest consumers are normally best understood as individuals whose interests are associated with economic goals, while citizens normally have collective status with interests inhering in cultural and political goals.[59] Consumer interest centres on 'wants, individual, private benefits, language of choice, short-term focus, regulate against detriment and plan to roll back regulation', while citizen interest centres on 'needs, society, public benefits, language of rights, long-term focus, regulate for public interest and continued regulation to correct market failure'.[60] The policy making on consumer issues, in their opinion, may need to reflect *both* the consumer interest and the citizen interest – not only the economic but also the political and cultural goals – at the same time, and not just focus on the economic realm in policy making.[61] Parker shares some of the views with Livingstone and Lunt on the consumer citizen relationship in his study of environmental protests in the 1990s, where he argues that consumer interest and citizen interest are indeed inseparable – that the political status of citizenship in some circumstances may in effect converge with the status of consumer as an economic agent.[62] Consumers, in his view, are not always individuals who make their own choices, because modern consumption practices linked to personal lifestyle and identity have largely and significantly connected consumers to other members of the society. As a result, consumers may prioritise community values (the citizen interest), at the expense of some of their individual economic interests (the consumer interest).[63] On the other hand, Parker also argues that the status of consumers may also be utilised as a tool for putting up resistance to free market policies, because protests or political actions expressed through market mechanisms – the strategy of using consumer power – tend to be more tolerated by governments than traditional forms of protest.[64] One reason Parker givers for the state's tolerance of such politicised consumer tactics, is that the state may rely on the individuals, the consumer-citizen, to regulate and pressure private business where market regulation is problematic for political reasons.[65]

The concept of consumer citizen has provided a new way to view consumer protection. Nevertheless, it has emerged from the experiences of the more developed markets in the western world and finds its importance in consumer protection in those societies. In this book, I try to explore the meaning of the consumer citizen in the Chinese context and consider its place in consumer protection in China. The question arises, are there any 'consumers' in China who regard themselves as 'citizens' with interests and entitlements that are respected in PRC law and practice? If so, how do they assert their consumer rights and interests in the context of the various possible methods, both legal and non-legal (social and political), available to them? In exploring this issue this book will offer research findings

[59] S Livingstone and P Lunt, 'Representing Citizens and Consumers in Media and Communications Regulation' (2007) 611 *The Politics of Consumption* 51 at 56.

[60] ibid.

[61] ibid.

[62] G Parker, 'The Role of Consumer-Citizen in Environmental Protest in the 1990s' (2007) 3 *Space and Polity* 69–72.

[63] ibid at 69.

[64] ibid at 70.

[65] ibid.

which suggest that the notion of 'consumer citizen' in the China context finds some expression in the role of 'professionals' in China's consumer dispute practice – that is, 'professional complainants' or 'litigants', who make a living from pursuing consumer issues as 'repeat players' on the one hand, but who may also have a more general social and political agenda on the other. The book argues that these professionals are the kind of actor in China who most closely approximates to the concept of 'consumer citizen', and the development of this kind of distinctive figure is shaped in part by the slowness of the re-emergence of civil society in 'socialist' China (itself a controversial issue).

IV. Fieldwork and Research Methods

This research is an empirical study of the functioning and experiences of the current consumer complaint and redress system, in one city in the People's Republic of China. The approach taken in my empirical research, as suggested above, has been primarily qualitative and inductive. Continuous fieldwork over a twelve-month period (September 2013 to August 2014) was conducted in Shenzhen, and used qualitative techniques, including extended case studies of consumer disputes.

During fieldwork, I collected data from various sources.

First, I was able to secure considerable amounts of empirical material in the field through participant observation. I spent more than three months in the Shenzhen Consumer Council, going to the office every day in the same way as ordinary members of staff. I was able to observe the actual practice of consumer dispute resolution, to learn about the real experiences of consumers when they brought complaints to the Council, and understand better their perceptions of how their grievance was being handled. During my stay in the Consumer Council, I observed on-site mediation meetings and conducted interviews with the parties (the consumer and the defendant business) after these meetings. I chatted with staff on a daily basis, discussed consumer matters with them, and also participated in their working meetings. As time went by, I became fully trusted and even handled some of the mediations myself, covering for staff members on leave. In a similar manner, I spent three months in the Market Supervision Administration (MSA) bureau,[66] which gave me access to worksheets and internal official reports, and opportunities to have discussions with officers on consumer protection practices and policies. For another couple of months, I then conducted research in one of the district courts in Shenzhen, while at the same time, paying visits to local MSA offices as well as to some Non-Governmental Organisations (NGOs).[67] These activities enabled me to take a close look at the situations in consumer complaint and redress, and to get in touch with the complainants, as well as sometimes even be the 'insider' – the 'mediator' – and talk to parties to consumer disputes directly.

Secondly, I conducted in-depth interviews in the main organisations where consumer disputes are resolved: the district courts, the Shenzhen Consumer Council, the municipal

[66] See ch 3 for a detailed account of the structure and work of the MSA.

[67] Not surprisingly, given China's reluctance to allow NGOs to operate, I only identified a few NGOs relevant for consumer protection. The Consumer Council, if it is to be seen as an 'NGO', is best characterised as a governmentally-organised NGO. See 'Introduction to the Field' in ch 2.

and local offices of the regulatory body (namely, the Market Supervision Administration) that handle consumer complaints.[68] Inside these bodies, interviews were conducted with aggrieved consumers, and also with the judges, lawyers, staff, and officials. Some interviews were arranged with well-informed informants in the organisations, and some of these interviews lasted for more than two hours, or even a whole morning or afternoon, as local officers seemed to be willing to talk about their experiences. Some other interviews were conducted after settlement meetings. This was often a process of following up issues and ideas developed during the periods of fieldwork, and enabled me to secure feedback from consumers, exploring their experiences with the redress schemes, and some with other consumers who had experienced problems, relying on other contacts of various types.

The interviews were semi-structured, as this approach not only provided the opportunity for me to ask the respondent's views on the consumer issues with which I am concerned, but also allowed me to pick up interesting points in the interviewees' comments, and follow them up by asking further questions. This style of interview was particularly helpful to me in eliciting consumers' accounts of their own experiences, as well as the local practices by the official. In any event, in the social conditions of China today, to use a formal interview approach might well have been counterproductive, with interviewees unwilling to commit their time and trust to a process which would involve answering very structured questioning.

Such flexibility – relying on informal interviews to secure a good deal of data – was important in my approach, because empirical research remains a sensitive process in China today. There are a whole range of factors which help us to explain this sensitivity but they include the fact that China remains essentially a party-state, with a broad concept of 'state secrets'. The administration of justice system (*sifa zhidu*) is located in the 'Politics and Law' ('*Zhengfa*') field, and thus operates within the authority of both the state and the CCP. Also, there is often a wide discrepancy between the 'law on the books' and the tolerated practice, giving rise for example to phenomena of '*qian guize*' or 'hidden rules' about which people are often reluctant to talk because they may themselves have doubts about the legality of following such rules. The technique of 'snowballing' – encouraging initial interviewees to introduce other potential respondents – was important in this context, and enabled me to build up a strong network of well-informed informants who were helpful in identifying on-the-ground practices. This sort of approach is important in a society such as that in China today, where there is often a lack of trust of strangers.

Thirdly, I was able to conduct interviews with both local 'professional' consumers, as well as more high-profile individual 'professional' consumer rights activists such as Wang Hai and his 'followers' – perhaps, as we have suggested above, China's version of the 'consumer citizen'. My fieldwork in the various places had already given me some experience of these followers in the systems of consumer complaint and redress. These people, as will be demonstrated in several of the chapters which follow, are regarded as the professionals in consumer complaining and reporting, and they are the 'consumers' who most frequently

[68] The Market Supervision Administration of Shenzhen Municipality is a department of the local government in Shenzhen which regulates all the market activities in local districts. It was established in 2009 as part of what is officially called 'Super-Ministry System' reform in Shenzhen, which consists of several departments, attached institutions and work units, and other institutions under its direct supervision. It regulates various areas directly or indirectly related to consumer welfare, including food safety, competition, intellectual property, etc. It has established an online complaint platform for aggrieved consumers to make complaints to the local authorities.

use the consumer complaint and redress channels. By following closely the work of some of these professionals – who allowed me to follow their trips to the supermarkets, observe how they negotiated with shop-owners and managers, attend meetings with their friends, join their 'We-chat' groups and so on – I was able to gain important insights. By using the snowballing technique, I was introduced to other professionals and had further chances to interview them, observe their court hearings, and so on.

Fourthly, data was collected from the media (local newspapers including their investigative journalists, with whom I already had some good contacts, TV programmes, the Internet, etc). I also attended several important local workshops and conferences on consumer issues when in the field. Thus, for example, one workshop in which I participated, held in Wuhan by an NGO in 2014, looked at the issues involved in requesting disclosure of government information. The workshop involved well-known 'activists', including consumer activists, who reported on their experience of using the scheme of requesting 'disclosure of government information', and how they achieved their goals through the disclosure system. In December 2014, I attended the 21CN.com's annual conference on consumer complaints, attended by a number of leading figures in the consumer protection field, in which I gave a short speech on online dispute resolution.

V. Structure of the Book

Chapter two explores the Chinese economic and social context for consumer protection, the general features of the consumer protection 'laws', current developments and key issues in consumer law-making in China. In order to set the scene, the chapter discusses several concepts important for this book. First, the concept of 'the consumer' in China. What is the nature of the 'consumer'? How is the consumer defined in the Chinese Consumer Protection Law 1993, revised 2013, and how is the idea of 'the consumer' understood and treated by the legal enforcement bodies, the court and other social actors in practice. Secondly, the concept of 'consumer citizen' is considered – which this book argues is to be found in China in an emergent class of professional 'consumers' (the professionals) – as will be discussed in some detail in chapter five. Thirdly, the concept of 'rights and interests' (*quanyi*) is explored, particularly, how the Chinese understanding of this set of concepts differs from that of the west, and how this may affect Chinese consumers in seeking redress.

Chapters three to seven discuss findings primarily based on my fieldwork. chapter three analyses data gained on consumer protection bodies, namely, the Shenzhen Consumer Council and the Market Supervision Administration Bureau, and examines in some depth their structure, operations and approach to dispute resolution. It shows how consumers choose the forum for securing redress, what processes they have gone through, and how these bodies handle consumer complaints and reports. Also examined in this chapter is the manner in which Chinese understandings of 'mediation' are culturally distinctive. The chapter shows that the preferred style of mediation is one that is strongly interventionist and judgmental in regard to the conduct of the parties.

Chapter four offers case studies that show the manner in which consumers decide on their dispute resolution forum, how they make complaints and how their grievances are typically handled. The chapter provides detailed accounts of how consumer cases are mediated in the Shenzhen Consumer Council, and analyses the language used by the consumers, the business defendants, and the mediators.

Chapter five, the longest chapter of the book, looks at the development of a new category of actor in consumer protection in Shenzhen – the 'professional' consumer or complainant. These persons are usually non-lawyers who possess expert knowledge about consumer complaint and redress. The chapter explores their style of complaining and reporting, the grievance redress strategies they use and how their strategies work in the negotiation with the businesses, the risks they may face in their practices, the background of the professionals and their mixed motives in entering this 'work', and so on. What is more, the chapter shows how the officials regard the professionals, and the interactions among the officials, the professionals and the defendant businesses. Through the discussion of the professionals, the chapter also reveals the problems of the local bureaucracy, the central-local relationship, and the barriers to effective enforcement of consumer regulations and product standards. It is argued that the 'professional' consumer is the closest approximation on China to the notion of 'consumer-citizen'.

Chapter six discusses how consumers seek redress through the courts. It explores the relationship between civil litigation, administrative litigation and other forms of court-focussed access to consumer justice in China. Like the preceding chapter, it gives much attention to the 'professional' complainants who are the most frequent users of the courts in consumer disputes, and explains the strategies by which they achieve their compensation goals. The chapter also provides a study of a normal consumer case in which a lawyer represents the consumer, in order to illustrate how consumer cases are handled in the courtroom, the language used by the judiciary in the hearing and the interaction between the parties.

Chapter seven explores the social and political methods that consumers use to safeguard their rights and interests, showing how new, more public, avenues are increasingly used. Such avenues include the media, accessing government information, Chinese Communist Party pressure, and the emerging processual possibility of public interest litigation. This chapter also explores the growing importance of online dispute resolution platforms, which are developing in response to the increasingly popular phenomenon of online shopping in China. It also draws the reader's attention to the importance of the fact that China has not yet established an ombudsman system – neither in general nor specially for consumer issues.

The concluding chapter (eight) reflects on the findings of the empirical research.

2

Consumer Protection in China

I. Introduction

This chapter introduces the social and legal context of the empirical research used in the present study. It considers in particular the ways in which consumer rights and interests are protected by laws and policies in contemporary China. The chapter first explores consumer protection issues that arise in China as a result of problems in the PRC's complicated social and economic transition to the 'market'. Next, it looks in greater depth at the 'consumer citizen' concept, in which consumers pursue a more explicitly political agenda in their quest to secure their economic and civil rights and interests as consumers, and explores its relevance for China. This is followed by an introduction to the field, the city of Shenzhen, in Southern China, where in-depth ethnographic research was conducted.

II. The Chinese Context

As I have argued in chapter one, consumer protection is often needed in market economies, because of the limitations of the market, especially in terms of provision of adequate information, and the availability of user-friendly, affordable private law remedies. These put the consumer in a disadvantaged position when bargaining with producers or sellers. In the case of China which, since 1980, has been increasingly committed to a market-based economy, this justification is also relevant. At the same time, some of the experiences of consumers in post-Mao China differ from those in western countries, largely because of the transitional nature of the economic system (socialist planning to the market), as well as other social factors, such as Chinese cultural attitudes (including, as we shall see, approaches to dispute resolution).

A. Economic Reform and Law Making

By adopting Deng Xiaoping's policy on reform and opening-up in post-Mao China, the Chinese Communist Party (CCP) has encouraged extensive economic reform that is steadily, but somewhat uncertainly, transforming a centrally controlled planned economy into a market-oriented commodity economy. Despite the political difficulties of 1989, following Deng's inspection tour of Southern China in early 1992, economic policy has sought to liberate China's productive forces through the market.[1] Later, in 1993, the concept of the

[1] R Keith and ZQ Lin, *Law and Justice in China's New Marketplace* (London, Palgrave, 2001) 7.

socialist market economy was officially embraced in an amendment to the Constitution, and this has formed an ideological and legal basis for policies designed to create a better market place in China.[2] The Deng-inspired economic reforms, however, have attempted to combine the virtue of market and plan, as China has attempted to maintain socialist principles of distribution, and with the state still owning the means of production and controlling directly many of the basic economic structures.[3] The current Chinese economy is, therefore, perhaps best characterised as a market economy in a socialist state. Indeed, the official constitutional characterisation of the situation since 1993 is that China is developing a socialist market economy.

The post-Mao economic reforms have gradually shifted the emphasis from state planning, production, work and comrade workers to a world of market and consumption.[4] Consumption was repeatedly referred to by Deng as the 'motor of production', and policies were pursued in a spirit of expanding domestic market demand in order to secure greater economic efficiency.[5] The Consumer Protection Law introduced in 1993 (revised 2013) was an attempt to 'protect the most vulnerable elements of the society against the harsh conditions of market competition',[6] and has been officially regarded in China as one of the key 'economic laws' (*jingji fa*) for liberating productive forces. However, because there has been a high level of dissatisfaction with the products appearing on the Chinese domestic market and rising expectations of improved standards of living on the part of many consumers, the range of legislation relating to consumer conduct was expanded to include other types of economic law (eg the Law for Countering Unfair Competition 1993 (revised 2017)).[7] Some other laws may also be relevant to consumers on the specific issues, such as Law on Product Quality 1993, revised 2000, Advertising Law 1994, revised 2015, and Anti-Monopoly Law 2007. It is worth noting that the Tort Liability Law of PRC 2009 was promulgated much later than most of the other 'economic' laws dealing with consumer issues. The establishment of a tort liability law has enabled consumers to seek better tort remedies through new mechanisms, such as those found in its product liability provisions. The Food Safety Law 2009, revised 2015 was promulgated in response to serious food safety scandals and is another important item of legislation relevant to consumer affairs.[8] As Chinese people

[2] See Art 7 of the 1993 amendment of 1982 Constitution.

[3] I Hsü, *The Rise of Modern China*, 6th edn (Oxford, Oxford University Press, 2000) 841–43.

[4] E Croll, *Desires and Destinies: Consumption and the Spirit of Confucianism* (School of Oriental and African Studies, University of London 1997) 1–2.

[5] ibid. Also, the current Premier, Li Keqiang, emphasises that 'consumption has become the primary growth driver' in the economy. See Mengjie, 'Li Keqiang: China's Economic Structure Has Been Steadily Upgraded' (*Xinhua Net*, 12 September 2017) www.xinhuanet.com/english/2017-09/12/c_136603740.htm.

[6] See n 1 at 13.

[7] OHM Yau, *Consumer Behaviour in China: Customer Satisfaction and Cultural Values* (New York, Routledge, 1994) 2–4.

[8] One of the most remarkable food scandals has been in the dairy industry. The problems of tainted milk powder products eventually led to the abolition of the important 'State Inspection Exempted Product' system first established in the early 1990s – a system that gave the right of exemption from quality inspections to the top-quality or globally competitive products with a long-standing quality record. Xinhua News, 'Quality Watchdog Cancels Inspection Exemptions for Food Producers' (*Xinhua News*, 18 September 2008) news.xinhuanet.com/english/2008-09/18/content_10070801.htm. The milk powder scandals have also highlighted the difficulties consumers face in seeking redress for infringements of their rights. Parents of victims were offered a one-off compensation if they agreed to waive their right to sue the offending company. See eg N An, 'The Tainted Milk Powder Incident – Hope in the Midst of Despair' (*Human Rights in China*, 11 January 2011) hrichina.org/en/content/4957.

are increasingly turning to online shopping, China's first E-Commerce Law was published in August 2018, in force January 2019. The E-Commerce law has largely strengthened the responsibilities of online businesses and the third-party e-commerce platforms, as well as addressing issues such as consumer fraud, privacy, intellectual property theft, tax evasion, promotion of competition, cross-border commerce, and so on. The growing corpus of law is intended to regulate better issues in competition, to enhance consumers' confidence in the commodities and services, and to thereby encourage the consumer spending that the Chinese leadership seek to encourage so as to sustain overall economic growth.[9]

B. The Emerging Concept of the Consumer in Socialist China

China's transition to a socialist market economy has altered the lifestyle of people in terms of working, purchasing, consuming, receiving education and so on. As a result, the socio-economic and political classification that labelled the general public as 'comrades' in every aspect of life, has gradually given way to the perception of the public as 'consumers'.[10] The consumer is a rather general class that exists in almost any type of market economy. However, in China, the concept of consumer (*xiaofei zhe*) has emerged in the context of a market economy with socialist features, and the socialist-influenced understanding of the consumer differs from that found in more firmly 'capitalist' systems. Much of the early Chinese-language discourse on the consumer and consumer law in China characterised the consumer on the basis of the Marxist analysis of ownership of means of production: because the means of production are owned by the working people in China's socialist system, socialist production serves to satisfy the needs of the working class, and therefore any protection given to the consumer is valued primarily as a way to promote socialist production.[11]

In some of the older literature published in the 1980s, when China was still seen as possessing a 'commodity economy' (*shangpin jingji*), rather than practising a socialist 'market economy' (*shichang jingji*), scholars believed that only in a socialist state could consumer activism (*xiaofeizhe yundong*) play a full and effective role. This was because the purpose of socialist production was consumption by 'the people', and so 'consumer activism' promoted the general welfare, contributing to China's socialist system, rather than representing a form of political dissent.[12] The belief was that under 'capitalism', although consumer

[9] See n 1 at 13.

[10] Croll, Desires and Destinies (n 4) 2.

[11] See eg MY Li Mingyi and ZC Wang, 'Tan Weihu Xiaofeizhe Quanyi' (A Discussion on the Protection of Consumer Rights and Interests) (1987) 3 *Beijing Shangxueyuan Xuebao (Journal of Beijing Business School)* 47; HQ Yu, 'Cong Xiaofeizhe Quanyi bei Sunhai de Xianzhuang Tan Xiaofeizhe Quanyi Baohu Wenti' (A Discussion on the Protection of Consumer Rights and Interests from the Perspective of the Current Situations of Consumer Rights and Interests Infringement) (1994) 4 *Guizhou Shangxueyuan Xuebao (Journal of Guizhou University of Commerce)* 33; YS Li, 'Shilun Woguo Xiaofeizhe Suopeiquan de Xianzhuang he Wanshan' (On Current Situations and Perfection of Consumers' Right to Claim in China) (2012) 28 *Sichuan Jiaoyu Xueyuan Xuebao (Journal of Sichuan College of Education)* 45.

[12] See eg SP Guo and JC Shi, 'Xiaofeizhe Yundong de Chansheng yu Fazhan' (The Emergence and Development of Consumer Activism) (1987) 3 *Beijing Shangxueyuan Xuebao (Journal of Beijing Business School)* 45. The term 'yundong' is here translated as 'activism' as this approach seems the most appropriate in the context of consumer welfare. However, it should be pointed out that ordinarily the term is translated as 'movement', conveying the sense of the mass political mobilisation that Mao used as an instrument of social control and political correction. The term has come to acquire a broader meaning in post-Mao China.

activism may reduce exploitation of the consumers to a certain extent, it is unable to change the capitalist nature of society in which consumers (the working class) are trapped, so that they are inevitably exploited by the owners of the means of production.[13] Chen and Huang hold the view that, as a legacy of this sort of thinking, the daily lives of Chinese people until recently had a 'productivist' feature. Bequeathed by a socialist state planning mentality, the importance of production continued to be over-emphasised in China long after the more market-orientated reforms were initiated in the early 1980s. Within this 'productivist' context, there was a lack of purchasing power for consumers, as well as only a limited development of a 'consumer culture'.[14] However, they also note that more and more Chinese consumers have been influenced through the media, overseas visits and so on by western consumer culture. Indeed, from a sociological point of view, we can identify, from the late 1990s onwards, a distinctive kind of Chinese consumer – one who is to be found in the affluent class that has emerged as the 'new rich' in the 'reforming' China.[15] These people have an unprecedented interest in consumer goods and enjoy lavish spending, in an attempt to show off their new-found socio-economic status, promote business ties and so on.[16] The general increase in living standards that has been brought about by the economic reforms has also encouraged a more widespread interest in consumer goods, so that there is a real sense in which the 'comrade' has now become the 'consumer' in today's China – and somebody whose rights and interests as a consumer are entitled to protection.

Other, more 'modern' perspectives, found in the recent literature explain the concept of consumer in terms of the 'rights and interests' (*quanyi*, abbreviating *quanli* (rights) and *liyi* (interests)). In fact, it should be pointed out that this expression is used in many social laws,[17] some of which are even specifically entitled 'rights and interests' (*quanyi*).[18] Some commentators, such as Keith and Lin, believe that the policy fashion of expressing rights and interests together in this way is an important aspect of human rights development in China.[19] They suggest that an interest is 'a value that is subjectively determined and pursued', and to pursue personal interest is indeed an activity of pursuing the individual human needs. Keith and Lin also take the view that reliance on the combination of 'rights and interests' may also be informed by political factors – the Chinese leadership believes that incorporating 'interests' into the law generates greater public support for law, especially as the term 'interests' (*liyi*) seems to have a subjective nature, implying that it is not something objectively generated by the state.[20] It thus avoids the restriction placed on 'rights' in Article 33 of the 1982 Constitution which declares, inter alia, that 'rights' and 'duties' are

[13] ibid.

[14] X Chen and P Huang, 'Xiaofei Zhuyi Wenhua yu Zhongguo Shehui' ('Consumer Culture and Chinese Society') (2000) 12 *Shanghai Wenxue* (*Shanghai Literature*) 59.

[15] D Goodman and X Zhang, 'The New Rich in China: Future Rulers, Present Lives' in D Goodman (ed), *The New Rich in China: The Dimensions of Social Change* (London, Routledge, 2008) 1.

[16] ibid. Also see the discussion on conspicuous consumption in T Veblen, *The Theory of the Leisure Class: An Economic Study of Institutions* (New York, Macmillan, 1902).

[17] See further my comments in ch 8, on 'social law', as analysed by Xingzhong Yu.

[18] eg Law on the Protection of Consumer Rights and Interests 1993, Law on the Protection of Rights and Interests of the Elderly 1996, and Law on the Protection of Women's Rights and Interests 2005. These laws seem to have a function of providing protection to the vulnerable groups of citizens affected by the uncertain social consequences of economic reform.

[19] See n 1 at 11.

[20] ibid at 12. 'Rights' are generally considered as given by the state in China. See explanation on 'rights' in 'The Consumer as Citizen in China' of this chapter.

'reciprocal' in nature. Also, this broad concern to offer protection for interests, as well as legal rights, is a reflection of the development of a more pluralist society in China, in which the concerns of specific groups can no longer be assumed to be exactly the same as the concerns of the state.[21]

In the old state-planned economy period (1949–79), collective interests were prioritised and well protected. As a consequence, the pursuit of individual interests was discouraged and society was based on the principles of 'obligation fundamentalism' (that is, the 'people' were expected to perform duties rather than enjoy rights as individuals).[22] The economic reforms, in bringing about the emergence of the concept of the consumer, have gradually shifted the emphasis from *collective* interests and obligations to the rights and interests of *individual* consumers. However, the debates in China on the relationship between state and society have also suggested that the protection of 'rights' entails the state playing a more active role in combating 'persisting "feudal" dimensions of authority' – which I take to mean that the state should more actively seek to change the thinking and the conduct of bureaucrats, so that they practise good governance rather than acting like old-style paternalistic and all-knowing leaders.[23] But such protection of personal rights and interests has its limits, as it should not infringe the interests of others – particularly, the common interests of the public.[24] Overall, the emerging concept of consumers has gradually replaced the socialist identity of the individual as a 'comrade', living and working in the planned economy and fulfilling extensive obligations rather than enjoying rights, autonomy and consumer satisfaction. But at the same time, the legacy of what is called 'productivism', the entrenched thinking of obligations fundamentalism, an inclination to limit rights in the public interest, and the persistence of traditional authoritarian attitudes clearly complicate the picture. As we shall also see, continuing deep state penetration of the economy is another significant complication.

C. Law on Protecting Consumers' Rights and Interests

Despite the existence of private law remedies such as those found in contract and tort, the Consumer Protection Law remains the most important law that provides consumers with rights against the malpractices of producers and sellers. The making of the 1993 Law on Protecting Consumers' Rights and Interests (the 1993 Consumer Protection Law) is largely considered as the legislative response to the prevalent practices of sale of counterfeit and inferior commodities.[25] Its enactment followed a series of local legislative efforts to provide consumer protection codes. With the subsequent rapid development of the socialist market economy and the development of new commercial practices, consumer complaints seem to be gradually expanding from the traditionally problematic areas of fake and inferior

[21] ibid at 3.
[22] ibid at 23–24.
[23] ibid.
[24] R Peerenboom, 'Rights, Interests, and the Interest in Rights in China' (1995) 31 *Stanford Journal of International Law* 359, 367–68.
[25] YG Liu, 'Qiche shu Shechi Xiaofei Pin? Mai Siche "Xiaofeizhe Quanyi Baohu Fa" Guan Ma' ('Are Automobiles Luxury Goods? Is Buying Private Cars within the Scope of the Law on Protection Consumers' Rights and Interests') (*Xinhua News*, 13 December 2006) auto.zjol.com.cn/05car/system/2006/12/13/008046639.shtml.

products, to more complicated or expensive areas such as purchases of high-value objects (eg automobiles and houses), online shopping, and abuse of market power by state-owned enterprises.[26] The Consumer Protection Law, first established more than two decades ago, has sometimes failed to address these emerging issues.

As a result, the 1993 Consumer Protection Law was carefully revised in 2013, in response to the impact of the rapid economic developments that occurred in the preceding two decades. The 2013 revised Consumer Protection Law bears some features that have enhanced the protection for consumers' rights and interests and has dealt with the new types of consumer dispute (such as disputes over online purchases) that have emerged in recent years. As mentioned in chapter one, fieldwork for this study was conducted from the end of 2013 until end of 2014, when the law had only recently been revised and put into effect.[27] Most of the practices that the author investigated in the field thus took place when the new law had yet to make much of an impact, and so its introduction does not affect significantly the main discussion of this book, which, it should be pointed out, is focussed on consumer dispute processes at the local level. The discussion on the national legal framework presented here aims to help the reader to better understand the Chinese legal context, as well as assist us in identifying the likely trajectory of future developments in consumer dispute resolution in China. As at the time of the final drafting of this book (Summer 2019), the consumer dispute resolution framework in China had not gone through any major changes subsequent to the 2013 revision. A small exception is perhaps the embryonic development of public interest litigation in the consumer field, which will be examined in chapter seven in this book.[28] The present work thus offers analysis of the actual functioning of consumer dispute resolution mechanisms at the local level in a Chinese city on the basis of intensive participant-observation fieldwork, a research approach that because of China's sensitivities remains quite rare.

One area of national law that, however, has a significant relevance for my analysis is Article 49 of the 1993 Consumer Protection Law, the introduction of which was something of a milestone in consumer protection in China, in the sense that through that provision, punitive damages were introduced into the law for the first time. As we shall see later in the present study, this provision has been important in encouraging an important form of consumer activism in the PRC. The revision of the Consumer Protection Law in 2013 has further strengthened the effect of this article. Article 55 of the revised law now provides that:

> Business operators that practice fraud in providing goods or services shall, on the demand of consumers, increase the compensation for their losses by an amount that is three times the payment made by the consumers for the goods purchased or services received, or in the amount of 500RMB if the increased compensation is less than 500RMB.

[26] SS Shi, 'Renmin Weihe Buzai Xinren 3.15' ('Why People No Longer Trust 3.15') (2010) 6 *Zhejiang Jingji* (*Zhejiang Economy*) 39. Also see discussion below on the debates and problems with the definition of the 'consumer' in law.

[27] In force, 15 March 2014.

[28] Legal responsibility for representing consumers in the court has been given to the provincial level of Consumer Council by the revised Law, and so the public interest litigation has not yet affected much of the local system for handling consumer disputes.

Compared to Article 49 of the old law, where consumers could seek punitive damages equal to twice the purchase price of the defective product, the new law has clearly increased the amount of compensation that might be awarded to an aggrieved consumer bringing suit. Also, the second paragraph of Article 55 extends the possibilities of compensation by adding that:

> Where business operators knowingly provide defective goods or services for consumers, causing the death of, or serious health damage to, the consumers or other victims, the victims shall be entitled to demand the business operators to compensate for the losses … and to demand punitive damages of up to twice the losses suffered.

The possibility of compensation for losses suffered is not something that the old law supported.

The 2013 revised law also introduced for the first time a 'cooling off period' for consumers buying online products. Article 25 stipulates that 'Where business operators sell goods via the Internet, or by television, phone, mail order, etc., consumers are entitled to return the goods within seven days upon receipt thereof and are not required to provide reasons.' Article 44 has clarified the responsibility that the e-commerce platforms should take, 'Providers of online transaction platforms that know or should know that sellers or service providers use their platforms to infringe upon the legitimate rights and interests of consumers but fail to take necessary measures shall bear joint and several liability with the sellers or service providers in accordance with the law.' This provision is another breakthrough in the sense that consumers who fail to identify the small online seller (perhaps to be thought of as web-based versions of the small street vendor) but who did register with the e-commerce platform, are now able to ask for compensation from the platform (typically, very large companies) where they made the purchases that left them aggrieved.

The 2013 revised law has touched upon the growing issue of the regulation on the usage of personal information by the business operators, Article 29 provides:

> Business operators shall collect and use the personal information of consumers in a lawful and proper manner in accordance with the principle that information collection or use is genuinely necessary. They shall expressly state the purposes, methods and scope of information collection or use, and obtain the consent of the consumers whose information is to be collected. To collect or use the personal information of consumers, business operators shall disclose their information collection or use rules, and shall not collect or use information in violation of laws or regulations, or in breach of the agreements between the parties concerned.

This Article is the first attempt to tackle the unfolding issue of misuse of consumers' personal information in China, an issue that is particularly important given that many consumers are dealing with the telecommunication companies that dominate the market and which are predominantly state-owned.[29]

[29] XC Li, 'Hexie Shehui Shiyu zhong de Woguo Xiaofeizhe Quanyi Baohu Wenti Yanjiu: Guowai Xiaofeizhe Quanyi Baohu zhi Kaocha ji Jiajian' ('Analysis on Chinese Consumer Protection in the Perspective of Harmonious Society: Study and Lessons Learned from the Consumer Protection in Foreign Countries') (2010) 11 *Faxue Yanjiu* (*Chinese Journal of Law*) 75. The Cybersecurity Law of the PRC, published in 2016, has provided further regulation on the use of personal data.

Another important change, touched on in later chapters, is that the law gives standing to consumer associations to file public interest lawsuits for aggrieved consumers. Article 47 provides that:

> The China Consumers' Association and the consumer associations established in all provinces, autonomous regions and municipalities directly under the Central Government may bring lawsuits to the people's courts against activities detrimental to the legitimate rights and interests of a large number of consumers.

Although the right to represent consumers in the court is confined to the provincial level of consumer associations, this provision has opened the gate for taking collective actions for consumers through the scheme of public interest litigation, and may well have long-term importance.[30]

D. The Concept of the 'Consumer' in Chinese Law

An important feature of Chinese consumer protection law is that the subject of protection by the law – the consumer – only has an unclear definition. Because the definition is somewhat vague, it has indeed given local courts considerable discretion of interpretations thereby directly affecting the scope of issues to which the consumer laws apply.

Three issues in the definition of the consumer have been of particular concern and debated fiercely within China. First, should the state enterprises and institutions in charge of purchasing goods for employees be regarded in the law as 'consumer'? Article 2 of the 1993 Consumer Protection Law provided that 'The rights and interests of consumers in purchasing and using commodities or receiving services for daily consumption shall be protected by the present law'. Perhaps not surprisingly, the revision of the Consumer Protection Law in 2013 did not touch this Article – which remains the same in both versions of Consumer Protection Law, indicating that the legislator chose not to further clarify the definition of 'consumer' in the law. This wording means that the law does not adequately distinguish individual consumers from collective consumers (eg, a work unit that purchases goods for employees for their daily consumption purposes). Indeed, many city-level consumer protection regulations have provided a more detailed definition of 'consumer', which covers situations in which 'organisations' purchase goods for consumption purposes.[31] Although in some provincial regulations, direct mention of 'organisations' as 'consumers' has been removed, the regulations often try to avoid providing a detailed definition of 'consumer', so as to avoid any conflict with the 1993 Consumer Protection Law. For example, in an early version of the regulations on protection of consumers' rights and interests in Shanghai, it is stated that both 'individuals' and 'state enterprises and institutions' (*danwei*) are under the protection of the consumer regulations.[32] However, in the revised version of the local regulations published in 2002, the term '*danwei*'

[30] The possibility of using public interest litigation procedure was first introduced by the 2012 Civil Procedure Law (Article 55). However, it was not until the revision of the Consumer Protection Law in 2013, and its new provisions assigning the body to represent consumers, that such a scheme became meaningful in practice.

[31] Similar definition of the consumer which includes organisations can be found in provincial regulations on consumer protection of Hunan (1997), Henan (1995), Guizhou (1994), Heilongjiang province (1995).

[32] Regulations of Shanghai Municipality on Consumer Legitimate Rights and Interests Protection (1994 Amendment), Art 2.

meaning 'state enterprises and institutions' or work unit, has been abandoned. Instead, the regulation has maintained the usage of the term 'consumer' as the subject to be protected, without giving a precise legal definition of the term.[33] In the latest revision of these Regulations (2014), the use of the term 'consumers' in Article 2, remains unchanged, without any further differentiation between individual and *danwei* consumers.

A consumer is commonly understood in many jurisdictions to be a natural person who purchases goods for non-commercial purposes – an understanding that does not include 'organisation'. This understanding can be seen in consumer laws in various jurisdictions.[34] Wang Xiaoming suggests that the practice of considering 'organisations' as 'consumers' in China, is a legacy of the PRC's socialist planned economy where state organisations control personal consumption.[35] This practice has continued, where *danwei* often purchase goods and distribute them to employees as a form of welfare, or pay for services enjoyed by the whole organisation.[36] In this regard, some commentators, such as Shen Shang, argue that 'organisations' should be regarded as 'consumers' in law, because the collective form of consumption – '*danwei*' consumption – has become a special type of consumption in China.[37] Liu also suggests that we should consider the nature of the consumption made by *danwei* when applying the law, and only when *danwei* purchase goods for daily consumption should they be regarded as equivalent to an individual 'consumer'.[38] Liu goes even further, implying that embracing the idea of *danwei* as 'consumers' helps consumers to fight for their rights and interests under the law, since consumer groups can enhance their bargaining power when they bring lawsuits against producers.[39] A recent comment by the Higher People's Court of Beijing reveals that the judiciary tends to characterise *danwei* as 'consumers', at least in the circumstances where the *danwei* (company) purchase products for individuals for their personal consumption, albeit as a welfare responsibility.[40]

On the other hand, many commentators are opposed to the idea of a broad definition of the consumer that would include the *danwei*. Wang Xiaoming, for example, explains that the understanding of consumers as individuals is consistent with international practice that

[33] Regulations of Shanghai Municipality on the Protection of Consumers' Rights and Interests, adopted at the 44th Session of the Standing Committee of the 11th Shanghai Municipal People's Congress in 2002, Art 2, (revised in 2014).

[34] eg the EU Unfair Terms in Consumer Contracts Directive characterises the consumer as 'any natural person who, in commercial practices covered by this Directive, is acting for purposes which are outside his trade, business, craft or profession'.

[35] XM Wang, 'Woguo Xiaofeizhe Quanyi Baohu Fa zhong Xiaofeizhe Gainian de Jieding' [The Concept of Consumer in Chinese Consumer Protection Law]' (2010) 8 *Beijing Lianhe Daxue Xuebao (Shehui Kexue Ban) (Journal of Beijing Union University (Humanities and Social Sciences))* 76.

[36] ibid.

[37] S Shen, 'Cong Wang Hai Xianxiang kan Woguo "Xiaofeizhe Quanyi Baohu Fa"' ('Analysis on the Problems of "The Law on the Protection of Consumer Rights and Interests" from the Wang Hai Phenomenon') (2005) 24 *Changchun Shifan Daxue Xuebao (Journal of Changchun Normal University)* 45.

[38] ZD Liu, 'Danwei yeying Shiyong "Xiaofeizhe Quanyi Baohu Fa"' ("The Law on the Protection of Consumer Rights and Interests" should also Apply to State Enterprises and Institutions) (2005) 3 *Guojia Faguan Xueyuan Xuebao (National Judges College Law Journal)* 95.

[39] ibid at 96.

[40] The case comment shows that Beijing judges distinguish *danwei* purchases by looking at the purpose of the purchase – in one case the judge supported the food processing company's claims for compensation for fake mooncakes, because the mooncakes were bought for the workers as part of the company's welfare system. See B Xu and J Qu, 'Goumai le Shangpin, jiu Shuyu Xiaofeizhe le me?' ('You become a Consumer, When You buy a Product?'), published on 19 March 2018 on *Beijing Fayuan Wang (Beijing Court Network)* bjgy.chinacourt.gov.cn.

defines consumers as individual 'natural persons'.[41] He disagrees with the practice of including 'organisations' as 'consumers', because individual consumers are usually in a vulnerable position, with little bargaining power compared to the manufacturers, but this is not necessarily the case for *danwei* or work unit purchases.[42] In fact, the above example of the change in wording of Article 2 of the consumer protection regulations in Shanghai, where direct mention of '*danwei*' in the scope of protection under the law was taken out, may well show a tendency to abandon the old-fashioned concepts used in a state-planning period, and the willingness to adopt gradually the modern concept of the consumer. The 1993 Consumer Protection Law was intended mainly to protect individual consumers, and in section two the law identified the rights that consumers possess, some of which 'organisations' are not able to enjoy.[43] For example, Article 14 in section two provides that '[T]he consumers enjoy the right, in purchasing and utilizing commodities or accepting services, to have their human dignity and nationality customs and traditions being respected.' *Danwei*, or state enterprises and institutions, do not have 'human dignity' nor are they carriers of 'nationality (that is, ethnic minority) customs and traditions'.

Secondly, there is the 'intention' issue: should the purpose of consumers when buying products be investigated, to see whether it is consistent with the purpose of 'consuming the product'? The consumers who are protected by the current Chinese Consumer Protection Law are those who purchase goods for consumption purposes.[44] This definition of consumer excludes 'commercial practices' from consumer activities. However, setting the purpose of consumer law as protecting only consumers who purchase goods for their own personal consumption, may be too restrictive – it may for example exclude new types of consumer activity which cannot be characterised as 'purchase to consume'. The Wang Hai phenomenon is a very good example of these difficulties. Wang Hai is a 'consumer' who has made extensive use of the double-price damages provision (Article 49) in the 1993 Consumer Protection Law in order to obtain compensation. He did this by intentionally buying goods that he could see were likely to be counterfeit. The revised Law has kept this provision (now, as Article 55) but has also increased the amount of punitive damages to three times the price of the product, and if the damages so calculated fall below 500RMB, then the award made against the defendant may be increased to 500RMB.

Wang is a controversial figure in China today, with some commentators arguing that he is a 'professional litigant' rather than a 'true consumer'. Wang Hai's purchasing conduct was not regarded as consumer behaviour by some local courts, on the basis that his motives in knowingly buying defective goods and then seeking compensation does not fit into the definition of buying for 'daily consumption' as provided by the law.[45] However, some observers argue that so long as Wang Hai does not purchase defective goods so as to 'make a profit', his motivation

[41] Wang, 'Woguo Xiaofeizhe' (n 35) at 77. Also see I Ramsay, *Consumer Law and Policy*, 3rd edn (Oxford, Hart Publishing, 2012) 17; C Scott and J Black, *Cranston's Consumers and the Law*, 3rd edn (Cambridge, Cambridge University Press, 2000) 8. Ramsay has defined the scope of consumer law in his major study of the consumer as being primarily for the purpose of protection of the end-user of consumer products and services. Similarly, Scott and Black, in their major analysis of consumer law in the UK, characterise consumers as citizens who 'enter transactions to obtain products and services from commercial enterprises'.

[42] ibid.

[43] See Section two of Consumer Protection Law 1993.

[44] See Art 2 of Consumer Protection Law 1993.

[45] See eg QQ Xie, 'Jiehe "Wanghai Dajia An" Jianyi Falü Jieshi Buquedingxing de Yuanyin' ('Discussion on Reasons Causing Uncertainty of Legal Interpretation on Cases in Relation to "Wang Hai Phenomenon"') (2010)

in buying the goods should not be relevant, because what really makes one a consumer is that one's conduct is 'non-business' in nature. If Wang Hai knowingly purchased defective goods in order to make a 'profit' through compensation, then there may be a problem.[46] In addition, Wang Xiaoming believes that Wang Hai's conduct in singling out counterfeiting products and then asking for double-price compensation by invoking Article 49 of the 1993 Consumer Protection Law, was indeed very helpful in cracking down on the illegal business of counterfeiting, as well as more generally safeguarding consumers' rights and interests.[47] So, the litigious conduct of Wang Hai has benefitted the public interest, and this was clearly the drafters' intention when crafting the provision on punitive damages in Article 49.

The 'intention' check has been raised constantly in food cases brought by the Wang Hai type of anti-counterfeit professional plaintiff, who is often seeking ten times the purchase price in punitive damages.[48] Indeed, the court seems willing to regard the professionals as proper consumers. This attitude is shown in the 'Provisions of the Supreme People's Court on Several Issues concerning the Application of Law in the Trial of Cases Involving Food and Drug Disputes' (2013) where Article 3 states:

> Where, in a dispute arising out of quality problems with food or a drug, the buyer files a claim against the manufacturer or the seller, and the manufacturer or the seller argues that the buyer purchased the food or the drug knowing that it had quality problems, the people's court shall not support the argument.

One commentator, citing observations made in a recent judgment in Qinghai, (Shandong Province) suggests however that if the court does not accept the claim, the situation will become difficult: Consumers of all kinds will not give much attention to spotting counterfeit products. As a result, the selling of counterfeit products will flourish, and this outcome would be contrary to the spirit of the Consumer Protection Law.[49] Another concern with this vague definition of consumer, namely that the consumer is a person who purchases for daily consumption purposes, is that it may exclude consumers who purchase high-value or 'luxury' products, including top-range automobiles. Liu considers that this is a dated perspective. What was once a luxury is nowadays often socially defined as a necessity. When the Consumer Protection Law was originally introduced in 1993, for example, automobiles were regarded as luxury items, with exceptionally high value: they were a social rarity.[50] However in today's China, although the motorcar is still a valuable item, automobiles are much cheaper and more popular than those of 1993. Automobiles may be regarded as a

Huainan Shifan Xueyuan Xuebao (*Journal of Huainan Normal University*) 58. Xie also observes that in order to avoid the risk of getting a case withdrawal, activists like Wang Hai now try to back off from the frontline in court, but instead give support to a 'real consumer' through their knowledge and court experience.

[46] LP Wang, 'Shiyi Xiaofeizhe Gainian de Falü Jieding' (Discussion on the Legal Definition of the Concept of Consumer) (2006) 4 *Jing Ji Shi* (*Economist*) 81.

[47] ibid.

[48] Ch 5 below provides details of the professionals' practices.

[49] GD Zhang, '"Pola Panjue Tuxian Falü Dandang"' ("Vigorous Judgement Shows the Responsibility of the Law")' *People's Court Daily*, 13 April 2019, Section 02.

[50] Liu, 'Qiche shu Shechi Xiaofei Pin?' (n 25). Also see LY, Wang, 'Lu "Xiaofeizhe Quanyi Baohu fa" de Shiyong Fanwei' ('On the Scope of Application of the Consumer Protection Law') (2013) 2 *Falü Shiyong* (*Journal of Law Application*) 76. Wang, a judge from the Supreme People's Court, agrees that those buying automobiles should be considered to be 'consumers'. Whilst she is opposed to applying the Consumer Protection Law to other controversial areas such as real estate, hospital services, and public higher education, she also holds that for private higher education, the Consumer Protection Law should be applied.

daily necessity today, and consumer purchases of automobiles as meeting the needs of daily consumption, rather than luxury goods. Some argue that automobiles can also serve commercial purposes and it is important to distinguish between the purchase of automobiles for home use and for commercial use.[51] Nevertheless, since the Chinese legal system nowhere provides particular protection for those who buy automobiles, it might be worth trying to broaden the consumer protection provisions so as to provide clear rules on the purchase of automobiles, and to better resolve disputes concerning post-purchase problems with cars.

Thirdly, should the legal definition of consumer be expanded to include some particular relations of consumption, such as the farmers purchasing agricultural commodities, people going to hospital for medical treatment, and so on? Article 54 of the 1993 Consumer Protection Law provides that 'The present Law shall be applicable *mutatis mutandis* to peasants' purchase or application of means of production used directly in agricultural production.' The 2013 Consumer Protection Law has retained this provision as Article 62. This provision has, in fact, expanded the scope of the Law to include farmers as a special type of 'consumer'. Wang Liping suggests that although most farmers are intermediate consumers, in China, because they are usually individual owners of small-scale farming enterprises, their bargaining power is as weak as individual consumers when they buy production goods from large companies.[52] Some scholars also suggest that it is necessary to keep farmers as agricultural producers within the scope of the consumer protection system because there is nothing else in the Chinese legal system that gives farmers effective safeguards against sellers of inferior seeds, pesticide and chemical fertiliser; while on the other hand, they also call for the establishment of a law focussed particularly on the protection of farmers' rights and interests.[53]

Another important issue in the definition of the consumer in law relates to whether the Consumer Protection Law should regulate relevant aspects of the doctor-patient relationship. Wang and Zong argue that access to medical services has become a fundamental need, or in the other words, daily consumer conduct by members of society which naturally falls into the scope of Consumer Protection Law.[54] They go on to argue that medical institutions are regarded as 'business operators' in the Consumer Protection Law – Article 3 defines 'business operators' as those who provide goods and services to consumers – therefore, medical institutions providing services to customers (patients) are business operators and they even make profits from their activities.[55] In addition, Wang and Guan take the view that services that combine features of both 'commodity' and 'social welfare', such as publicly provided medical services, fall within the scope of consumer protection because service users are charged fees for these services.[56] Indeed, it is in this spirit that both Hunan and Zhejiang Provinces have characterised 'patients' as 'consumers' in their local regulations on consumer protection.[57]

[51] Liu, 'Qiche shu Shechi Xiaofei Pin?' (n 25).

[52] Wang, 'Shiyi Xiaofeizhe' (n 46) 83.

[53] See eg Shen, 'Cong Wang Hai Xianxiang' (n 37).

[54] CY Wang and M Zong, 'The Legal Relationship between Medical Establishment and Sick Men' (2001) 18 *Journal of Suzhou Teachers College* 27. Also see Art 2 of Consumer Protection Law.

[55] ibid. Also see Art 3 of Consumer Protection Law.

[56] QX Wang and B Guan, 'Jingji Fa Shiye xia de Xiaofeizhe Dingwei' ('Positioning the Consumer in Law from the Perspective of Economic Law') (2002) 9 *Fali yu Shiwu (Jurisprudence and Vocational Work)* 12.

[57] ibid at 13.

As the definition of consumer in the law remains unclear, it seems that local practice, or local level legislation, has often adopted a working definition of 'consumer' so as to include actors who are considered as 'vulnerable' in an economic relationship, such as farmers and patients, who are traditionally not regarded as consumers, but who suffer from a power imbalance in their business relationships. In this sense, the Consumer Protection Law seems to have been used as a law to provide solutions for complaints from vulnerable actors in the economic field because no other rules dealing with such complaints have been drawn up and put into effect. The conceptual difficulties that we have noted above are also interesting in that they suggest that the transition from characterising the citizen as producer to seeing the citizen as consumer has not been a straightforward process.

III. The Consumer as Citizen in China

As noted in chapter one, in many jurisdictions around the world, the concept of consumer citizen has become increasingly important in the protection of consumers. Since every citizen is a consumer, a citizen's political and social rights are also relevant and should not be lost from view when dealing with the economic rights that he or she pursues as a consumer. This may mean that the consumer is willing to draw upon his or her 'citizen's rights', including fundamental rights such as rights of freedom of speech, access to public information, taking collective actions, and so on, to secure their individual consumer rights.

Although the term 'consumer citizen' has become an important concept and branch of study in the consumer protection discourse worldwide, it has not been an important one within the academic literature on China. Hooper is one scholar that has discussed – albeit briefly – this subject within the context of China. He makes reference to the 'consumer citizen' in China by attaching it to the growing rights consciousness among consumers and the efforts that the state has made to enhance popular awareness of such rights. As he notes, the 'growing consumer rights consciousness in China, together with the willingness to exercise those rights, have been linked substantially to the government's creation and promotion of laws and avenues for the assertion of consumer rights'.[58] Hooper stresses – as we have noted above in the discussion of the 'rights and interests' in consumer law – the PRC concept of citizenship involves a strong emphasis on citizens' obligations (or collective interests) rather than rights – 'citizens perform their duties, in return, the government gives them their rights'.[59] Particularly in the old planned economy period, when obligations and collective interests were prioritised by the party-state over the pursuit of individual rights and interests, citizens were not thought of in terms of their individual rights. Similarly, Tian and Dong use the term 'consumer citizen' only very vaguely and their argument on consumer citizenship in China mainly focuses on exploring consumers' changing rights awareness. They limit their focus, however, so that they see the civic consciousness of the Chinese consumer as being expressed in substantial part by the selective nationalist attitudes (sometimes positive, sometimes negative) to western brands in China. Chinese consumers favour

[58] B Hooper, 'The Consumer Citizen in Contemporary China,' (2005) *Working Paper No.12, Centre for East and South-East Asian Studies, Lund University* 1, 15.

[59] ibid at 3.

those brands where either the brand (or a country associated with that brand) is one that has helped China in the past or is seen as a part of China's wealthy and powerful future. They reject brands that are associated with failures in China's past or regarded as unimportant for China's future prosperity and strength.[60] They too fail to identify any specific consumer rights-pursuit conduct that is also part of their performance of citizens' rights. In fact, the existing literature has failed to offer a clear vision of what a 'consumer citizen' is in China. The empirical evidence on consumers' pursuit of justice presented in this present study supports the view that there is a group of people who are indeed consumer citizens in China or bear similar qualities to consumer citizens as generally understood in the relevant literature. Thus, there is value in exploring how – if at all – the concept of 'consumer citizen' is to be found in a socialist context such as that of China and thereby bring the China case into the international academic discourse on this topic.

Despite its weaknesses, some of Hooper's discussion on the understanding of 'rights' in China has some important points to make. As he suggests, the official understanding of rights in China, specifically citizens' rights, continues to be different from more international understandings in several respects. Thus, rights still tend to be understood as gifts of the state in China, rather than something naturally given as a matter of birth.[61] This may also help us to explain why 'rights awareness' has hitherto been weak among Chinese citizens. A second difference in the official conception of rights, as Hooper suggests, is that 'rights' as perceived in China are relatively limited in another sense – these rights are primarily concerned with the social aspects of citizenship, and do not extend to the political aspects of citizenship.[62] The Chinese government has promoted consumers' rights awareness during the post-Mao reform era, through educational and propaganda strategies as well as enacting consumer protection laws and creating consumer associations.[63] The state has officially characterised consumers as citizens with 'rights and interests' to be protected, who are encouraged to use legal processes ('weapons') to assert their rights.[64] Hooper's view is fairly positive, and he sees the government as making great efforts in ensuring that consumer rights and interests are well protected, despite the limited understanding of rights from a comparative perspective.

Nevertheless, when compared to more 'developed' societies, the notion of consumer-citizenship in China remains relatively nascent. It seems that Hooper has also noticed the limits of his study and points out that '[T]he major theme [of this paper] is that, in the area of consumerism, people are asserting rights not vis a vis the state, which is the focus of much of the debate about the nascent growth of civil society in China, but vis a vis the market, with the endorsement and encouragement of the state.' I would further argue that even though consumer rights are being promoted by the state, the official policies seem to only cultivate citizens' awareness of already-bestowed rights. There is no evidence that the state encourages consumers' struggles for new rights through a political agenda and rights-assertive process. The meaning of citizenship in China is

[60] K Tian and L Dong, *Consumer-Citizens of China: The Role of Foreign Brands in the Imagined Future China* (Abingdon and New York, Routledge, 2011).

[61] Hooper, 'The Consumer Citizen' (n 58) 3.

[62] ibid.

[63] ibid at 6–10.

[64] See Arts 1 and 6 of the Law on the Protection of Consumer Rights and Interests 1993.

largely restricted by the official, narrow, concept of rights, and the limited room allowed for Chinese civil society to challenge this understanding. Indeed, the restricted official understanding of citizens' rights in general may be seen as stifling the development of the consumer movement or consumer activism in China, through which consumers as interest groups might actively participate in the discussion of the forming of consumer law and policies.

In contrast, there is an increasing acceptance internationally of consumer protection as something of a fundamentally important rights principle, especially given that every person is a consumer from time to time and consumer welfare has become a significant feature of 'modern' society.[65] The development and protection of international human rights may also promote the protection of consumer rights in a sense that some of the fundamental human rights include the rights that individuals enjoy as consumers. For example, the right to physical and mental health, provided by the International Covenant on Economic, Social and Cultural Rights (ICESCR), implies that consumers need to be protected from dangerous products.[66] China has signed and ratified the International Covenant on Economic, Social and Cultural Rights, but has not yet acceded to the International Covenant on Civil and Political Rights, which may mean that the classical civil and political aspects of international human rights, such as the right to freedom of expression and the right to freedom of assembly and association, remain uncertain in China. Chinese consumers may find it difficult to air their voice or participate in discussion of consumer law-making, because these citizens' rights have not been given genuine meaning by the state. It may well be the case that in due course consumer protection in China comes to stress not only the protection of individuals' economic and social rights, but also citizens' civil and political rights. Such a development would be helpful if consumer groups are to become a countervailing force to industry or even the powerful government in the search for better protection of the interests of the consumer.

In China's consumer protection regime, and especially in the party-state's encouragement of the use of punitive damages, we see potential for the 'economic consumer' to also act as a 'responsible citizen' and promote the public interest. In both the 1993 and 2013 versions of the Consumer Protection Law, there are provisions which specifically encourage aggrieved consumers to bring suit in court. Such suits do have a public interest dimension to them in as much as the punitive damages awarded are primarily intended to encourage higher product quality and safety standards. For example, as we have noted above, Article 55 of the revised Consumer Protection Law (2013) provides that punitive damages have been increased to a minimum of 500RMB, or to three times the amount of the consumer's costs in purchasing a defective consumer product. This compares favourably to the punitive damages of twice the sale price of the defective good under the 1993 law. Also, as we have also noted, punitive damages in cases where product defects cause death or severe damage to consumers' health have been increased. Moreover, relevant local regulations have been put in place so as to encourage citizens to report the selling malpractices of businesses to the state's economic regulator. Such encouragement includes rewarding those who have

[65] I Benohr and HW Micklitz, 'Consumer Protection and Human Rights' in G Howells et al (eds), *Handbook of Research on International Consumer Law* (Cheltenham, Edward Elgar Publishing, 2010) 19.

[66] ibid at 21. Also see Art 12 of ICESCR on the right to health.

successfully spotted product safety issues, and those who provide evidence that helps the regulator to crackdown on illegal business conduct.[67]

The nature of some kind of consumer citizenship in the PRC is likely to bear unusual and distinctive features when compared to ideas about consumer-citizen found in many other societies, especially those in which the recognition of the importance of citizenship, particularly, the recognition of the citizen's individual rights, is relatively high and well-developed. So, in the present study, attention will be given to the issue of if and how the legal developments noted in the preceding paragraph have perhaps helped to generate some form of consumer activism despite a political environment in China that is generally hostile to the idea of a strong and autonomous civil society, and therefore also to robust understandings of the nature of consumer citizenship that have emerged elsewhere in the world.

IV. A Brief Introduction to the Field

Fieldwork for the present study was conducted in Shenzhen, China, a city located in southern Guangdong Province and adjoining Hong Kong. Shenzhen became a Special Economic Zone (SEZ) in 1980, one of the first four SEZs to be established in the post-Mao era of economic reform. These SEZs enjoy a relatively high degree of autonomy in trade and investment matters. Prior to its changed status it was only a small market town, but now has a population of more than 15 million people – many of whom are migrants from other parts of China – and is one of the most important centres in the Pearl River Delta economy. It is a major financial centre host to many key Chinese companies (including high-tech enterprises), and a very important container port.

Shenzhen has sub-provincial administrative status. It comprises ten districts, and my fieldwork was mainly concentrated in Futian District and Luohu District – located at the heart of the city, the site of Shenzhen's Central Business District, and the site of its Municipal Government – because that is where the headquarters of the Shenzhen Consumer Council is located. Although geographically in Guangdong Province, massive migration from other parts of China into Shenzhen means that Putonghua ('Mandarin') is the main language used in government, business, media and so on, although the local dialects of Cantonese and Hakka are often used in daily life as well. The city's population is young, with an average age of less than 30 years. Shenzhen and Hong Kong enjoy close business, trade and social links, and at the border crossings every day one might see Shenzhen residents hurrying back from Hong Kong laden with consumer goods because of worries about the authenticity of many products sold in China. Other residents will be taking children across to school in Hong Kong to 'consume' a more global education.

Shenzhen is one of two cities in China which have their own stock exchange (the other is Shanghai). Its major industries include telecommunications, computers manufacturing and electronics. ZTE and Huawei – famous domestic telecoms equipment producers and suppliers in China – are examples of telecommunications giants who have located themselves in Shenzhen. Shenzhen has a large retail sector – multinational retailors such as Wal-Mart, Carrefour, and Tesco, as well as domestically famous retailors such as Vanguard, Rainbow

[67] The report and reward scheme will be discussed further in ch 5.

Department Store and Ren Ren Le all have large local branches in the city. Many of the daily consumer products sold in Shenzhen are imported from manufacturers located in various parts of China.

The Shenzhen Consumer Council (SZCC) is the most important consumer dispute resolution body in Shenzhen. It is one of the many local organisations that operate within the national network of Consumer Associations, and it accepts professional guidance from its leading institution at the national level – the China Consumers' Association (CCA).[68] Besides the SZCC, the regulatory body for many economic activities in Shenzhen, the Market Supervision Administration (MSA) bureau is another important body where consumers can seek mediation services for resolving disputes over claims against businesses. The MSA holds sanctioning power over illegal business practices, and citizens are encouraged to report product issues and provide useful information to the MSA, so as to help it to stop illegal business practices that cause harm to the public. The MSA was previous known as the Shenzhen SAIC (State Administration on Industry and Commerce) – a regulatory body that can be found at different levels throughout China. It has extensive functions and powers to regulate the market, and these are dealt with greater depth in chapter three.

The People's Court is the forum of last resort for consumers. It should also be pointed out that whereas a number of jurisdictions elsewhere in the world have been developing a consumer protection ombudsman system in recent years (in large part as an alternative to the courts), there is no such avenue available in China. The People's Republic has yet to introduce any kind of ombudsman system, making it one of the few jurisdictions anywhere to lack this form of access to justice. The present study shows that the Consumer Council in Shenzhen is perhaps locally (and indeed, nationally) the closest equivalent to the ombudsman. It is an umbrella CDR entity in a sense that it provides comprehensive mediation services to consumers on different kinds of dispute, as an alternative to the courts.

It might surprise the reader to learn that there are no local NGOs specialised in promoting the protection of consumer rights and interests in Shenzhen. Establishing NGOs in China is very difficult legally, and most NGOs found in Shenzhen are focussed on other issues, such as environmental problems, rights of the disabled, and labour rights. One 'quasi' NGO that does, to some extent, works on consumer issues, is a pro-bono legal service provider registered with the Futian Office of the Shenzhen Judicial Bureau (*sifa ju*).[69] This provider has established a group of pro-bono lawyers who deliver free legal service to those whose income is higher than the criteria for receiving legal aid, but who are still financially unable to hire a lawyer. One of its goals is to handle cases with public-interest elements, such as consumer cases against telecommunication giants, the China Mobile, China Telecom, and China Unicom.

Shenzhen is an especially good location for studying consumers' grievances and their experiences of attempting to secure redress for their grievances. Here, the economic reforms have been deep and far reaching and have resulted in specific attention being given to the position of the consumer – many consumer complaints are made to, and handled by, various administrative bodies, consumer associations and courts, and are widely reported in the

[68] See CCA's website for more information about the China Consumer Association at www.cca.org.cn.

[69] See an introduction to the work of the Wider Probono Legal Service Centre at www.probonochina.com/en/index.php?m=content&c=index&a=lists&catid=2.

media. Of central importance in this system is the Shenzhen Consumer Council, the study of which is at the heart of the present work.

V. Conclusions

This chapter has introduced the relevant literature, identified some important issues in the notions of 'consumer' and 'consumer citizen' in the PRC post-Mao context, and outlined the main consumer laws that form a backdrop for the account which follows of the findings of my field research on consumer dispute resolution. Given the gap between formal legal rules and actual social practice in China, I decided that rather than focus on national law through a doctrinal research lens, it would be more productive to explore how China's consumer protection regime actually functioned at the local level and was experienced by ordinary people making their everyday purchases and pursuing their grievances when those purchases went wrong. Fieldwork in China has thus primarily focused on providing local-level data and analysis of consumer redress and access to justice, local efforts at consumer activism and case studies of consumer protection in action.

3

Extra-Judicial Processes for Handling Consumer Disputes

I. Introduction

This chapter aims to explore two main questions: what are the main extra-judicial mechanisms for resolving consumer disputes in Shenzhen, and how do they function on a daily basis?[1] Particular attention will be given to the city's Consumer Council, one of the most important local organisations for handling consumer complaints and redress in Shenzhen outside the court system. The chapter is divided in two parts. The first part focuses on explaining the main processes set up by the consumer organisations for dealing with consumer disputes – the 'Three-Consumer System'. These processes are probably best described as a first-level of dispute handling, in which an initial response is made prior to a dispute reaching the hands of a specific body. The second part then looks at the dispute processing system within the Shenzhen Consumer Council – the manner in which disputes are logged and filed, distributed and then handled by the Consumer Council's staff, both in theory and in practice.

Thus, the chapter initially explores the primary *fora* that consumers use to pursue their grievances in Shenzhen, the organisations that deal with these grievances when they become disputes, and the workload and the relationship between the various relevant organisations. The primary *fora*, my fieldwork shows, consist of the Consumer Council (the Council, or the 'CC'), the Market Supervision Administration (the 'MSA') bureau and the Hotline Centre (the 'Centre'). These *fora* are in practice referred as the 'Three-Consumer System' (*sanxiao tixi*) and are fully government-funded. One important contribution of this part of the chapter is that it explains the manner in which these organisations cooperate with each other. Such cooperation is important because all three *fora* share one very important portal for consumer complaints. This is known as the 12315 portal, containing both a hotline and an online complaint platform. The chapter examines on the 'Three-Consumer System', giving close attention to its rules for allocation of work, its efficiency and effectiveness, and offering a case flow analysis which demonstrates the sequential processes of any given case.

In the following part of the chapter, the analysis will explore the manner in which disputes are distributed amongst the staff members working in the Shenzhen Consumer

[1] The factual materials in this chapter, as in other parts of the book, are up to date as of September 2014, when I completed the main phase of my field research. It should be added here that subsequent to this fieldwork I was able to follow up certain issues in short term visits, and I indicate in the text where this is the case.

Council. It identifies the type of dispute processes used by the staff to handle the disputes, and considers how these processes may affect or even bring about different outcomes of the cases. It should be added here that this chapter does not provide detailed accounts of how consumers themselves experience and view these dispute processes. Instead, an analysis of specific cases of consumer complaint handling is provided below in chapter four, so as to explore complainants' interaction with the defendant business and the mediator, in the negotiation or mediation processes. This chapter thus offers an introductory examination of the steps that an actual case needs to go through before it reaches the hands of a 'grievance manager' or 'handler'.

The 'Three-Consumer System' of extra-judicial processing of consumer complaints and redress, as this chapter will show, seems to be a preferred route by the consumers, many of whom feel uncomfortable pursuing their grievance by litigation through the courts. The 'Three-Consumer system' has probably become the easiest and fastest way of resolving consumer complaints in Shenzhen. However, my findings show that the same type of case going through the Three-Consumer system may end up having reverse results, and this is perhaps because the handling of cases relies heavily on the activities of the particular individual staff member who is in charge of the case. In addition, a number of new problems – for example, those to do with online shopping – greatly complicate the picture, and make it difficult for the Consumer Council to put in place definitive structures and processes.

This chapter offers a picture of the most important extra-judicial dispute processes that an aggrieved consumer will likely go through if she or he seeks redress for his or her grievance. It provides new and important empirical data on the functioning of one of the principal non-court-based mechanisms for consumer access to justice.

II. Consumer Bodies and the Complaint System in Shenzhen

As noted in the chapter introduction, the main consumer redress processes in Shenzhen are of a regulatory nature. They constitute a 'Three-Consumer System' consisting of the Consumer Council, the MSA (particularly, the Consumer Protection Department, CPD) and the Hotline Centre.[2] The term 'system' is used here in only a very loose sense. For those working within the 'system', the insiders, the expression 'Three-Consumer System' is simply a convenient way to refer to the three organisations collectively, particularly at meetings. Nevertheless, these bodies are by no means the only channels for handling a consumer complaint. For example, a problem of food poisoning may also be reported to the Bureau of Food and Drug Administration of Shenzhen Municipality. The 'Three-Consumer System' is perhaps the most basic and overarching type of avenue for handling consumer complaints in Shenzhen. It is intended to deal with all kinds of consumer problems, and to function as the most important extra-judicial procedure for aggrieved consumers seeking to voice their concerns and to secure some kind of redress.

[2] The Hotline Centre is also referred to as 'the Information and Advisory Centre'.

A. The Hotline Centre

This system was only established a decade or so ago, and it has since gone through several reforms and changes. It started life as the 12315 hotline – a nationally accessible telephone number for making consumer complaints. The '12315' is a unified telephone number for the consumer complaint, accessible throughout China. It was established and operated by the regulator – the State Administration for Industry and Commerce (SAIC, *Gong-shang Ju*) at the national level, and the analogous departments within local governments (such as the MSA in Shenzhen). The general telephone number of the hotline is the same across the whole country, but with the consumer using the local area code when making the exact phone call complaint. The actual hotline, accordingly, is in reality managed by each local regulatory body. In 2005, a call centre was specifically established in Shenzhen, with the aim of handling telephone calls from not only the 12315 hotline, but also the 12358 hotline which had been established (nationwide) for filing complaints about the excessive prices of products.[3] This later internally became known as the Hotline Centre (hereinafter, the Centre) which is the entry portal for most of the complaints (*tousu*) and reports (*jubao*). Before its establishment, it was not possible to talk of a 'system'. The evolution of something approaching a 'system' (as insiders understand it) probably started from the Shenzhen SAIC, and then incorporated the Consumer Council, and then later the Hotline Centre to help deal with phone calls from aggrieved consumers and others made to these two bodies. With this development, the 'owner' of the hotline – the MSA, previously known as the Shenzhen SAIC – extended its capacity to receive and handle complaints. The Centre is now an active player in the consumer complaint and redress processing system, as every complaint made by a telephone call will be initially handled by Centre staff. The number of such calls places a significant pressure on the staff. As one former staff member (now an officer in the MSA) jokingly complained to me, 'You can't leave your seat for too long [in this job], even for a toilet visit, and you [certainly] don't have much time for lunch.'[4]

As a portal, the Centre primarily performs two functions: first, it registers each complaint and creates a *gongdan* (a work sheet of registered complaint) with a summary of the complaint and some personal contact details of the complainant. This resembles the application form that a consumer needs to fill in when making a complaint in person. It merely contains some very basic information regarding the dispute – it cannot be a sophisticated document, as each operator probably cannot spend more than five minutes for one phone call. The *gongdan* will be uploaded to an Office Automation (OA) system and be seen by staff working in the 'Three-Consumer System'. The second, and key role that the Centre plays, is to provide advice to consumers. As a staff member in the MSA describes this aspect of Centre work, 'perhaps as much as half of the consumer complaints are withdrawn or otherwise dealt with by a phone call to the Centre, and thus do not proceed to the departments for further handling'. We can see from this that an operator in the Centre is not

[3] See news report, 'The Opening of Shenzhen 12315/12358 Centre for Complaints and Reports' (Shenzhen 12315/12358 Shensu Jübao Zhongxin Qiyong) (*Shenzhen Commercial Daily*, 11 January 2005) news.sina.com.cn/c/2005-01-11/06274782547s.shtml.

[4] The author was also during fieldwork told by Centre staff that the performance of the operators was linked with the number of the phone call complaints that they received and registered, so that the more complaint calls the operator receives, the better the payment that she or he gets.

simply a 'note-taker', she or he also needs to be a good 'listener', and even an 'advisor'. At the same time, since the operators do not appear to have an extensive knowledge on consumer matters, the advice they can provide aggrieved consumers is rather limited. In fact, their advice is mainly concerned with procedural matters. What the operators are concerned with most seems to be recording the message provided by a consumer in a fast and relatively precise way. Nevertheless, the advice that they do give clearly has an effect, and that is probably why approximately one half of all complaints made by telephone go no further.

In addition to these two main functions, the Centre is the place where consumers track the progress of their complaints. Since most consumers cannot reach the exact handler of the complaints by telephone, they must ring the Centre for an update. But there is some reassurance here for the consumers that their complaints are not 'lost in the system'. A consumer can pay a visit to the Consumer Council in person and ask about the progress, if she or he insists on knowing what progress has been made regarding his or her complaint.[5]

B. The MSA and the Consumer Protection Department

The Market Supervision Administration (MSA) of Shenzhen municipality is one of the most important state agencies in terms of economic regulation, and is an important public body in the system of consumer complaint and redress. As a relatively new bureau in Shenzhen, MSA was transformed and reorganised from the department for 'State Administration for Industry and Commerce' (SAIC), a major regulator that can be found in many other cities in China. The idea behind the SAIC in Shenzhen is to create a super-ministry bureau, which administers the activities in the economic field and maintains 'good order' in the (socialist) market economy. It regulates economic actors and their activities in most fields of industry and commerce. The MSA has not only retained all the administrative functions of the former State Administration for Industry and Commerce' (SAIC), but is now also expanded to include the functions of supervision on quality and technique (functions of the former Bureau of Quality and Technical Supervision), intellectual property (functions of the former Bureau of Intellectual Property), prices (functions of the former Bureau of Prices), catering (including food and sanitary issues), alcohol, and so on. According to the 'Temporary Provisions on Administration of Industry and Commerce' (1995), which inter alia, deals with the powers and functions of SAIC, the MSA, as a successor body to the SAIC in Shenzhen, has the power to enforce national laws, as well as making administrative regulations under the legal framework on matters within its jurisdiction.[6] The MSA has three levels of administration in Shenzhen: the municipal level, the district level of MSA bureaus, and local MSA offices (previously known as SAIC offices) across the whole city.[7]

[5] However, this is not done by most of the consumers, as the time and money they spend on paying a visit to the Consumer Council may exceed the amount of their claim.

[6] See Temporary Provisions on Administration of Industry and Commerce [Gongshang Xingzheng Guanli Zanxing Guiding], published by the State Administration of Industry and Commerce in 1995. Copy on file with the author and available upon request.

[7] The local offices are largely created by the amount of commercial activities in an area and the perceived need for such an office. For example, one of the MSA local offices is located in the nationally well-known street for electronic appliances – Hua Qiang Bei. The geographical coverage of the Hua Qiang Bei office is not very substantial, but the workload it bears is probably the highest of all the offices.

When complaints are collected and registered as *gongdans* in a shared automation office (OA) system, they will be forwarded to the Consumer Protection Department (CPD) of the MSA or the Consumer Council for a further allocation. Before going to the field, it seemed to me that the CPD was a forum where complaints are dealt with, and where mediation was arranged and carried out to resolve disputes. However, as I found out later, in the course of my fieldwork, it is probably best to describe the CPD as a place for lodging the complaints, as its primary task is to distribute *gongdans* to different local MSA offices, rather than handling the complaints per se.[8] The complaints accepted by the CPD are those which fall within the jurisdiction of the MSA. Although the CPD does not handle any complaints, it acts as a liaison office for collecting and distributing consumer protection matters between the local MSA office at the street level, the MSA bureau at the district level, and the municipal MSA bureau. A local office has to deal with matters within the MSA's jurisdiction in its territorial area and, thus, it has personnel whose role largely corresponds to the function of the departments in the MSA bureau.[9] In terms of access to consumer justice, the main function of a local MSA office is to handle the general consumer disputes allocated to it by the CPD. However, local MSA offices also deal with matters such as company registration and the annual renewal of business licences, which are not consumer-related and do not appear in the 'Three-Consumer System'.

Before the new Consumer Protection Law was revised in 2013, and came into force on 15 March 2014, complaints made to the MSA bureau (or in other cities, the local Bureau of the SAIC) were termed *shensu*, which is to be distinguished from the wording of the complaints made to the Consumer Council, namely, *tousu*. This is because in Chinese the term *shensu* carries the meaning of making complaints to a body with public authority. However, the new law has not adhered to this distinction, and uses *tousu* to describe *both* the complaints made to the MSA bureau and those to the Consumer Council. Despite this indistinct terminology, making complaints to these two organisations is regarded in the Consumer Protection Law (whether the 1993 original version, or the 2013 revised version) as two of the five channels by means of which a consumer may seek redress.[10]

[8] The *gongdans* are first allocated to the MSA bureau at the district level, and then to the local MSA offices. The Consumer Protection Department used to perform more important tasks, such as collecting data and constructing reports on consumer complaints, providing working guidance and legal advice on consumer matters to local MSA officers, etc. Some of these tasks have been shifted to other MSA departments (such as the Regulation Department). Some have been removed and not continued by others.

[9] This re-arrangement of the personnel in the local office has also created many problems. The MSA was established as a result of the 'super-ministry reform' in Shenzhen in 2009. Since that development, there have been problems associated with re-arrangement of personnel in the local MSA office. Given that the former SAIC has merged with other departments, the former SAIC local office was subsequently given the same role that its superior plays – meaning that it has had to expand its jurisdiction to deal with matters that were previously dealt with by other organisations. For example, before the reform, a local SAIC office did not deal with food safety cases, as these would go to the food safety department at the district level. However, there was no organisation such as a 'food safety office' at the street level. The super-ministry reform, therefore, has given the reformed SAIC office – the local MSA office – the function of a food safety office, while at the same time, did not add in new personnel specialised in food safety issues. As some staff in the local MSA office stressed, 'we have had to learn new things from the start, since we had never dealt with them before'. This may help to explain why the local MSA officers are often so annoyed by the activities of so-called 'professional complainants' (that is, repeat complainants and informers), especially as they may not possess as much expertise as the professionals on matters such as food safety. They find themselves too easily outfoxed by the repeat players.

[10] See Art 39 of the current Consumer Protection Law (promulgated in 1993, as revised in 2013).

Although this change of name may seem to be a minor matter, it does affect some practices. Previously, the way to distinguish a complaint, whether it is made to the MSA or the Consumer Council, was largely by the name. If a consumer said, 'I want to *shensu*', the operator would assume that she or he would like to make a complaint to the MSA (an administrative department). However, if a consumer said, 'I want to *tousu*', the complaint would most likely have been sent to the Consumer Council, even though the consumer did not particularly stress that she or he wants the complaint to be dealt with by the Consumer Council.[11]

C. The Consumer Council

At the very heart of the 'Three-Consumer System' is the Shenzhen Consumer Council (SZCC), also known as the 'Shenzhen 315'.[12] The SZCC is a fully government-funded organisation that handles most of Shenzhen's consumer complaints. The establishment of the SZCC is largely a response to the consumer protection demands in China in the late 1980s, when the state declared that there was a need to establish consumer associations across the whole country. The Consumer Association, abbreviated as *xiaoxie* in Chinese, is a nation-wide organisational network for protecting consumers' rights and interests. At the top, there is the national *xiaoxie* called in English, the 'China Consumers' Association'. The *xiaoxie* network extends to various administrative areas – there are *xiaoxie* at provincial, municipal and district levels of China. However, some of them do not share the same name, in a sense that they are not strictly called *xiaoxie* or 'Consumers' Association'. For example, a 'Consumers' Association' (*xiaoxie*) in Shanghai is indeed called 'Shanghai Consumer [Protection] Council', in Chinese, 'Shanghai Shi Xiaofeizhe Quanyi Baohu Weiyuan Hui'. Similarly, in Shenzhen, the Shenzhen Consumer Council is also a 'Council' rather than an 'Association'.

The Consumer Council in Shenzhen consists of a 'secretariat' at the municipal level, and branches in the local area. Generally, when the name 'SZCC' is used, the speaker is referring to the municipal 'secretariat' only. The district consumer councils, on the other hand, are normally called by their district names.[13] For a long time, it has not been clear to consumers and others in China as to just what type of organisation a Consumer Council or Association really is. In the 2013 Consumer Protection Law, Article 37 states that a consumer association is a 'social organisation' (*shehui zuzhi*), which has a duty to protect consumers' rights and interest.[14] The 2013 Law has to some extent clarified the 'nature' of the 'Consumer Council', but does not provide enough detail for us to understand what a 'social organisation' means in practice. Is it a public or a quasi-public body? Are staff regarded as being administrative personnel of the local government, in receipt of a governmentally-funded stable salary

[11] This practice has confused consumers in several ways. Further details about consumers' perspectives on these practices will be explored below.

[12] I have heard this name used by both ordinary citizens on the street and consumers who visit the Consumer Council with complaints. The domain name of the CC's office website – 'sz315.org' – also reflects this characterisation.

[13] For example, the consumer council in Luohu district in Shenzhen is called the Luohu Consumer Council. Therefore, hereinafter in the paper, SZCC only refers to the municipal level body.

[14] See Art 36 of the 2013 Consumer Protection Law. The old law addressed it as a 'social entity' (*shehui tuanti*).

and associated welfare benefits? The status of the organisation is probably a matter that is decided on an area-specific basis, and is largely decided by the relevant local government. It is reported that the 'secretariat' of the Consumer Council network in Shenzhen – that is, the SZCC – has recently been formally recognised as a 'work unit' (*danwei*) by the Shenzhen government.[15] In this sense, the SZCC has become a relatively independent organisation, given that its previous status was that of 'an institution attached to MSA' (*guakao danwei*). Nevertheless, this formal designation of status does not make much difference in practice – either as a 'work unit' or an 'attached institution', it is a public body supervised by the MSA.[16] It is also worth noting that the status change merely affects the municipal 'secretariat' of the Consumer Council network, the SZCC, while the status of the district Consumer Councils (district CCs) remains unclear – or in another sense, they enjoy the general status given by the law as 'social organisations'. A knowledgeable member of staff in one of the district Consumer Councils has advised me that 'only the head (of the district CC) and several decision-makers belong to the "personnel establishment of the work unit" (*shiye bianzhi*), the others are contract-based workers and do not receive the same benefits as public servants [of a work unit]'.

The funding is rather different as well. As a 'work unit', the SZCC receives funding directly from the municipal government. But for a district Consumer Council, funding largely comes from the local government's budget. The relationship between the SZCC and district Consumer Councils is interesting. On paper, these are relatively independent bodies: the district Consumer Councils are not 'branches' of the SZCC, and so they do not 'enforce' decisions made by the SZCC, and retain autonomy over matters within their own territory.[17] Nevertheless, the SZCC provides working guidance to the district Consumer Councils. There is no obvious hierarchical structure of the two levels of the Consumer Council, but my sense gained from fieldwork experience is that, in practice, a hierarchy does exist. For example, in meetings, the director of the SZCC normally gives 'instructions' and the representatives of district CC respond in a very positive way. It seems that the staff in the system tend to regard this 'hierarchy' as a type of voluntary but directed cooperation – if there are any new rules created by the SZCC, the district CCs need to follow them.

Another important aspect of the relationship between the two levels of Consumer Council is the portal function of the SZCC. Claims collected by the Hotline Centre are first passed to the SZCC, and then they are distributed to district CCs by the SZCC, and this is similar to the role of the Consumer Protection Department of the MSA. What is more, the SZCC has created its own 'portal' for consumer complaints which includes a web page based complaint portal, and a mobile application, the '315 Xiaofei Tong'.[18] But as a complaint management

[15] SZCC has recently formally become a 'work unit' (*danwei*). See news report 'Shenzhen shi Xiaoweihui Huo Shiye Danwei "Mingfen" Xietiao Xiaofeizhe Gengyou Diqi' (Shenzhen Consumer Council has Obtained the Title of a 'Work Unit' Making it Stronger in Negotiations for Consumers (*Yangcheng Evening Post*, 08 August 2014)) sz.people.com.cn/n/2014/0808/c202846-21924485.html.

[16] In the news report in n 15 above, it seems that the SZCC has gained much more independence on itself, as the word 'attached' does not appear in the name. But in fact, this change only gives a better name to the SZCC, by which its nature as a 'work unit' is clearer to the public.

[17] There are different practices in district CCs. Some have developed a system of complaint management that works effectively and is praised by the SZCC, in which case they act as a role model to other district CCs.

[18] The idea of this mobile app was introduced during the time I stayed in the SZCC, and it has since then continued to develop, and to be tested and modified. Now the technology is more mature, and it has become a relatively separate system from the 'Three-Consumer System', as the complaints are received by the SZCC directly and are circulated within the Councils only.

body, or indeed an 'ADR body', the SZCC itself also deals with various consumer complaints. There is a distribution of work between the SZCC and the district CCs. Generally speaking, claims filed against large businesses, such as China Mobile and China Unicom, chain supermarkets and department stores, are more likely handled by the SZCC, while the others are sent to the district CCs according to the location (postal address) of the business.[19] In addition, there are channels offered by district Consumer Councils for consumers to bring complaints that fall within the geographical boundaries of their jurisdiction.

D. The Flow of Work within the 'Three-Consumer System'

As mentioned above, a complaint may come to the Consumer Council from a variety of channels, and of these – the 'Three-Consumer System', a shared platform by the Hotline Centre, the Consumer Council and the MSA – is probably the most vibrant and important channel. It is worth clarifying that it is the function of these institutions in terms of consumers' access to justice that is of central concern in this chapter. However, it should not be forgotten that the MSA (as a regulator) and the Hotline Centre (as a general phone call enquiry centre) are endowed with many other responsibilities.

It is not surprising that *gongdans* are distributed several times before they reach the hand of an individual staff member. To begin with, there is the matter of the manner in which *gongdans* are circulated within the 'Three-Consumer System', in other words, how does the Hotline Centre (the collector of *gongdan*) distribute *gongdans* between the Consumer Council and the MSA? As complaint channels, the Consumer Council and the MSA may provide similar complaint handling processes, but they have different functions: the MSA is a regulatory body while the Consumer Council is not. The primary rule for the distribution of work perhaps lies in distinguishing the responsibilities of the two bodies. My sense of these matters is that there are some rules or informal practices, which give shape to this process. First, the system works on the basis that it is the consumer's request that activates the system. When she or he decides that she or he wants to bring a complaint to the Consumer Council or the MSA, then that is what triggers off the dispute resolution process. As mentioned earlier, before the new Consumer Protection Law came into force, the terms for 'complaints' for the Consumer Council and the MSA were different, as one was called '*tousu*' (for a complaint made to the Consumer Council), while the other is called *shensu* (for a complaint made to the public authority, the MSA). In practice, the way that the consumer characterises his or her complaint – whether he or she wants a '*tousu*' or '*shensu*' – may well decide the processual track of the complaint, because staff of the Hotline Centre often refer the complaints to the organisations simply by the terms used by consumers, even though it is not the consumer's intention to initiate that particular process.

Secondly, there are agreements between the Consumer Council and the MSA, according to which certain types of case are allocated to a particular organisation. A good example is the complaints that come from online shopping. Through talks with staff in the SZCC,

[19] The SZCC has established a 'fast settlement' channel for businesses that are well known and large, and this receives a relatively high number of complaints. Complaints to these businesses are kept by the SZCC and go through the 'fast settlement' channel instead. Details about the channel are provided below in the Section on 'Dispute Processes in the SZCC'.

I got to know that there are meetings held regularly between the 'Three-Consumer' organisations. One of the relatively recent meetings (held during my fieldwork) is about the distribution of *gongdans* on online shopping matters. The outcome of the meeting seems to be that the SZCC are in charge of most of the online shopping complaints,[20] and since then, *gongdans* concerning online shopping matters have been largely forwarded to the SZCC, with some further forwarded to the district Consumer Councils. In particular, due to an increasing amount of online shopping complaints in the then current year (2014), the SZCC later established a special 'working group' for dealing with online shopping complaints. As a result of further meetings on the issue of handling online shopping complaints, the Three-Consumer organisations have agreed on making the 'working group' responsible for all the online shopping matters, in the hope that it can relieve the workload pressure on district Consumer Councils and local MSA offices.[21]

Thirdly, complaints that indicate a breach of law or regulation are likely to be forwarded to the MSA rather than to the Consumer Council. Nevertheless, much is down to the way that consumers present their complaints, which means consumers need to point out in their application which organisation they would like to turn to for help. However, complaints that carry a requirement of the intervention of the administrative department may still be sent to the Consumer Council because consumers cannot tell the difference between the two bodies. This is obvious when staff in the Consumer Council reply to the complainant that what he or she claims is beyond the scope of the 'authority' of the Consumer Council, and therefore, he or she is encouraged to bring a complaint to the more 'powerful' administrative body, the MSA (or other administrative bodies), that can give administrative sanctions.[22]

After the CPD receives the complaints, they are distributed to the district MSA bureau, and further to the local MSA office. Generally, *gongdans* are distributed (forwarded) by the business' location as shown in them. Similar to the MSA, the SZCC distributes *gongdans* to district Consumer Councils in accordance with the location of the business, except those handled by the SZCC itself. With a shared Office Automation (OA) system, the dispute management bodies of the Three-Consumer System, including the SZCC, the district Consumer Councils, the district MSA bureaus, and the local MSA offices, are able to transfer *gongdans* in a very convenient way (simply by clicks).[23] There does not seem to be any standardised manual to guide them in the allocation of work. In practice, most matters are decided through daily communication, or in fact, sometimes through negotiations among the bodies. For example, whether it is okay to return a *gongdan* to the Hotline Centre and have it reallocated, is a matter that is often under discussion for one or more reasons (for example, that the *gongdan* has insufficient information, so that the complaint management body finds it difficult to handle the grievance).

[20] I also learned that this *gongdan* distribution arrangement was suggested and facilitated by the new head of the SZCC after he took office (that is, roughly, from July 2013 onwards). The new head was previously a department head from the E-commerce department of the MSA, and has experience (as well as interests) in dealing with E-commerce (online shopping) matters.

[21] The rapid growth of online shopping complaints indeed has caused many problems to the 'Three-Consumer System'.

[22] It may well be an excuse made by the Consumer Council staff so as not to handle some of the more tough cases. Further details are offered in the following Section below.

[23] Only staff in certain senior positions in the organisation are given the authority to transfer the *gongdan*.

E. Problems in the System as Perceived by Consumers

The Three-Consumer System has provided an important channel for consumer complaints. Nevertheless, there are various problems, particularly perceived by the users of the system, the consumers. One of the core issues is that consumers are often very confused with the function and authority of the complaint management bodies when they make complaints.

This issue is manifested in several ways. Complaints received by the portal (the Hotline Centre) end up in two different routes – the Consumer Council or the MSA – based on the consumer's request. As staff in the Hotline Centre normally spend a very limited time on each complaint phone call, they are likely to forward the complaints to different bodies merely by the complaint names used by consumers – those who have said 'I want to *shensu*' are likely to have their complaints dealt by the MSA, and those who have said 'I want to *tousu*' are to be sent to the Consumer Council.[24] The wording that a consumer uses to address his or her grievance would likely affect the outcome that she or he can secure from the complaint, and also may involve a waste of time in approaching the wrong complaint body. It happens that some consumers are so confused with the function of the bodies, that even though they address their grievance as '*tousu*', as this is a more general term in Chinese for any unhappy experience, their intention is to have a powerful administrative body deal with their complaint. They consider that an administrative body is able not only to help them get compensation, but can also impose some form of negative sanction on the other party in order to stop (say) an illegal commercial practice. Complainant consumers are often very angry when they make complaints, and invariably urge the 'government' (specifically, the administrative body) to take action to prevent similar things from happening in the future. They initially have high expectations regarding the outcome of their complaint. But later, when the complaint is transferred to the Consumer Council – a body that does not possess any administrative power, but shares the same 'face' as the administration – some consumers are not very happy. They are told by the Consumer Council that it cannot help them to achieve their hoped-for outcome, and the aggrieved consumer becomes frustrated. Some may even be asked to start a new complaint with different wording – that is, addressing it as a *shensu* rather than a *tousu* on the phone, so that the operator will be able to send the complaint to the MSA rather than to the Council.

To a large extent, the Consumer Council in Shenzhen resembles some of the consumer ADR bodies in European countries:[25] It provides various ADR processes to consumers, without any charge or fee, with a portal to receive consumer complaints. However, this is a public body – not only is it fully publically funded, but its structure is also hierarchical and bureaucratic in nature, especially now that the SZCC has been officially recognised as a 'work unit'. A problem with this, however, is that the lack of clarity means that many consumers are so confused that they even assume that the Consumer Council is another governmental department, and is in effect a regulator. Most of such aggrieved consumers consider they are using the regulatory redress scheme rather than a public-funded ADR-type service. Given this misunderstanding, it is perhaps not surprising that consumers may

[24] See the difference between '*shensu*' and '*tousu*', as explained in the text above.

[25] See C Hodges, N Creutzfeldt and S Macleod, *Reforming the EU Consumer ADR Landscape: Implementation and its Issues* (Report of the Third Oxford Consumer ADR Conference, Oxford, October 2014).

expect something more than an award of compensation from the Consumer Councils when they bring a complaint. They seek, also, action from the authority to investigate and crack down on illegal business practices.

In terms of handling the grievance, both the MSA and the Consumer Council provide mediation services, and their styles are very similar. As a member of staff at a local MSA office explained to a complainant, '[w]e cannot guarantee a result that is in your favour, as the mediation process is conducted on a voluntary base, and getting compensation is very much down to the business's willingness to let you have it. We cannot force a business to compensate you'. But there may be a 'psychological' difference in complaining to these two institutions – many aggrieved consumers assume that there is a higher chance of getting back his or her money if the grievance is channelled to the MSA. Indeed, theoretically speaking, the MSA dispute processes are regulatory redresses, which should be more 'powerful' – as this may include some sanctions that will stop businesses from harming consumers through their misconduct or negligence. However, what consumers are primarily concerned with is not about helping to maintain a clean and orderly market, or other responsibilities of the administration. They care primarily about securing redress in their own case, and they think the MSA's array of sanctions means that defendant businesses will make more concessions in an MSA mediation.

It seemed to me that consumers tend to consider that the reason why the MSA emphasises its role as an impartial 'mediator' (rather than a regulator), is to avoid responsibility for a mediated outcome that does not really satisfy the parties. It may be that the authority, as it claims, tries to be impartial on the matter. While in practice, it may well be that the authority can actually impose subtle 'pressure' on a defendant business so that it will behave better. From what I observed during fieldwork, the consumers do believe in the MSA's capacity to exert pressure, and there is a good reason for such belief. The local MSA (SAIC) office is given so much authority in the system, and it administers issues relating to the 'defendant' business over almost every aspect of its commercial activity. As a result, businesses generally do not wish to cause any trouble for the MSA. If a consumer is tough, and robustly annoys the MSA office, it is very likely that the MSA will then persuade the business to make some concessions so as to calm the consumer down, in the spirit that the business is doing a 'favour' for the MSA and expects to remain in the 'good books' of the MSA. The business has good reason to believe that if the business does not 'obey' MSA wishes, the MSA officer may create obstacles for the business on other administrative matters. As some MSA staff described the situation to me, 'the business (in the local MSA's jurisdiction) are living under the same sky as the MSA officers – even if they do not see each other when they bow, they do see each other when they look up.'[26]

III. Dispute Processes in the SZCC

This part of the chapter explores the manner in which a complaint goes through the relevant processes within the SZCC. The SZCC receives complaints from various channels: a phone call to the 12315 consumer hotline; a complaint form filled on the SZCC's official website or

[26] This is a Chinese saying, *di tou bu jian, tai tou jian*.

through the *Xiaofei Tousu Tong* mobile application, and other communication means such as sending letters and paying visits to the Consumer Councils in person. According to official data, the Consumer Council (including the SZCC and other district Consumer Councils) deals with more than 20,000 complaints (cases) each year, and a substantial number of them were dealt with by the SZCC. The number of cases dealt with by the Consumer Council surpasses the number of consumer cases that the courts deal with annually in Shenzhen. The Consumer Council has indeed helped a great deal to reduce the workload of the court, since most of the grievances are settled within the Consumer Council and do not proceed to litigation.

A. Complaint Acceptance

As a portal for grievances brought to the Consumer Council, the SZCC accepts complaints, and distributes a portion of the *gongdans* to the Consumer Council in each district. A particular member of staff working in the Complaint Department of the SZCC is in charge of the distribution of *gongdans*. He or she is able to see all the *gongdan* that are forwarded to the Consumer Council by the Hotline Centre. Also, for paper-based complaints, such as those made by letter, or by complaint forms filled on site, the staff member needs to key into the computer the information contained in the paper and to create a *gongdan* in the system. As a complaint management body, the SZCC also deals with part of the registered complaints that are received by it. The same person working in the Complaint Department is in charge of the distribution of *gongdans* among staff members in the SZCC. Because of this combined function of the SZCC, if a case is accepted by the SZCC then this means that it is a case that may be circulated within the Consumer Council system, and is possible to be dealt with by one of the district Consumer Councils. Accordingly, the case acceptance standards of the municipal council and district councils are probably not very different, despite the fact that some cases involve businesses operating over the whole city, while other cases only concern local matters that have arisen within that district.

The types of case accepted by the SZCC cover a wide range. In terms of value, claims ranging from several hundred RMB upwards are handled. Some complaints may not even contain any monetary claim, as consumers only want an apology from the 'defendant' business. Although there is no financial cap on the claims, nevertheless, the vast majority are relatively small claims. During my stay in the SZCC, I observed successful settlement of cases in which the agreed compensation was above 10,000RMB, and have witnessed housing complaints with claims for refund of money handed over for residential property purchases for up to several hundred thousand RMB. On the other hand, many complaints against the telecommunication companies such as China Mobile, can be as small as 5 or 10RMB, as they concern grievances over relatively minor matters such as the excessive charge of a monthly plan or phone calls.

The case acceptance system is in fact very informal and flexible. There are no clear guidelines as to what constitutes a suitable case for handling by consumer council processes. Cases accepted by the SZCC cover almost every aspect of consumption, including home and electrical appliances; houses and apartments, interior decoration and building materials; services (such as telecommunication, travel, education, matchmaking and so on); and, grocery and daily necessities.[27] In theory, the SZCC is supposed to accept complaints that are made by 'consumers' – as defined in Article 2 of the Consumer Protection Law 2013 namely, that a consumer is a person or organisation who purchases goods or receive services for the daily consumption purposes.[28] This means that in law the SZCC may refuse to deal with the types of complaint brought by those that may not be considered as a 'consumer' by the law,[29] such as grievances regarding provision of medical services and purchases of property. However, in practice, the standard of case acceptance of the SZCC seems to be broader than the scope of the Consumer Protection Law (which is supposed to be the dominant law for determining the standard). It is shown that complaints concerning medical services or purchases of property are sometimes accepted by the SZCC, but there are some restrictions. As a staff member in the SZCC has explained the matter to me, generally, complaints accepted by the SZCC concern simple issues, such as unreasonable charges of medical services or purchases made due to misleading advertisement of properties. The more complicated cases, such as complaints that concern the duty of care of a doctor that are not easy to classify, are likely to be refused and the consumer is instead encouraged by the SZCC to take their case either to the court or to relevant regulatory bodies of hospitals.

My observation of the working practices of the SZCC, revealed that there are probably some shared understandings of how best to handle certain types of claim. One such understanding is perhaps that the acceptance of a case is shaped by the SZCC's ability to provide meaningful help. As for cases which require expertise in a certain area, the staff members in SZCC simply feel that they do not possess the expert knowledge to handle them. It also seems that cases accepted by the SZCC are mainly disputes focussed upon contractual issues, where the consumers' main claim is to seek monetary compensation. Another shared understanding is that if a claim is clearly based in an assertion of illegality – that a seller or a producer has broken the law in causing the problem – then the likely decision would be to forward the complaint to the MSA (the Consumer Protection Department), because the SZCC does not hold any administrative power to close down the illegal business; or, to accept the case while explaining to the consumer that the SZCC can only help them to get compensation through mediation. Also, it seems that for the matters that are difficult to decide, the final decision on whether or not to accept a case for Consumer Council processing often is a matter for the Consumer Council leaders' personal judgement. When difficult cases occur, the staff member in charge of *gongdan* first discusses such a case with the head of the Complaint Department and seeks his permission on the acceptance decision. He or the head of the Complaint department may later consult other department heads (often, it is the head of the Legal Affairs Department), or eventually, the vice-head or head of the SZCC on the matter.

Therefore, there can be exceptions on case acceptance from the general understanding, as long as permission is granted by the SZCC 'leaders'. An exception can be made, for example, on a complicated grievance that the complainant has tried almost every possible complaint channel before he comes to the SZCC and they all fail completely to resolve the

[27] The list is created with reference to the semiannual report provided by the SZCC in October 2013.

[28] Art 2 of the 1993 Consumer Protection Law provides that 'The rights and interests of consumers in purchasing and using commodities or receiving services for daily consumption shall be protected by the present Law'.

[29] See the discussion on the legal definition of consumer in ch 2.

problem (in a sense that the complainant did not achieve his or her goal for the complaint).[30] On an exceptional basis, the SZCC may even accept a case that has already been litigated. I have seen complaints in which consumers have gone through the litigation processes on the same matter, but failed to have the judgement enforced by the defendant business; or, situations where consumers have secured a judgement but considered it unfair, and instead, hope to get a fairer outcome through a mediation process under the assumed 'authority' of the SZCC.

Staff members in the SZCC take the view that Shenzhen's neighbour, Hong Kong, has taken a very different approach to the acceptance of consumer complaints. One staff member in particular, who is in charge of cross-border complaints in the SZCC, informs me that the policy of the Hong Kong Consumer Council is to accept mainly large impact cases, while the Shenzhen Consumer Council policy is to accept cases of all kinds, and most of the cases handled tend to be 'small matters'. A good example that he provides is consumer disputes which arise in the border area (a shopping street) between Shenzhen and Hong Kong known as *Zhong Ying Jie* (or Chung Ying Street).[31] As a border street, the jurisdiction of the shops in *Zhong Ying Jie* are divided in two – half of the shops fall within the jurisdiction of Shenzhen, while the other half come under the jurisdiction of Hong Kong. However, in practice, the vast majority of cases have gone to the Shenzhen Consumer Council because they do not reach the threshold for filing a complaint to the HK Consumer Council. Since most of the shoppers come from the mainland, when they fail to make a complaint to the HK Consumer Council, they will instead have a complaint registered in the Shenzhen Consumer Council, even if the dispute arose in a shop within the HK Council's jurisdiction.

It is worth noting that a large number of disputes that the Consumer Council has dealt with recently, do in fact arise from online shopping. These disputes involve various problems. One of the most annoying problems that the SZCC faces is that the address and contact information of online sellers provided by consumers are very hard to reach, or may even not exist. As a result, it is very difficult to settle them by the traditional dispute resolution methods of the SZCC – that is, by mediation on-site or through phone calls. So at this stage, as staff in the Council suggest, they are more like a point for collecting information of such disputes, rather than actually resolving them.

B. Hejie

In recent years, the SZCC has established a special channel for the 'fast settlement' of consumer disputes. The channel is called '*xiaofei zhengyi hejie tongdao*', meaning the 'amicable settlement channel for consumer disputes'. This channel is used by businesses that have come to enjoy a good reputation for fair trading or a willingness to cooperate in order to

[30] I would think that the purpose for accepting these cases is in fact to avoid any more social problems created by the complainant.

[31] *Zhong Ying Jie* is a shopping street created in the colonial time of Hong Kong right on the border between Shenzhen (mainland China) and Hong Kong. The shops there mainly sell imported goods, such as luxury foreign-brand watches and handbags. *Zhong Ying Jie* was very prosperous before 1997 because of the restriction for Chinese people going to Hong Kong to shop. Now it is still an important shopping street that sells various goods coming from Hong Kong.

settle claims against them. Such businesses are given the title of '*hejie shifan qiye*', meaning 'a demonstration business for amicable settlement'. The SZCC has created a rule that complaints made to the businesses with the channel are to be handled by the SZCC. As mentioned earlier in this chapter, most of the businesses within this channel (that is, the '*hejie shifan qiye*') are large and reputable businesses, such as state-owned enterprises, China Mobile, China Telecom and China Unicom. They are actively encouraged by the SZCC to take part in this 'fast-track' settlement system. The number of complaints against a business is also one of the SZCC's reasons for putting that business into this fast settlement channel. Large businesses normally receive more complaints than small streetside businesses, and have a business model that is more systematic and responsive to consumer queries, so that meaningful negotiation with such businesses is much more likely to happen.

The 'amicable settlement channel', *hejie tongdao*, is primarily where a negotiation process is carried out under the supervision of the SZCC. The Chinese term for the basic nature of this process, *hejie*, is a difficult term to translate in the sense of identifying its precise meaning. The term *hejie* is often translated as 'conciliation' in official documents in China. However, in this context, I see *hejie* as a facilitative style of mediation process offered by the *hejie tongdao* (amicable settlement channel), with the parties being given 'light-touch' third-party assistance with their otherwise bilateral negotiations, and without involving a direct evaluation by the third party mediator. It therefore differs from *tiaojie* (mediation), for the latter can involve a much more evaluative style of 'mediation', as that process is understood in ADR discourse, as well as sometimes also being more facilitative in style.[32]

The process of *hejie* is used initially, and only if it fails will the SZCC management of the dispute move to a *tiaojie* or mediation process. So, there is a sequential or staged handling of the case. When a consumer makes a complaint to the SZCC against a business with the settlement channel, a *gongdan* containing the information of the registered complaint is forwarded to the business through the SZCC's office automation (OA) system. The settlement channel thus clearly saves enormous amounts of time and labour of the Consumer Council. With such a channel, basically, staff members only need to click on the computer to forward the *gongdan* to the defendant business. The business is then required to contact the consumer, initiating the 'negotiation', without direct intervention by the SZCC. The Consumer Council staff will sometimes make a telephone call to the business if the latter's response is delayed, or ring the consumer to check the progress, but is not likely to provide any guidance or advice that would affect the decision-making of both parties. The facilitation provided by a staff member is very minimal, and focuses on procedure matters. In this way, the staff member who handles the complaint in the SZCC plays the role of a remote facilitator or 'case supervisor', rather than directly assisting the parties to resolve their differences as a neutral third party intervener.[33] In Riskin's terminology, the SZCC intervention

[32] In the mid-1990s, Leonard Riskin introduced the distinction between the classical model of mediation in which third party mediatory intervention was primarily limited to facilitating communication between the disputing parties, and the emerging practice of 'evaluative mediation' in which the mediator offered assessments or evaluations of the parties' positions, predicted likely outcomes if the case went to court, offered possible settlement solutions and so on. See, L Riskin, 'Understanding Mediator's Orientations, Strategies and Technique: A Grid for the Perplexed' (1996) 1 *Harvard Negotiation Law Review* 7.

[33] It seems that what a staff member actually does is to facilitate the negotiation process – essentially playing the role as a 'facilitator'. However, because of the public nature of the SZCC, the effect of the facilitation is more persuasive than that by a private body, so in a sense, he or she may seem more like a 'supervisor' of the process.

in the *hejie* process is not only facilitative in nature but also very narrow in scope. During this *hejie* process, indeed, it is often the business party rather than the SZCC who offers a settlement plan for resolving the consumers' grievance.

One may wonder, what is the difference between *hejie*, in which the disputing parties' exchanges are facilitated by the SZCC, and the kind of negotiation that happens when consumers use the in-house redress scheme of the business? The answer to this question lies in the relative effectiveness of supervision by the SZCC. From my fieldwork observations, I learned that it is often the case that, within a company, there are two differing sets of personnel dealing with consumer complaints. One set comprises those people who are responsible for dealing with complaints that come from the SZCC through the settlement channel. These people tend to be employees in higher positions within the business than those employees who deal with complaints that come directly from the consumers. Moreover, my feedback from aggrieved consumers with whom I discussed these matters was that the employees whom they face when using the company's internal complaint scheme are often less polite, less willing to compromise, and have less technical and commercial knowledge about the relevant issue. What is more, a consumer who fails to get compensation in the business internal complaint scheme, and then learns of the SZCC's *hejie* process, may in fact be able to secure a favourable result if she or he then brings a complaint through the *hejie* settlement channel 'set up' by the SZCC. This often happens when the consumer is not clearly right as a matter of law, but because the business has become tired of the case and fears that further trouble may arise, particularly as the progress of the case is now being monitored by the SZCC, decides it is best to make some concessions and to reach agreement with the complaining consumer by offering a modest sum of money in compensation.

There may not be a strict and clear line between a *hejie* process and a *tiaojie* process. However, it is worth mentioning that the staff in the Council do not see themselves as 'mediating' (in the sense of *tiaojie*) in the *hejie* process. The *hejie* process is perhaps intended primarily for the convenience of the staff members so as to reduce their workload, and is probably described in terms by the staff on the basis of their allocation of work – with some doing little more than clicking the mouse on their computers, but others being a little more interventionist and making a couple of telephone calls or more. Nevertheless, from an analytical point of view, it is clear that the *hejie* process is not simple bilateral negotiation between the parties, as the parties move through the resolution process and construct their agreement in the shadow of the facilitative and narrow supervision of the SZCC.

C. Tiaojie

Tiaojie is the most important dispute process in the Consumer Council. In the Council, there are two types of *tiaojie*, namely, *tiaojie* via telephone and on-site *tiaojie*. As mentioned earlier, the *tiaojie* process is a mediation process, although in the SZCC context it covers quite a diversity of mediatory style. In the *tiaojie* process, sometimes the mediator may be quite evaluative and interventionist in approach, giving the parties his or her opinions on the position of the parties and making suggestions for the case when it seems appropriate during the mediation session. This approach is perhaps encouraged by the fact that there is no explicit ethical norm requiring that the mediator be impartial. However, at other points in the dispute handling process, the SZCC mediators may be primarily facilitative in the intervention. Moreover, individual mediators have their own 'orientations' or preferred style of mediatory intervention. Thus, in the SZCC *tiaojie*, the mediator may be willing to offer opinions and suggestions quite readily, so that the general style is both evaluative and, in Riskin's terminology, broad in nature, but at other times, is content to be a facilitator of communications between the parties. Whatever approach the mediator takes, the core in a *tiaojie* is by no means a mere facilitation of the conversations. At any point in the exchanges, the mediator can interrupt to distinguish right from wrong, educate the parties on their conduct, like a parent or guardian, or as happens most of the time, nudge the conversation forward in the consumer's interest and persuade the business into making a further compromise on the deal to satisfy the aggrieved consumers.

i. *Tiaojie via Telephone*

In this process, the mediator, usually the staff member handling the case, will initiate the contact with the consumer. There are two further situations: if the complaint is one against a large business with the settlement channel, this process normally comes after process of *hejie* – amicable settlement – which means that efforts to achieve an agreement have been attempted at least once by the parties (sometimes twice, if the consumer has gone through the in-house redress scheme offered by the company), but failed. If the complaint is not one against the large business with the settlement channel, the complaint will then be mediated (*tiaojie*) immediately after it has been registered.

The mediator normally first makes a telephone call to the consumer, listens to his or her version of the story and gains as much information as she or he can about the dispute. Since a large number of complaints are made to the Council through the 12315 hotline, the complaint is written down (recorded) not by the staff in the SZCC but, rather, by the operator from the Hotline Centre. Staff in the SZCC can only read the limited information provided in the *gongdan*. It is sometimes the case that what is written on the sheet is rather different from what is claimed by the aggrieved consumer, and this is probably down to the mishearing of information by the Centre's staff, since they each normally do not spend more than five minutes on the phone for each complaint. After the complaint has been recorded, the SZCC staff member will seek a solution primarily in terms of the consumer's interests. With the consumer's claims and some possible solutions in mind, she or he then rings the business, seeking to negotiate a settlement deal.

So, one may find that, in this process, it is almost impossible for the 'mediators' to talk to both parties at the same time. Mediators have to talk to the parties separately (use caucusing) throughout the whole resolution process. In order to help to overcome this problem, the SZCC is considering some processual innovations: there are suggestions for the creation of an online mediation room (*zaixian tiaojieshi*) using increasingly popular 'chatting software', or even to use an ODR website to mediate disputes. This would also be helpful in saving time and money. However, making phone calls is still considered by consumers as the most convenient way to make complaints and resolve disputes, especially for senior citizens who do not know how to use the Internet, and in fact, most of the complaints received by the Consumer Council are from phone calls. The SZCC is contemplating these innovations, but as of the time my fieldwork was completed in late 2014, it had not yet established any such schemes.

ii. On-Site Tiaojie

On-site *tiaojie*, as the term suggests, is a process in which the disputing parties are gathered together in the SZCC for face-to-face *tiaojie*. This is the most traditional type of *tiaojie* practised by the Council, and shares some of the features of the dispute resolution processes used in *renmin tiaojie* (people's mediation, that is, community mediation) in China.

These features include: first, the *tiaojie* is in every aspect, very informal. Mediators are not required to have special expertise, nor to receive mediation training, and any member of staff in the SZCC may mediate. The *tiaojie* process and outcome is conducted on a voluntary basis.

Secondly, the mediation agreement can be easily revoked or withdrawn – if one party (usually the consumer) is not satisfied with an outcome, then she or he walks out of the venue. Also, his or her civil right to litigation is preserved, as is the right to bring the same complaint to the SZCC again. This randomness has indeed caused many problems in the SZCC. In addition to the problem of repeat complaints, the business may also delay the enforcement of the mediated result. In particular, because sometimes the mediator did not initiate the drafting of the written mediation agreement (*tiaojieshu*), and the parties have only an oral agreement, this normally reduces the incentive for enforcement of the terms of the agreement.

Thirdly, and as we have indicated above, the style of the mediation is largely dependent on the mediator. In technical terms, the mediator can choose to be more 'facilitative' or more 'evaluative' during the *tiaojie* process. These two styles may be used in turn within one mediation at different stages of the *tiaojie* process, or may be applied to different disputing consumers and businesses with different personalities. Also, some mediators are broader, and others narrower, in the scope of their intervention – and this too can vary at different points in the *tiaojie* process.

Normally a mediator will decide on his or her own principles for conducting mediation. There are Council principles pasted on the wall of the mediation room – however, they are more of the nature of 'moral' principles than legal norms, and in effect, neither the mediators nor the parties really pay much attention to them. The most fundamental and unchangeable principle for the mediator, as I would conclude the matter, is this: 'to resolve a dispute so as to prevent from complaints being made to the Consumer Council again'.

IV. Conclusions

In this chapter, we have examined the principal features of the approach of the Shenzhen Consumer Council to handling consumer grievances, and its associate bodies in the Three-Consumer Complaint System, the Hotline Centre and the Market Supervision Administration Bureau. As a gateway for consumer complaints, the Hotline Centre is more than a passive receiver of complaints. It also guides consumers through the complaint procedures. The manner in which it records the complaint story and creates a *gongdan* (a work sheet of registered complaint) may determine whether or not the complaint is sent to an appropriate complaint management body as the consumer hopes. In terms of complaint handling processes, the two complaint management bodies, that is the MSA and the SZCC, are quite similar – both provide mediation services of an informal nature. However, they are also two rather different bodies, as the MSA is a regulator while the SZCC is not. What often causes problems is that consumers cannot easily distinguish between the nature of the SZCC and the MSA, as both of them are public-funded and they share the same complaint portal. Often aggrieved consumers are disappointed to find that the SZCC does not have the necessary regulatory authority by means of which the seller of a faulty article might be made not only to redress the consumer grievance, but is also subjected to regulatory or even criminal sanctions. When making complaints, consumers believe that either of the two bodies – the MSA or the SZCC – should be able to use governmental authority to help them to secure favourable outcomes. In reality, it is only the MSA that possesses this regulatory power. The aggrieved consumers' misconception tends to give them unrealistic expectations about the results they can obtain from the complaint system. In the later stages of the complaint process, these inflated expectations can come to impede the narrowing of differences between the consumer and the defendant business in the negotiation or mediation processes. The problem, at the most fundamental level, arises because many ordinary Shenzhen residents continue to hold the view that the role of government is much more than simply to create a level playing field. The strong powers of government in China should be matched by broad social protection responsibilities, and so it does not seem natural to many aggrieved consumers that the government should set up a body such as the Consumer Council with 'mere' dispute resolution functions. It should also have regulatory teeth.

The chapter has also explored the manner in which the system handles consumer complaints. As we have emphasised, the strong continuing emphasis on governmental power and responsibility is one of the most important factors encouraging consumer views of the SZCC as a crucially important avenue for securing consumer justice. As outlined in this chapter, disputes are handed by the system in terms of their size and their complexity, and by a sequential mix of processes – most notably, by facilitated dialogue between the parties and then mediation if negotiations fail.

4

Consuming the Consumer Council: Complainants' Experience

I. Introduction

As earlier chapters have shown, the Consumer Council has become an important channel for consumer complaints in Shenzhen, and provides various kinds of consumer redress schemes for bringing together the parties in order to assist them to resolve their problems. In this chapter, the research shifts from the organisation to the consumer complainants themselves. It offers a detailed account of consumers' experiences with the dispute processes of the SZCC – the language which consumers use to express their grievances, the way they conduct themselves and respond to the other side in negotiation, the feelings they have about what is going on in the dispute handling process and the obstacles they may well encounter in their attempts to secure access to consumer justice.

Among the various complaint handling processes provided by the SZCC, on-site mediation is probably the most important statistically. It is also the most vibrant and approachable forum for observing the manner in which consumers pursue their grievance in the Council. As an example, I have selected one mediation meeting for analysis of the language used by the consumer, her performance, and the interaction in the mediation meeting between the consumer and the businesses against whom the consumer has brought a complaint. The reasons for selecting the case are not methodologically rigorous. It has been chosen because it illustrates aspects of consumer grievance handling within the SZCC that in my observational experience seem to be among the most important.

The chapter then explores the types of complainant and the processual problems they face when bringing their grievances to the Consumer Council (including both the SZCC and the district councils). Here, too, specific cases will be given as examples for illustrating important aspects of the complaint handling process. The types of complainant and the processual problems faced are crystallised inductively from my intensive participant observation conducted in the SZCC, through which the author has direct contact with most of the aggrieved consumers. Thus, what this chapter provides is primarily a close look at the consumers, while in some exceptional situations, perspectives from the staff members of the SZCC may also be drawn upon, especially where I do not have full access to some of the stages of an unfolding case.

II. Case Study of On-site Mediation

In analysing the case below, the present study draws loosely on Gulliver's developmental model of negotiation and mediation, as this provides a good general model for examining the progress of a dispute handling process.[1] Essentially this approach sees dispute resolution as moving through sequential phases (not all of which may necessarily be completed or pursued rigorously in the suggested order): forum (in this case, the SZCC), agenda (the parties decide on what it is they will agree to talk about), the opening statements (usually the most expansive of claims, and often involving venting), narrowing of differences (in which the parties become more cooperative), preliminaries to final bargaining, final bargaining, agreement and celebration and enforcement of award.

A. The Dry Cleaning Case

Ms Lu was a very loyal customer at her local dry cleaning shop – one of the branches of the XYZ Dry Cleaning Company located near her home. However, a recent event (which took place on 18 October 2013) in the shop had made her unhappy and troubled about the service provided by the business, and as a result, she filed a complaint against the Dry Cleaning Company online through the SZCC's website.

The complaint was accepted, and it came to one of the staff in the SZCC for handling. Because the defendant business is one of the 'large complaint receivers' (*tousu dahu*) – which also means that it is most likely a 'repeat player' – it had an already-established fast settlement channel with the SZCC, and the case had initially gone through a fast settlement, that is, a '*hejie*' process. However, as recorded on the complaint flowchart of the Office Automation (OA) System (the computer based working platform shared by the Three Consumer System bodies), while the defendant business had attempted this initial negotiation with the complainant, the parties had in fact failed to reach an agreement. The Company noted in the OA system, '[w]e rang the client several times, but the client made unreasonable demands, and the phone calls were cut off by the client [in the end]. Now we decline to negotiate with this client anymore'.

As Ms Lu described her grievance in her complaint form, a dress that she had taken to the shop for dry cleaning had been damaged during the cleaning process and could hardly be worn anymore. So, the problem was goods damaged while in the care of the company ('naming'), and the company was at fault ('blaming').[2] She then secured an oral agreement with the shop staff: she could bring in some clothes for dry cleaning for free, as a way to compensate her for the damage caused to the dress ('claiming').[3] A few weeks later, she brought five items of clothing to the shop for dry cleaning. The staff took all of her clothes. However, only two garments were formally recorded on the receipt given to her as being taken in for cleaning. Ms Lu was worried that the staff would forget about the other three garments, so she insisted that they too be added to the receipt. As a result, the staff inserted an additional sentence 'plus two leather jackets and a coat' in an empty space on the receipt.

[1] P Gulliver, *Disputes and Negotiations: A Cross-Cultural Perspective* (New York, Academic Press 1979).

[2] That is, the 'grievance' that had emerged out of a 'perceived injurious experience', to use the terminology for dispute development to be found in W Felstiner, R Abel and A Sarat, 'The Emergence and Transformation of Disputes: Naming, Blaming, Claiming …' (1980) 15 *Law and Society Review* 631.

[3] ibid.

After a week or so (on 13 September), Ms Lu visited the shop again, giving the staff some more clothes. While paying the charges, she checked the balance on her membership card, and discovered that her credit balance was down by more than 100RMB. The staff explained to her that the reduced credit balance might be the result of an error by the computer of their company. Ms Lu initially believed this to be the case. However, at the same time (in the shop), she rang a senior member of staff in the company and asked for an explanation, just to be sure. She did not get a reply immediately, but was told to wait for a few days so that the company could check the situation for her.

After that, Ms Lu paid several visits to the shop to collect her cleaned garments. The latest visit she made, on 18 October, was to collect her final item, one of the leather jackets, and also to ask about the credit situation on her card for one last time. When checking the condition of the leather jacket, she discovered two small holes in the back of it, which she believed had been caused by carelessness during the cleaning process. She then found out that there was another receipt, drafted after her first visit, containing the information on the other three garments – two leather jackets and a coat. She took a look at the newly discovered receipt, and was shocked by the fact that her leather jackets had been recorded incorrectly as 'artificial leather jackets'. What is more, on making another phone call to the company about the problem of the reduced credits on her card, she learned that the company's view was that 'lost money' was in effect her own expenditure incurred on the day when the unknown receipt was drafted. In other words, she had in fact been charged for garments which the parties had agreed would be cleaned without charge. She was very angry about this development, as it did not make any sense to her – she had not visited the shop on the day in question, and her signature was not on the receipt.

Ms Lu had a fierce row with the staff in the shop. She described on the complaint form this turn of events in the following terms:

> I was trying to collect my leather jacket (on that day). The staff member serving me in the shop behaved in a very bad manner. He started shouting at me, calling me 'shameless' (*buyao lian*). Then he even kicked the red plastic chair that I was about to sit on, and he almost made me fall over as a result. The leather jacket was my personal belonging. But he did not let me take it back, and even telephoned some friends, ordering them to 'take care of' me (*shoushi wo*). I felt my personal safety was threatened, so I had to call 110 (the police). With the help of the police, I got back my leather jacket, but it was then that I discovered that there were now two holes in it and some obvious tarnish on the back of the jacket.

The mediator, a staff member in the SZCC in charge of handling cases at the mediation stage, was given the case when the parties failed to reach an amicable settlement by themselves. As I observed in the office, normally he – as would other SZCC colleagues in a similar position – would make a phone call to each party to hear their versions of events again and to try to narrow down their differences over the phone. If the disagreement is still significant, he would then seek the parties' willingness to participate in face-to-face mediation. Ms Lu's case was one such case. The on-site mediation of Ms Lu was scheduled for two days after the business's reply in the fast settlement system (that is, one week after the registration of the case).[4]

[4] The time varies significantly, depending on the timetable of both parties, and the workload of the mediator. In this case, it was very fast. There are some guidelines setting out the general schedule. As the SZCC working

On the day of the mediation meeting, two staff members from the business side, a female business representative (Ms Peng) and the male shop assistant (Mr Sun) who had had a row with the complainant, arrived first. Ms Lu, a middle-aged lady who speaks with a strongly northern Chinese accent, arrived several minutes late. The parties sat around a large square meeting table, with one party on each side. The mediator, Mr Li, who was also the case handler, sat at the other side of the table in between the parties. The atmosphere was rather casual and relaxed. When both parties were ready for discussion, the mediator first gave some words of hope and encouragement, and encouraged good conduct during the mediation without specifying any particular ground rules: 'Today we are here to solve the problem … Hope that you can all be more tolerant and understanding (of each other)'. He then kicked off the meeting by asking the complainant to describe her grievance. So without clearly defining the agenda, as one might expect from the Gulliver developmental model, Mr Li got things going by asking the complainant orally to restate her case.

Indeed, in the following almost a quarter of hour, Ms Lu explained in some detail and with some passion what had happened to her, focusing particularly on the arguments that she had with the young shop assistant. She described her grievance in a very meticulous way – she recalled the time she visited the shop down to the exact minute; how she addressed the young shop assistant and how he answered; how she took pictures and sent them to the senior staff in the company for support; how the police came and urged the shop assistant to return the damaged leather jacket to her; even how the two guys who wandered around the shop were dressed (and whom she assumed had been called to the scene by the shop assistant), and so on. She re-emphasised what she saw as key facts – that she did not sign the unknown receipt, did not show up in shop when the unknown receipt was formed, did not know the leather jacket was recorded as an 'artificial' leather jacket, and so on. She even believed that the missing credits were indeed consumed by the shop assistant, as she was so surprised to find out that they were not caused by a computer error. However, it seemed that some of the facts were still confusing for her, so that for example, on one hand, she said on 3 September she brought the five items to the shop for free cleaning, but later she referred to the event as happening on 4 September. She had presented the receipts several times to the mediator, but could not remember when she had and had not done so. At various points she raised her voice, showing that she was extremely angry (her anger seemed to me quite genuine) with what had happened to her and which she was now recalling. This was the 'venting' conduct which, as Gulliver points out, is often found when aggrieved parties make their opening statement.

Ms Lu's account was barely interrupted, except that the mediator asked her at several points to clarify some 'missing facts': for example, 'did he give you anything [other than an oral agreement] for your damaged dress', or 'did you take a copy of the receipt for the cleaning of the five items, since now you have issue with one of these items, namely

guideline states, 'staff member must inform the complainant of acceptance of the complaint within 2 days' … 'the settlement process should last no more than six days … if parties fail to reach an agreement, staff member should seek their agreement for mediation', and 'the mediation of the case must be finished by within 10 working days'. The guideline also gives the staff member extra days for handling cases at each stage, if the case is considered to be complicated. In practice, there is no strict limit of the time spent by the staff member on a specific case.

the leather jacket'.[5] In other words, the mediator was quite skilfully allowing Ms Lu to vent, while at the same time trying to get her to be more precise about the facts of the dispute, as she had experienced them. The business representative and the shop assistant, at this stage, did not say a single word. After hearing the story from the complainant, the mediator offered a few thoughts, which seemed like both a very polite expression of his opinion and an attempt at facilitating the parties' mutual understanding of each other. He spoke to the shop assistant:

> Well, Mr. Sun, let me tell you something. Doing business means that you need to wear a smile all the time … Ms. Lu lives in your neighbourhood and she often comes to your shop. Not just her, she probably has friends or family who live nearby and come to 'consume' in your shop too … I would suggest you do not call her names. And even if you have called her [bad] names, I don't think you should [make the matter worse and] shout at her nor ask her to get out of the shop. This is not what 'doing business' should be about.

He then asked the shop assistant to respond to the complainant's allegations.

Mr Sun, the shop assistant, explained to the mediator that the terms of oral agreement for free cleaning were not as Ms Lu had assumed them to be. Mr Sun gave her a free cleaning option equivalent to 200RMB – which was, in effect, a 'ten-times' monetary compensation for the damaged dress, according to trade standards, rather than free cleaning of 'five items' as had been claimed by Ms Lu. He continued his explanation by claiming that the leather jacket had mildew when it was received in the shop, and had been returned to the factory for re-cleaning several times already.

The mediator addressed him, giving him some friendly advice, 'If this [the above mentioned matter] happens again, you should probably write down the problem, such as, there is mildew and the mildew cannot [easily] be wiped off, and then ask the consumer to sign the piece of paper.' Mr Sun explained his failure to carry out this course of action:

> This person [Ms. Lu] is a regular customer, a loyal one. Before this, we had pleasant conversations like old friends, about domestic trivia (*jiachang*), and so on. I never thought about keeping any proof [about the mildew problem] … I am the sort of person, you know, [who is good], you're good, I'm good, and everybody's good … I am not at all a cunning person … The day she brought her six items to my shop[6] … it was very late. She took out three items, the two leather jackets and a coat, and asked me to clean them for her for free, but I said the price for these three would be more than the amount of money allowed for in the compensation, so she would have to pay the excess price.

However, later in the mediation meeting Ms Lu argued that the shop assistant, Mr Sun, did not explain any of these qualifications to her, nor was she aware of the 200RMB limit for free cleaning. It was further revealed that, according to Mr Sun's explanation, he tried

[5] Ms Lu submitted the receipt to the shop assistant, in order to collect her clean laundry. As she got back all her clean laundry (including the leather jacket with damages), she would not be able to keep the receipt anymore. She also answered to the question that, normally, consumers checked the clean clothes in the shop, and if there was a problem, they would argue with the shop assistant right away and had it solved on site. She had not thought about copying the original receipt for claiming for damages (she found out the damages after she submitted the receipt for collecting). The receipt was in the hands of the shop assistant, and it was later presented in the mediation.

[6] The two parties had different stories about the number of items Ms Lu had brought to the shop, but this did not obstruct the flow of negotiation between them. This is because the focus of the case was on the claims brought by the complainant, which was indeed about compensation for the damaged leather jacket.

to reduce the price by recording the three free-cleaning items on another receipt (the unknown receipt). He put down the 'leather jackets' as 'artificial leather jackets', so as to keep the price down to 200RMB on paper (or, more specifically, on the unknown receipt). But, in fact, he had sent the leather jackets to the 'leather department' of the cleaning company's factory, and asked the factory staff there to do him a special favour, using the cleaning process for genuine leather. He also claimed that he had to make a phone call to the company manager, and to the factory staff, in order to secure their agreement to this 'ruse'. He could not draft the receipt on the same day when Ms Lu visited the shop because it was too late in the evening, and the money in Ms Lu's membership card had indeed been used for the cleaning of some of her other items.

When the shop assistant, Mr Sun, was telling his version of the story, the complainant consumer, Ms Lu, kept interrupting and arguing on some facts, and it seemed that the mediator was letting her do this. A fuller story had unfolded with the shop assistant's response, and she clearly was in disagreement with his version of events. However, from my observer's point of view, some of the facts recounted by the parties were rather blurred and confusing, and even offered a contradictory picture. I suspect that there were mainly two reasons for the lack of clear communication: first, the parties chose not to reveal those facts which spoke against themselves, as they were trying to be defensive and therefore 'strategic with the truth' in the mediation.[7] Secondly, the mediation took place some time ago, and so the parties did not always remember their story about the dispute very clearly.[8] On the other hand, the accuracy of the factual background did not seem to bother the mediator too much. Indeed, his strategy was to try to stop the parties from dwelling on and elaborating factual detail. He addressed them, for example, saying 'well, it is no use that you keep arguing about what has happened (*chepi*)'; 'I told you that the more you argue (*che*), the less productive you would be'; 'You two don't trust each other now. You have lost the trust you had before. Nothing is worth arguing about now'; and so on. I suspected, too, that the mediator himself did not have a firm grasp of the history of the unfolding dispute. It seems to me that at this stage, since the consumer had done a great deal of venting, the mediator was willing to shift his third-party intervening style so that it became less evaluative and rather more facilitative: he was not inclined to encourage the parties to dwell on the facts and think in terms of who was 'right' and who was 'wrong' but, rather, to think of solutions and the future of their relationship.

After hearing the parties' arguments over the same issues for some time[9] – the unknown receipt, the missing credit from the membership card and the ruse or 'trick' of recording of the leather jacket as an artificial leather jacket – the mediator managed to ask the complainant to re-state her claims in the complaint. This was, perhaps, when the agenda of the mediation meeting was first truly formed. The 'agenda' of the mediation meeting turned out to be the complainant's claims – in other words, what the consumer hoped to achieve in the mediation meeting. As far as I could tell, a clear agenda had not been formally set up before or early on in the meeting, and in fact, the complainant was

[7] For example, Ms Lu denied that she brought six items to the shop, while the shop assistant claimed she did. When the shop assistant revealed that she used a pen to jab him during the row, she said she had never done it firmly.

[8] Ms Lu herself had confessed that she could not remember some of the details when she was telling the story.

[9] At this time, it was nearly halfway through the mediation meeting, which in its entirety lasted two hours.

allowed to make demands for as long as the meeting continued.[10] In reply to the mediator, Ms Lu emphasised her primary demand – to get the business to repair the two small holes in the back of her leather jacket. However, the business representative, Ms Peng, did not agree with this. There was thus another round of vigorous argument regarding this requirement.[11] The second demand, which Ms Lu proposed a while later, was to return to her in the form of cash the 'missing credits' taken from her membership card. While the business representative showed willingness to refund the credits, she said she would only allow them to be returned to Ms Lu's membership card, as some special discounts had been credited to Ms Lu's membership card when it had been topped up earlier. During the remainder of the mediation session, the parties were negotiating over these two requirements. Most of the time was spent on the first requirement, because the business stressed that it was unable to repair the leather jacket sufficiently well as to return it to its original condition, as Ms Lu had demanded. Thus, agreement was hard to reach. The impasse seemed so unlikely to be removed that that the mediator, Mr Li, proposed to end the mediation session. Ms Lu agreed to give up her claims and to exit the mediation process provided by the SZCC, so Mr Li fetched a 'mediation termination' form for Ms Lu. However, just at the moment before she filled it in, as a last attempt, Mr Li brought up the fact that the business was actually willing to meet Ms Lu's second demand (albeit in a modified manner). Ms Lu, finally, showed her willingness to accept the deal. Ms Lu's first demand, on the other hand, was brought to the table for discussion again. After several rounds of discussion, which focused on the techniques used for repairing the leather jacket and the risk of having uneven colouring on the two holes after the repair, Ms Lu agreed to allow the Dry Cleaning shop to re-process the leather jacket. In addition, she demanded a 200RMB voucher in compensation, a possibility which had been previously proposed by the mediator, as a further reparation, given that the repair might well cause uneven colouring in the area of the two holes.

B. Some Remarks on the Case

The mediation meeting turned out to be a success in the sense that two parties reached an agreement, albeit at the last minute. Ms Lu's conduct struck me as, overall, much more rational than it was emotional. Although she sometimes raised her voice to make points, she did not pursue this aggressive behaviour throughout the mediation process. Also, as we can tell from her complainant experience, she was a first time complainant – she was a one-shot player rather than a repeat player in the SZCC complainant process, and so initially she was not very trusting of the mediation. She did not wish originally to bring the matter to the SZCC, and would not have done so but for the fact that the shop assistant called her names

[10] In this case, Ms Lu had in her mind the number of requests she would make, so there was no new request coming out of blue in the mediation. However, the consumer can always change their mind in the mediation meeting, and it would not be a surprise if some of the requests were not expressed in the complaint form. Complainant consumers can negotiate everything regarding the case in the mediation meeting.

[11] The parties had perhaps spent 1/3 of the meeting time on agreeing on the method used for repairing the leather jacket.

and otherwise treated her badly in the shop.[12] In a telephone interview with me after the mediation meeting, Ms Lu described her experience in this way:

> The man's (the shop assistant) attitude made me so angry ... I don't think it is a problem of his service in the shop, but rather, there are some issues with his personal quality ... If I didn't call the police, I would never be able to get back my leather jacket. Also when I called the senior staff [for help], she said it was indeed my right to call the police, and asked to me call the police if I wanted to. Their arrogant attitude gave me such a bad feeling even though I know it was just a small matter.

She also expressed her feelings about the possibility of using the avenue of the court:

> The guy [the shop assistant] said, 'well let's meet in court'. He tried to use this possibility to pressure me (*ya wo*) or scare me (*xiahu wo*), but I don't think it is really worth going to court [so I ignored this pressure]. If we went to court, it would be making a matter as small as a sesame seed (*zhima da de shi*), into a matter as big as a water-melon (*xigua da de shi*). There are many unpleasant things in life. The [best] situation would be to get away from such a guy [and not go to the shop again].

What is more, her focus was throughout on compensation: she spent an enormous amount of time in the mediation arguing about the problem of repair of her leather jacket. She even suggested that if the leather jacket could not be repaired, the dry cleaning shop should pay her a sum of money that would enable her to purchase a new leather jacket. She brought up the possibility of 'media' exposure when her negotiating stance seemed destined to fail – she advised that she would post photos and text on the popular Chinese microblog Weibo, or expose the matter to 'First-hand Report' (*Diyi Xianchang*).[13] However, she gave me the impression that this was a strategic way to put pressure on the defendant business so as to secure a good outcome, rather than (say) a concern to reveal information for the public good or some other general purpose.[14] She, therefore, fits the profile of a fairly typical type of SZCC complainant, aggrieved consumers who have some understanding of consumer issues, are rational, willing to compromise and to solve problems, and truly in need of help from the SZCC.[15] In fact, Ms Lu herself was rather pleased with the complaint experience. In a post-mediation interview I held with her, she used the expression 'very positive' (*hen zhengmian*) to describe the role of the Consumer Council:

> I am so grateful for Mr. Li for helping me. At least to me, the impression I have of it is that it is very positive [beneficial to society] ... I thought the problem was about consumer protection, so I just turned to the Consumer Council for help. I did not think about seeking help from other organisations ... I was also aware that if we [the parties] were 'too serious' (*jiaozhen*) about the matter, then even Mr. Li could not help to solve it.

[12] She mentioned several times in the meeting that the 'key' was that the shop assistant called her names, would not let her take her jacket and kicked the chair she wanted to sit on.

[13] *Diyi Xianchang* is a popular news report programme in the area of Shenzhen, where various local issues are reported every day.

[14] The analysis here is in accordance with the analysis provided below on 'Different Types of Complainant'.

[15] According to SZCC staff members, some 90% of the complainants follow a course rather like the one described above. The remaining 10% that are 'difficult to handle' or 'problematic', such as repeat complainants, and also emotional grievants who resort to threats such as jumping from the building if they do not succeed in their complaint. Details of these complainants will be discussed in the below section 'Different Types of Complainant'.

It is also worth noting that during the mediation meeting, the consumer, Ms Lu, sometimes called the mediator 'the leader', instead of 'Mr Li', without perhaps realising her use of a more deferential and 'politicised' term of address. The moments that she used the term 'the leader' (*lingdao*) to address the mediator, as I observed, were those when she was losing the momentum and advantage in the argument – as if she was seeking 'help' from the assumed 'authority' to correct her disadvantaged situation.

The business party in this case was polite and cooperative during the mediation. As we can see from the above account, the entire mediation meeting was a very consumer-orientated process. The agenda, as also mentioned above, was basically just the complainant's demands. The complainant was allowed to talk freely. There were no 'turn-taking' rules set up by the mediator about the speaking order. Instead, proceedings were based on the approach which the mediator suggested at the onset of the meeting – the parties had come together to solve problems rather than to argue – and so the business should (and indeed did) give the complainant every chance to speak. What is more, in many cases, the success of the mediation really relies on how much the business side is prepared to compromise, which is something that varies from one case to another. I also observed that the result of the mediation may well be influenced significantly by the identity of the individual personnel of the business party who attended the mediation meeting: his or her personality, negotiation skills, comprehension of the matter, or even some personal feelings such as compassion, and so on, seem to me factors shaping outcomes.[16]

More generally, there is in effect a very high rate of business party participation in the SZCC's mediation. As discussed in the previous chapter, most of the defendant businesses that come to the SZCC are relatively large companies, especially those that have established a fast settlement channel with the SZCC. Normally, a senior member staff (most likely in a management position) is designated by the company to attend the mediation. The mediator may have been in touch with the individual staff member on various occasions, through phone calls or mediation on spot, as there may have been several cases against the same business in the past. In Ms Lu's case, the defendant business is one of the above mentioned kind. The mediator – I specifically asked him about this – was aware of the individual defendant company staff member's presence. The result of Ms Lu's case did not seem to be affected by the mediator's working acquaintance with the staff member of the business. However, in some other mediation meetings which I observed, such a relationship seemed to help the mediator to encourage the business to make further compromises – in particular, when the complainant seemed to be very 'stubborn' in responding to the mediator. Also, as the business is somewhat collaborative in its approach to the SZCC, and indeed has quite strong ties with it, so the issue of participation in mediation often lies on the consumer side. This is probably somewhat different from the situation in – for example – some European jurisdictions, where the willing participation of businesses against whom complaints have been made in mediation can be a problem that is difficult to overcome.[17] The complainant

[16] This observation comes from my experience of auditing in more than 20 face-to-face mediation meetings, and the daily conversation I had with the staff members in the SZCC.

[17] See C Hodges, N Creutzfeldt and S Macleod, *Reforming the EU Consumer ADR Landscape: Implementation and its Issues* (Report of the Third Oxford Consumer ADR Conference, Oxford, October 2014).

consumer has to balance the cost (especially of time, including time off from work perhaps without pay, transportation costs) that he or she may pay for coming to the mediation with the compensation that hopefully will result from the settlement. SZCC staff report, in response to questions on this issue, that those who are most willing to come to the SZCC for mediation tend to be housewives, senior citizens (retired people), and 'rich ladies' (who enjoy 'driving their BMW'[18] to the SZCC). Obviously costs are one of the main concerns for complainants, but it is also clear to me that the personality of the individual consumer is another factor that often determines whether she or he will attend an on-site mediation. In one case that I observed, the claim was extremely small, but the consumer wanted to get things right – he wanted an explanation about how things happened, and wanted the business to admit that it had done wrong.

During the mediation meeting in Ms Lu's case, some strategies were skilfully used by the mediator to facilitate agreement, compromise, and mutual understanding between the parties. For example, he allocated more time to the complainant than to the business, giving the 'consumer' a chance to express the grievance in detail and to vent her feelings. He proposed some compensation options for the parties, such as offering cleaning vouchers to compensate the damaged leather jacket. He kept bringing the parties back to the agenda – which, as they all assumed, was the complainant's claims,[19] and pushed the parties onto solutions. In addition, the mediator even provided a moderate evaluation on the case. He mentioned to the complainant that it would be very difficult for her to resolve the case in the court, since she would need to provide evidence to prove the facts, and so on. The mediator was also skilful in breaking the seeming impasse between the parties and then moving the parties promptly to an agreed settlement.

At a more general level, however, staff members (mediators) of the SZCC are inclined not to say anything against the consumer, even if the consumer's claims do not make much sense (this 'sense' is largely understood in terms of the law and the factual evidence). In order to avoid problems, staff members often express their opinions in a very soft manner, which comforts the consumers and gets them to understand situations for their own sake. In the above case, whenever the mediator tried to propose, persuade or stop something, he used expressions such as, 'Ms Lu, of course you have your right to go to the media … I am not trying to ask you to do anything, but maybe you can listen to my advice that …'

It happens that if staff members' mode of expression is too harsh, aggrieved consumers may accuse them of aligning with the business party rather than the complainant. In my interviews with aggrieved consumers, it became clear to me that they often expect staff members to be their ally rather than a neutral intermediary. This is because, in their view, the Consumer Council's mission is to protect consumers, and they see themselves as the

[18] The BMW is considered to be a very 'up-market' car in China, and in everyday conversation (and as in this case) given the affectionate Chinese nickname of '*baoma*' or 'precious horse'. As one Shanghai car dealer explained to the *Financial Times*, 'In China, so many people have got rich – so many – but they don't have that much experience, so they just follow what other people say,' he says. 'If their friend has a BMW 7 series and they do not, they can lose face.' P Waldmeir, 'Chinese Car Buyers Show Off with a "Baoma"' (*Financial Times*, 15 August 2011) www.ft.com/intl/cms/s/0/29fd0c30-c275-11e0-9ede-00144feabdc0.html#axzz3fmDnKFQn.

[19] This assumption comes from the fact that, first, the business is aware of the problems by reading the complaint form; secondly, the Consumer Council was regarded by consumers as a helper for them – an institution who will get the business to resolve their problems. The agenda was re-confirmed by the mediator, by asking the complainant to speak about what her demands or claims were.

weaker party for whom support was supposedly to be given by the SZCC.[20] In response to this perception, a common defensive technique used by the staff members who fail to satisfy aggrieved consumers' demands is to pass the case to other organisations for handling when they are able. This practice also seems to serve as a kind of 'right of appeal' as found in litigation, giving consumers some hope for their claims, so that they can carry on and feel more comfortable with a result that basically they are not happy with.[21] The staff members often spoke to consumers in the following terms, 'we tried our best but failed to help you to reach your goals … if you want to, you can try making complainants to the XYZ bureau. Their complaint hotline is 12345678 … and you still have your rights to [take your case to] the court'. One informant, a SZCC staff (a mediator), calls this technique '*dataiji*' – that is, 'playing *taijiquan*'[22] – meaning that the mediator feels it best to 'pass' [the buck] (*tui*), mimicking the motion of *taijiquan* (or Tai Chi), to other organisations. Indeed, he told me that he obtained this important skill from his informal 'master' when working in one of the district Consumer Councils.

III. Different Types of Complainant

Having considered in some detail one of the cases that came to my attention during the SZCC fieldwork, and given the reader a sense of the manner in which the SZCC handles the grievances that come before it, let us now look in a more systematic and analytical manner at the differing types of complainant who choose to bring their grievance to the SZCC. By what criteria are different types of consumer complainant to be characterised? The types offered here are derived from my observations on the conduct and performance of

[20] Indeed, I experienced this myself when I did some mediating. Thus on one occasion I was accused of favouritism by a consumer over the telephone. He said I was helping the business party in his case, as I had advised him that he should be more understanding of the issues, and that the problem is difficult to resolve to the satisfaction of both parties, and that there are limits to the extent to which a mediator can help one party. Some of the consumer complaints raised are comparatively small, such as a 10 yuan internet package. I learned that I had to be very careful not to be drawn into an expression of my own opinion in a telephone call to the consumer, especially if (say) the consumer had made a mistake about the package, but paid for it and then overused it, and wanted to claim damages for the original problem (say, poor labelling). Thus, I realised I needed to be more circumspect in the future, and make sure that next time I avoided this problem. Sometimes the problem is that the consumer did not read the contract carefully, and did not see that there was a provision in the contract saying that payment for the product, for example, a training course, would not be refundable. Staff from the Consumer Council would sometimes still find ways to help the consumer to get round the contract provisions, so as to help them get the compensation. As one staff member-mediator put the matter: 'so, blaming them does not help at all, because they will just come again and bother you'.

[21] As Shapiro has put the matter 'one of the principal virtues of a trial is that it provides an official termination to conflict, relieving the disputants of the necessity of further reciprocal assertions or retributions. But too much finality may be disturbing to the losing member of the triad. One of the functions of a "right of appeal" may be to provide a psychological outlet and a social cover for the loser at trial. For appeal allows the loser to continue to assert his rightness in the abstract without attacking the legitimacy of the legal system or refusing to obey the trial court. Indeed the loser's displeasure is funneled into a further assertion of the legitimacy of the legal system. Appealing to a higher court entails the acknowledgment of its legitimacy'. M Shapiro, *Courts: A Comparative and Political Analysis* (Chicago, University of Chicago Press, 1981) 49. See also, M Shapiro, 'Appeal' (1980) 14 *Law and Society Review* 629.

[22] *Taijiquan* is a kind of traditional Chinese shadow boxing, in which your hands move in circles as you push and pass [in the air] all the time.

consumers during the Consumer Council handling of their dispute. There are, in my view, three main differentiating variables at work that enable us to undertake this characterisation of the nature of complaints: style of complaining, procedural experience and strategic 'savvy', and the broad goals or motives in pursuing a grievance through the formal channel of the SZCC.

Now, many of the consumers who lodge their complaints before the SZCC do not display important aspects of all three variable characteristics. In many cases, one feature stands out as dominant, but some do exhibit two or more features. What is more, the unfolding process of making a complaint is not a static phenomenon – it flows with complainants' changes of mind, purpose, attitude and knowledge. As a result, a complaint may oscillate or shift between these features during the process. For example, a complainant may be more rational at the beginning of the process. As the process unfolds, he or she may become more emotional, and may even disregard their previous goal of obtaining some kind of compensation, and instead simply blame the other party – often venting his or her anger, especially when they sense there is little hope for them to secure a good outcome or to change the likely result. There is no absolute line between the categories. The complainants who belong to one type may also exhibit features of other types to a lesser degree. During the complaint process, the complainant may well shift perspective and goals, so it is the main feature of the complainants that I have used to distinguish them from other types, and even then this dominant feature may be more or less important at different points of time.

A. Style: Rational and Emotional Complainants

Roughly speaking, in terms of what we might call 'styles of complaining', my research shows that there are two main types of complainant, reflecting the extent to which they used 'rational' argument on the one hand, or emotional pressure on the other, in order to present their grievance. Therefore, state of mind or 'psychological condition' of the complainant is one important distinguishing criterion, and I argue that we may meaningfully contrast the 'Rational Complainant' from the 'Emotional Complainant' (or, perhaps preferably, 'Anxious Complainant').

The 'Rational Complainant' we have already encountered in our case study, as Ms Lu is one such rational complainant. She was unhappy with the shop assistant, but generally, she was aware of the details of the situation in which she found herself, and of the bargaining power she had. In addition, she had an understanding of the role of the mediator and the Consumer Council, and the offers provided by the business. However, not all the complainants are as rational as Ms Lu. In one extreme case, an 'Emotional Complainant', Mr Cheng, got very upset when his demand was not met – he even threatened to jump from the building window of the SZCC office's corridor which would almost certainly result in severe injury or even death. This resulted in a fireman having to come and rescue him.[23]

[23] I met Mr Cheng in the SZCC for his latest complaint, but the case for which he threatened to jump from the building occurred almost two years ago, so I heard his previous story from the staff member in the SZCC.

B. Procedural Experience: Repeat and Multi-Channel Complainants

The characterisation of complainants' procedural experience and strategic 'savvy' is a second differentiating variable. I highlight in particular two types within this general category: the 'Repeat Complainant' and the 'Multi-Channel Complainant'. It is worth noting that the Consumer Council also describe complaints/complainants in a way that enables them 'better' to handle case processing pressures. In their routine dispute resolution work, they speak about 'repeat complaints'. By 'repeat complaints', staff members refer to all the complaints that are attempted more than once, and they do not distinguish the different situations of repetition. They also speak about the big family of complaints (*tousu dahu*), which refers to businesses which receive the most complaints at the Consumer Council. They include the three main telecommunication companies operating in China.

First, the 'Repeat Complainant'. I noticed that there are in effect three types of repeat complainants: One is referred to locally as a 'hotspot complainant' (*redian tousu ren*) or 'professional complainant' (*zhiye tousu ren*), and I will discuss this type in some detail in chapter five below. This type of repeat complainant is regarded by CC staff as a kind of professional, looking to secure significant material benefits from their repeated and strategic presentation of grievance.

Another type of Repeat Complainant is not 'professional', but rather, comprises citizens who are keen to defend their own rights. These complainants normally lodge complaints only when they come across the matter in their everyday life, that is on an ad hoc basis, unlike the more systematic approach of the professional. Let us take, for example, a complainant called Mr XX. By searching his name in the OA system, I found that he had indeed brought several cases on different matters across an almost two-year time span, including various issues of mobile network and usage. However, he does not seem to represent the patterned conduct of the professional complainant. For example, he did not seek punitive damages in his compensation claims, asking only for a refund of the price he had paid for the item in question. In addition, the issues he brought up were seen as 'real troubles' and as not requiring much technical expertise to deal with – unlike issues brought up by the professional, which are more likely to be about matters such as misleading food certification on the package, or unclear information about the place of production.

The last type is the persistent complainant who brings the same case repeatedly, or who makes duplicate complaints by attempting several phone calls, each time typically presenting his or her grievance as a new and different inquiry, or adding further issues into the mix so that the revised complaint has novelty. These complainants raise the same case with the Consumer Council every now and then because they are not satisfied with the settlement or other solutions offered by the business. For example, in a case over some furniture of inferior quality, at the first time of handling the case, the complainant did not reach an agreement with the business, so he agreed to terminate the process of dispute resolution. However, almost one year later, the complainant made a complaint to the SZCC again, after making some further investigations, such as making phone calls to the local government and the industry regulator, but without offering much new evidence. Later, he made a follow-up complaint adding his new requests into the previous complaint.[24] In addition some complainants, particularly those buying electronic appliances in department stores, might make another complaint. This was especially so when there was a perceived lack of willingness by the defendant business party to abide by the terms of an agreed settlement. In one such case that I learned about, the complainant accused the business of failing to send people to fix his air conditioner, even though they had agreed orally over the phone to do so in good time. A separate complaint form was created for him by the SZCC, but the case number of the old case was referred to in the new complaint form.

Secondly, there is the 'Multi-Channel Complainant', who may be described as using something of a 'scattergun' approach in which complaints are simultaneously lodged with several organisations at the same time. Mr Hou was such a complainant, as we can see from his grievance over mobile data usage. His mobile data usage within a given period had gone up to more than 7GB (without any warning notice from the carrier), and as a result, he had to pay almost 2000RMB for his excessive mobile data usage. It was revealed in the mediation meeting that he had already taken his complaint to a local radio programme as well as making complaint phone calls to the local government. In another case over the cancellation and refund of a paid language course, Ms She, the complainant, had made a protest both to the Consumer Council and to the popular TV programme, the First-hand Report, at the same time. She told me that she was so worried about losing her money, that she felt she needed to lodge complaints to both forums, and she was waiting for responses. It turned out that, on the evening of the next day after she made a complaint to the SZCC (she visited the SZCC in person and I helped her with filling the complaint form), her story was shown on the TV programme, from which I learned that the journalist and Ms She had visited the private educational institution and argued with its manager for resolution of her case. Later, in a telephone interview that she agreed to give with me, she told me that she simply was pursuing her case with the first forum from which she received a reply. Apparently, the complaint she made to the SZCC had yet to secure a reply. The outcome, which was not shown on the TV but reported to me by Ms She, was that she was able to terminate the contract for the English language course, as the journalist and other staff of the TV programme helped her in negotiations and also her bank put pressure on the business, as she had intended to pay for her course by means of a bank loan.[25]

C. Goals: Compensation Orientated, Public-Interest Orientated and Anger-Venting Complainants

From observing many cases during my fieldwork, it is clear to me that it is possible to analyse complainants in terms of the goals that they broadly pursue in bringing a complaint. In this respect, we may speak of the 'Compensation Orientated Complainant' (whose main purpose is to get award for compensatory damages even when punitive damages

[24] Sometimes the operators of the Hotline Centre may combine the complaint forms, but it also seemed that if the new requests are so different from previous ones, they will be separated.

[25] Details of this case are provided in ch 7.

can be applied), the 'Public-Interest Orientated Complainant' (whose main goal is to draw public attention on the issue, but who in my experience is nearly always also very interested in securing a good outcome in terms of compensation), and the 'Anger-Venting Complainant' (who cares less about the result, but wants to express his or her anger at what has happened to them through the forum of the dispute resolution process). These goals may also relate to the level of consumer knowledge possessed by the complainant. It is more likely that the 'Public-Interest Orientated Complainant' has a better knowledge of consumer law than the other two types.

The Compensation Orientated Complainant is the most common type. Ms Lu in the above case study is a typical Compensation Orientated Complainant, whose main purpose is to get compensation for this one-shot complaint. I also came across a case in which the complainant seemed to have several demands, but in the end, it was the refund of what he paid for that really mattered. The complainant, Mr Ma, a senior citizen in his seventies, lodged a complaint against the TV station for false advertisement on a tablet PC. Along with the compensation demand for the tablet PC, Mr Ma also claimed in the complaint form that he wanted the TV station to stop broadcasting the advertisement, so that it would not cheat more people (especially old people like him). However, his attempt at blaming the TV station did not succeed, because the mediator failed to have a meaningful conversation with the TV station.[26] Nevertheless, the mediator successfully obtained the contact information of the manager of the defendant business. By contacting the manager, he helped Mr Ma get a refund for his tablet PC. In a post-mediation interview, Mr Ma seemed very happy about the result. It also appeared to me that the reason he blamed the TV station was because he could not reach the business in order to discuss getting compensation. He explained that he tried calling the defendant business many times, by dialling the 'after-sale service line' provided in the receipt, but the calls were all directed to the automatic voice of the 'purchase line' (so in fact, there was no effective 'after-sale service line' phone number).[27] He even made a significant compromise by paying the 'delivery fee' for returning the dysfunctional tablet PC to the business, in order to get back the rest of his payment as a refund.

With regard to the Public-Interest Orientated Complainants, some are real fighters for consumer rights and interests at the grass roots level, such as Mr 'Yang Jianchang', who has lately become a public figure.[28] His stories are widely reported and he has gained a reputation for his public-spirited actions. So much so that in due course he was elected as a people's representative (*renda daibiao*) in the Shenzhen People's Congress, and later moved into public service – he became the Director of the Luohu District Consumer Council. Another, perhaps slightly controversial example, is the professional complainant (or professional litigant if they bring the case to the court). These players originally used the Consumer Council

[26] The mediator informed me that he reported the false advertisement issue to the TV station, and the advertisement was removed. But several days later, Mr Ma told me in the post-mediation interview that the false advertisement was still there on several channels during noon time. Weeks later, I happened to watch it once on the TV too.

[27] As I found out later, Mr Ma was not the only plaintiff who bought the fake and dysfunctional tablet PC. There were in fact a handful of complainants who made complaints over the same type of tablet PC, but their cases ended up in difficult hands, and with different results. More details are offered in the last section.

[28] See eg 'Yang Jianchang, the Shenzhen Figure: Consumers Called him "Justice Yang"' (Shenzhen Renwu zhi Yang Jianchang: Xiaofeizhe Chengta 'Yang Qingtian') (*Sohu News*, 6 September 2010) news.sohu.com/20100906/n274736381.shtml.

as their main stage for achieving their purposes.[29] Nowadays, however, they tend to use the MSA's complaint processes. Only a very few of them still make complaints to the Consumer Council. However, as noted above and as will be discussed in the chapter below on professional litigants, these people have mixed motives. Some of the professional complainants are 'compensation orientated' only – as they themselves admit, do not care about 'public interest' at all, as their purpose in pursuing a claim is to earn money. Others do fight for the public interest, but at the same time, they may well need to earn a living. So they are unlikely to abandon their hopes for financial reward even when pursuing a claim 'in the public interest'.

As with the Anger-Venting Complainants, especially when I mediated some cases myself, I found out that some people do not expect a quick solution, especially not from a phone call 'mediation'. The complainant is aware of the difficulties often involved in a case, but is basically looking for a forum in which to express his or her anger. For example, a man complained about the services of the telephone giant, China Mobile, as the problem of poor reception on his phone during an exhibition event caused him financial losses. He claimed that he lost thousands of money on his business, because of the breakdown of the network in the event, and he now asked for compensation for his lost business. His claim was unrealistic and the impression he gave was he did not really mean to claim compensation, as it would be impossible to secure such compensation. However, he made a complaint in order to vent his anger at his unpleasant experience, and it only cost him a little money to do so, as he only needed to make a phone call to the SZCC to get people to listen to him.

IV. Problems Faced by Consumers in the Complaint Process

By analysing the different types of consumer complainant, some fundamental issues in the complaint process are highlighted.

As we have noted in the case study of the handling of Ms Lu's grievance, a business like the XYZ Dry Cleaning Company is a repeat player. It has plenty of experience in dealing with customer complaints and disputes arising out of customer grievances. As a result, it can be quite adept at resisting pressure, and it was indeed quite reluctant to make concessions to Ms Lu in the case described above.[30] From the point of view of the 'persistent complainant' in particular, this means that bringing a complaint is often a 'draining' process – it really exhausts the complainants' energy and patience, so that the complainants get tired of being so persistent and may well give up in due course. Ms Lu refused to give in to this 'strategic

[29] As people in this group vary greatly, some pursue more of a public interest purpose; some pursue more private interests. It would be best to describe them as having 'mixed motives' rather than see them as having a single motive.

[30] One SZCC staff member reported to me that there was a case in which the complainant did not accept some of the terms in the compensation proposed by the business. He later exposed the matter to the mass media, but the business was not afraid of the pressure from the media. Instead, it withdrew its previous offer and refused to have further negotiation with the complainant. The business told the Consumer Council that since the matter was already exposed, it had nothing else to fear, and it did not want to cooperate anymore.

resistance' but even so, her case was only accepted at the last moment of the mediation, and with the help of a very skilful mediator.

Therefore, many complainants do come to the Consumer Council again and again on the same matter, hoping optimistically that this time they might win. However, in most situations they will not in fact be able to secure a 'better' result. Sometimes, they may even get a result that is actually worse than the first settlement offer made by the defendant business. Their persistence, however, has parallels in contemporary Chinese society: it probably resembles for example the stubborn conduct of property owners resisting government resumption of land at artificially low prices, stubborn patients with a medical treatment grievance (an increasingly important social problem in China today so that in recent times a system of special 'medical' dispute mediation committees has been established), and so on. On the one hand, this reflects a determination to try to get the authorities to be just and to do the right thing. As also mentioned earlier in this chapter, the Consumer Council tends to pass the unsolved issue to other public bodies as a way out, so that the complaint does not come to it again, and so that the complainant still has a sort of 'right of appeal' for his complaint to other bodies. However, some consumer complainants considered this as an 'act of omission' (*buzuowei*), a strategic practice of avoiding dispute handling responsibilities also found in some other administrative bodies. Complainants were disappointed that the Consumer Council in effect was giving up so easily on its duty to protect consumers' rights by simply putting unhappy consumers into another complaint process provided by another organisation. As a result, consumers have to spend time on a new round of complaint processes which may also mentally distress them.

The 'multi-avenue' approach also reflects the fact that there are many channels for making complaints – people can always make complaints to different organisations, and there is often no real final say on the matter (including even a judgement). People feel that there is always a way to be 'flexibly persistent' in their pursuit of their rights and interests. Or, to put it another way, there are many avenues for securing access to justice, but most of them have serious weaknesses and so when the complainant senses resistance in one avenue she or he will quickly shift to another. The Chinese style is to 'bang one's head' against multiple walls, rather than just one wall.

In the mediation-based process, the outcome that the consumer can get is often a compromised one. This means that the consumer complainant may not necessarily get what is offered by the law. An interesting observation is that a majority of the common complainants – excluding the professional – were unable to negotiate for punitive damages when they could have been awarded.[31] Some are simply not aware of the punitive damage; many have put the claim in their complaint form, but later in the negotiation, because the business is so tough in its response, they simply reduce their claim down to a refund of the money they spent on the product. This problem is exacerbated by the fact that there are so many counterfeit products in China. Particularly in Shenzhen, fake mobile phones are a major problem. In law, the complainant should be able to secure an award for punitive damages against the seller, but through the mediation process often is able only to secure a refund.

[31] Simply put, there are two main situations where consumers can ask for punitive damages. One is for counterfeit products (also misleading ads, etc). The other is for unsafe food. See Art 54 of the Consumer Protection Law 1993 and Art 96 of the Food Safety Law 2009.

This empirical finding has confirmed one of the main criticisms of an informal forum – the danger of abandoning rights for a compromised outcome, particular when one party is weaker than the other in terms of bargaining power. While even in court, if the case goes to court-annexed mediation, the result is probably not much different (as I describe below, in the court most consumer cases are also mediated, and consumers still do not get the compensation they seek, especially when they seek punitive damages).[32] So the law does not seem to be very useful in practice, except when it is skilfully used by the professional litigants, or for small matters over very small claims – even if it is three or ten times the purchase price, the compensation would not be significant, so the business is relatively willing to settle and pay up so as to avoid trouble.

It is also important to note that if the settlement agreement is reached through phone calls, it is often an oral agreement and sometimes difficult to enforce. The delay of enforcement and a passive attitude from the business may mean that the consumer has to spend time on pressing the business to enforce, or may even bring a new complaint, especially when the case was once closed due to a reached agreement, to ask the Consumer Council for a push for enforcement.

In addition, there may be a lack of consistency in decision-making. A same fact case can end up in different hands, and thus with different results. In the above mentioned case of Mr Ma, there were quite a few similar cases over the same product – the fake and dysfunctional tablet PC. Mr Ma made his complaint against the TV station, which according to relevant work allocation rules, would be dealt with by the SZCC. But in fact, there were two addresses of the business: one was printed on the package (an address in the Luohu district), the other was provided by the receipt (an address in the Nanshan district). The address of the business is primarily to be provided by the consumer when they fill in the complaint form, and the address he or she provides may decide the place that the complaint goes to. In the successful mediation of Mr Ma, the mediator of the SZCC had used his own local knowledge to obtain the contact of the manager of the company, and thus led to a success. However, this knowledge was not shared by mediators in the district Councils. It was found out that complaints dealt with by the staff in Luohu were terminated, because the staff could not get in touch with the business against whom a complaint is made; complaints dealt with by the staff in Nanshan, tended to be compensated less generously than Ma has received in compensation.

Mr Ma's case also revealed that it was sometimes difficult for the consumer to make meaningful contact with the defendant business. The basic method for a Consumer Council staff member to initiate the mediation process is to contact the business by phone. The Consumer Council has to rely on the phone call, as it does not go on foot patrol – unlike the MSA officials – nor visit the business's address. As a result, valid information such as the telephone contact of the business is very important to the mediation process, and the contact information is initially provided by consumers. Someone like Ma, who used to be a civil servant in the old SAIC, is probably more experienced than many other complainants. But still, he needed assistance with the explanation of some of the questions in the complaint form. In particular, in the column of the seller's 'business address', Ma was not so sure which address to fill in. What is more, in disputes of online shopping, some 90 per cent

[32] Details about this will be explained in ch 6 on the dispute processes in the court.

of the cases cannot be dealt with simply because the defendant cannot be reached by the staff member in the Consumer Council. The website provided by the consumer is closed down, and the contact is not answered. In these situations, most consumers can do nothing but give up their grievance.

V. Conclusions

As discussed above, consumers continue to face various difficulties and challenges in securing justice in China. In order to enhance the possibility of getting a satisfactory outcome, different consumers take different approaches to their disputes and might be characterised as sometimes engaging in 'forum shopping'. The categorisation of consumers' approaches is helpful in understanding how they go about their grievances and how these approaches may affect the outcome of their negotiations with the businesses. They continue to believe that the state is responsible for taking care of people's welfare, and that officials need to play an active role in securing compensation for them. In most situations, consumers are prepared to make compromises, though they may also have unrealistic expectations on the possible outcome that hampers the progress of a negotiation, and even bring up the complaint repeatedly. Despite the problems, public bodies, such as the Consumer Council and the regulator, are able to handle most of the consumer disputes to a reasonably satisfactory standard deemed by the consumer. The positive sides of their handling of the disputes, from the consumers' perspective, seem to include setting up mediation meetings in good time, often taking the side of consumers and empowering them, having good connections with large companies so that it is easier to persuade them to make good compromises to consumers, and no limits on disputes that have been dealt with somewhere else. Most importantly, the services are free and these extra-judicial dispute processes remain the easiest way for consumers to obtain at least some degree of justice.

5

The 'Professional' in Consumer Disputes

I. Introduction

This chapter explores primarily the experiences of a new 'class' or 'category' of 'consumer' in Shenzhen. We must immediately point out that whether or not the type of complainant focused on in this chapter is regarded as a true 'consumer' in the law is a locally (and, indeed, to some extent nationally) controversial issue.[1] There is much evidence that both this type of complainant and also the ambiguous manner in which such actors are regarded, are found more generally in China as a whole, though this chapter focuses primarily on the situation in Shenzhen, especially as I experienced it during my fieldwork.

In the bureaucratised world of consumer protection in Shenzhen, a figure has emerged who may well see himself as a consumer, but whose expertise gained through repeat playing of asserting consumer grievances and report results in officialdom characterising them as 'professional' complainants/reporters. These important figures are expert in both complaining and reporting in parallel, and often use or mix the two tracks of the consumer protection administrative processes strategically so as to maximise their interests or 'returns'.[2] I am going to call them 'professional complainants', or 'professional consumers', because this is the term frequently used by the local official, and is one that singles the process they initiate. There are other several terms that are particularly used by the official or the media dealing with them, but I will discuss this later in the chapter.

The difference between '*tousu*' (to complain, or complaint) and '*jubao*' (report), discussed in chapter three above is important: the term '*tousu*' is a complaint made by consumers seeking compensation for damages, and is usually resolved by mediation; while '*jubao*' is a process for citizens to report malpractices of the business, so as to urge the administrative department to investigate and punish the business for causing harm to the public.[3] Those who merely report an infringement of consumer rights or interests (ie, *jubao*) are not officially regarded as aggrieved consumers. The official's attitude is that *jubao* (to report malpractices) is independent from *tousu* (to seek compensation) – *jubao* only results in the fact that the company may get administrative punishments, so it does not mean that consumers can get compensation in this process. Indeed, the professionals who do this do not necessarily purchase the goods or services about which they lodge a report. However,

[1] As discussed in ch 2, the definition of 'consumer' in the law is rather unclear.

[2] See below for a more detailed analysis of these 'official' attitudes towards the professionals.

[3] The '*jubao*' process is important to the professionals because it provides monetary rewards to the person who makes the report and the report in effect helps the administrative department to deal with businesses' malpractices. Details are revealed in the section on 'Style of Complaining and Reporting'.

at the same time, there are official regulations – for example, those issued and implemented by the Market Supervision Administration Bureau in Shenzhen (hereinafter, the MSA) – which actively encourage reporting practices. Given this encouragement, it seems sensible to regard the 'reporters' as important players within the consumer protection dispute processing system in Shenzhen.

A fair amount of the data in this section is collected from conversations with officials in the MSA. However, this does not mean that the information they provide is necessarily very 'official' or in any other way significantly 'biased'. Our conversations were as between work colleagues rather than formal interviews. There is a good reason to believe that the official knows a great deal about the real life of the professionals, and can give a true account of the development of their practices, based on their experience of dealing with the professionals' complaints and reports. An important reason for this is the professionals pay regular visits to the MSA staff in their offices. They chat in some depth with the MSA officers, some of whom are regarded as 'friends' with whom they like to discuss both personal and professional issues in a relaxed way.

II. The 'Professionals' in Consumer Dispute Processes

A. Background

The 'professional complainant' is a relatively new characterisation, one mainly given by officials, especially those working in and around institutions such as the MSA and the Consumer Council in Shenzhen, to people who frequently assert consumer grievances, including through litigation. Their practices can be traced back to early 1990s when the Consumer Protection Law was newly established.[4] The 1993 Consumer Protection Law was for many years the major legislation governing protecting consumers' rights and interests, and in particular, its Article 49 gives consumers the rights to claim punitive damages when they have been sold counterfeit products or been misled by deceptive advertisement. In the early days of the reforms, the Chinese market was full of copied and fake products.[5] Gradually, a group of people started to make use repeatedly of Article 49 in various dispute processes so as to highlight selling malpractices, as well as to obtain a 'double' compensation. According to the CPL, the consumer can obtain a compensation which is double the price of the product – one amount as compensatory damages, the other amount is for punitive damages. One of the most influential figures, Wang Hai, has made extensive use of Article 49 of the Consumer Protection Law in his consumer dispute practices and has been characterised as an 'anti-counterfeit hero' by the media.[6] A news item reveals that in two years, he had claimed a total amount of compensation up to $13,000 by intentionally

[4] The 1993 Consumer Protection Law has been revised in 2013.

[5] This problem still exists, albeit to a lesser degree, at the current time.

[6] QQ Xie, 'Jiehe "Wanghai Dajia An" Jianyi Falü Jieshi Buquedingxing de Yuanyin' ('Discussion on Reasons Causing Uncertainty of Legal Interpretation on Cases in Relation to "Wang Hai Phenomenon"') (2010) 5 *Huainan Shifan Xueyuan Xuebao (Journal of Huainan Normal University)* 58.

buying goods that appeared fake and then seeking redress in court.[7] The 'Wang Hai phenomenon' as it became known swept China in the mid-1990s and soon many followers of Wang Hai started their own practice of buying counterfeiting goods primarily in order to secure compensation. At first, the mass media and the Consumers' Association spoke highly of Wang Hai for his achievement in singling out counterfeiting products and safeguarding the masses. As the number of Wang Hai's imitators increased, however, the mass media and the Consumers' Association gradually developed a more sceptical view on Wang Hai, and they even seeing him as 'a trickster' who makes money strategically from the law.[8]

Perhaps Wang Hai's initial efforts represent the start of this 'profession'. Some of my informants proposed the names of some other 'specialists' in this kind of consumer claimant as also being influential, but Wang Hai is by far the most famous figures among this kind. He is still 'practising' as a consumer rights advocate – here I am inclined to call him a 'rights advocate' rather than a 'professional complainant', because the activities he is involved in and the procedures he initiates are wide-spread and diversified.[9] The term that this chapter uses, 'the professional complainant' (*zhiye tousuren*), is more of a local description, particularly given by the local officials (in Shenzhen) from their procedural perspective, and in the absence of a good alternative it seems sensible to use it here.

The style of practice of these 'professionals' in the Shenzhen area, as many of my informants have pointed out, perhaps did not really get started in a meaningful way until the introduction of the Food Safety Law in 2009.[10] Their practices are regarded by the official as being of a similar nature to Wang Hai's anti-counterfeit practice – to manipulate the law, particularly, to ask for punitive damages in order to make profits from their consumer complaints. For like the Consumer Protection Law, the 2009 Food Safety Law has included a 'punitive damages' provision in order to protect consumers buying food products: Article 96 stresses that aggrieved consumers 'may claim for punitive damages which are ten-times of the price of the [defective] food product purchased'. The professionals seem to have turned in some numbers to the field of food safety, to continue their 'anti-counterfeit', or 'rights advocate' practices, as a result of the introduction of the ten-times punitive damages provision. In my searches of the complaint/report system operated by the MSA, I found that a majority of the cases (either complaints or reports) received were, and still are, on issues relating to food products – concerns relating to their packaging, food additives, accreditation, and so on. The areas of labelling, product information and additives in respect of food products have many problems. This is largely because the guiding standards (which must be followed by the manufacturers) for labels of food product are rather strict and high. The standards are made and published by the National Standardization Technical Committees (in food industry) where most people are laboratory scientists who do not know the commercial practices and the law very well. The standards are down to very detailed things, such as the size of the Chinese characters and line spacing that should be used on product

[7] 'Wang Hai, a Consumer Advocate in China' (*China Daily*, 26 July 2007) www.chinadaily.com.cn/china/2007-07/26/content_5443739.htm.

[8] ibid.

[9] I have interviewed Wang Hai during my fieldwork and was able to ask him questions about his recent activities.

[10] My informants have all pointed to this period of time as the beginning of their current style of practice (which in nature resembles Wang Hai's methods of obtaining compensation).

information. The standards are thus very difficult to enforce, and they are sometimes not even noticed by the manufacturers – many manufacturers do not even know the existence of these standards.

In something of a contrast to Wang Hai's early approach, which mainly used litigation and the courts to assert claims, the professional complainants in Shenzhen now more often use the city's administrative procedures to assert their rights and interests. My interviews with staff in the MSA and with the professionals themselves indicate that the MSA has received and still receives enormous numbers of complaints and reports from these professionals, and this has created manifestly significant pressure on the work of the MSA. According to official data, in 2010, the number of cases (including complaints and reports) filed by the professionals was 699; in 2011, it had gone up to 3,285; in 2012, it soared to 10,435; in 2013, it was even higher at 17,276. The number of cases officially recorded has thus increased almost 25 times in three years, and it had risen to 64,593 in 2016. As a member of staff in a local – and relatively small – MSA office described the situation to me:

> There are only three people in this local [MSA] office who are in charge of handling consumer complaints/reports, but we receive hundreds of complaints/reports from these professionals every month … Sometimes the complaints come in large numbers at one and the same time … There are still over a thousand 'un-dealt with' complaints in the system now.

Indeed, in developing their working practices, the MSA staff have created a list of 'professional complainants' whose names regularly appear in the complaint and report system, as well as a ranking of the number of complaints/reports that each professional makes monthly. There are some features commonly perceived by the MSA staff through their case handling experience as the standard to judge if the complainant/reporter is a 'professional'. These include, for example, first, whether or not the complaint concerns food label and product information (popular issues for the professionals and problematic areas which the professionals have often studied in some depth); secondly, whether or not the complaint or report was made through the internet, and is written in a format that is used by the professionals, with the laws and regulations quoted; and thirdly, is there a claim for punitive damages (another indicator).

B. Style of Complaining and Reporting

The professional complainants tend to bring complaints or to report malpractices against the business in order to get monetary 'compensation'. In fact, in most situations, whatever route they follow, a settlement agreement is reached where a sum of money is given to the professionals by the defendant business, so that the professionals withdraw the case and the business is exempted from administrative sanctions.

The simplest pattern of how the professionals approach negotiation is as follows: a professional complainant spots a certain issue or problem with the product, often a food product sold in the supermarket. The complainant then buys the product, and files a complaint or report against the business on the issue.[11] The MSA receives the complaint or report.

[11] The reason why I use 'he' here is because so far as I can tell, 90% or more of the professional complainants are men. There is only one professional complainant that I know who is a woman, and she is the wife of

If it is a complaint, it arranges mediation, calling the parties to attempt mediation in its office. If it is a report, the MSA sets up a case file, and starts an investigation, including checking the product on the spot (in the supermarket) and the product specifications provided by the manufacturer or wholesale distributor. The defendant business (in many cases a supermarket), after being informed of the complaint or report by the MSA, will first try to contact the professional complainant before it takes other action (including attending a mediation or providing certain evidence as required by the MSA). This is what the professional complainant is waiting for: it is his chance. He seeks a favourable settlement with the defendant business, in which an agreed sum of money will be paid to the professional complainant on the condition of returning the purchased products to the business. The professional complainant visits the business, gets the deal done, and then withdraws his complaint from the MSA, as well as returning the purchased products to the business, as if he did not spot any error with the product.

The above description shows us the basic processes at work. However, in reality, in many cases various matters arise and the situation becomes quite complicated. An important reason for such complications is that the professional complainants apply different strategies and negotiation skills in the complaint and report processes, largely according to the reaction of the MSA.

First, the professionals may file hundreds complaints and reports in a short time. According to the professionals, it is likely that the local MSA officers deliberately ignore their complaints or reports, since the officers assume that the professionals are doing this to make money. The officers either do not go and check, or claim that they have not found any problematic products. One strategy that the professionals employ is to file a large number of reports, usually reports rather than complaints, using different names. One professional, as I learned, used his relatives' names as 'reporters', in order to file reports over one issue that he spotted. Another professional has filed one thousand reports to a local MSA office using different names, but it was found out later by the relevant MSA official that these reports were all sent from the same computer IP. The professionals may also seek help from the internet, ask their net-friends all over the country to file complaints and reports for them. This is strategic, creating a heavier workload for local officers, so that the officers will more readily help them to negotiate with a defendant business.

Another tactic is that one professional may make hundreds of reports over 'one illegal act' against one local shop. This, indeed, has raised the argument between the professionals and the local officers, as to what constitutes 'one report'. Say for example, the professionals discovered that the price tags of 100 products (of different brands) in a local store were unclear. They made 100 reports against the store, and each report points to the unclear price tag of one single product. The professionals believe that these reports were made on different products in the local store, so they should be regarded as 100 independent

the man who is himself a professional complainant. They work together on this job. Also, as we can see from the job advertisement of the professional complainant, the job requires people who are ruthless, thick-faced and 'gutsy', and it is more likely – given Chinese socio-cultural attitudes – that men are seen to possess these qualities. Thus, the predominance of male 'professional complainants' may well reflect local gender stereotypes rather than any intrinsic lack of interest in consumer 'activism' on the part of women. The collaborative nature of 'consumer complaining' also helps to make it a 'man's world'.

reports over 100 problematic products. On the other hand, the MSA officers hold the view that this is indeed one 'illegal act' (or misconduct) – that the local store failed to check the price tags of the products before putting them on the shelf.[12] Regardless of whether this is found on one product in the shop, or thousands of products in different shops of the business, the business should only be punished once. Thus, MSA officers consider that the professionals deliberately divide one single illegal act (*weifa xingwei*) which they have spotted into hundreds of reports, so as to create more work burdens for the officials, instead of simply making one report to inform the official of the single illegal act. However, the professionals argued that the way they file reports is strictly consistent with the rules on reports that are published up by the MSA. Indeed, on the issue of what constitutes 'one report', the official's rules stressed that one report means that it is on 'the same product' of 'the same specification', for 'the same illegal act'.[13] Since the reports are made on different products, though they are of the same illegal act, they should be considered as different reports.

It is also clear to the local officers that some reports are made just for the sake of 'creating trouble'. For example, a report that contains no evidence of the product being sold in a store, such as a photo of the product on the shelf. Also, some of the stores listed in the report may not even exist anymore. MSA officers advised me that they went to one of the stores listed in a report against a chain store, but the store was closed for several months and could not for any reason be selling the problematic product. The officers later learned that the professional complainant just copied the list of the stores posted on the chained store company's website, without noticing that it had not been updated for a long time. However, again, the professionals argue that the administrative rules do not state that reports have to include an evidence for the malpractice, and in fact, it should be the MSA's job to confirm and investigate the business's behaviour.[14] Most professionals admitted that they developed such strategies just because they want to pressure the MSA, and get their help for a settlement deal with the business. In developing these strategies, they carried a very thorough study on the administrative rules, particularly, rules on the complaint and report procedures, so that they can exert pressure on the official in different ways – and their knowledge about the administrative rules is often much better than the official understanding.

Secondly, the professionals may pick up on what they consider to be procedural errors in any step of the MSA handling of their cases (usually, the report cases), and then request an administrative review (*xingzheng fuyi*) or bring an administrative lawsuit (*xingzheng susong*) in the Administrative Chamber of a People's Court against the MSA. The administrative

[12] This is the general view of the MSA official, but there are some officers who have different opinions. For different views of the official, see section below on Official Attitudes.

[13] This was reported to me by an MSA officer whom I interviewed. The officer also told me that the reason why the MSA introduced such a rule was for the purpose of protecting the business – the business may not receive punishments too often because the requirements for identifying an illegal act are strict (has to be on 'the same product' of 'the same specification', for 'the same illegal act'). However, the rule is now used by the professionals against the officers themselves.

[14] The MSA officers tried to establish a new rule which prevents reports being made upon little evidence (or clues). At the time when my interview was conducted with the MSA officers, they were involved in the first administrative suit brought by the professional complainants, on the rejection of reports lack of evidence. After some pre-trial conversations with the court, the official felt that they would lose the case, and it was unlikely that the court would support them on their new rule.

review or lawsuit may be brought by the professionals on issues at the following stages: first, accepting a report (whether an acceptance is decided, and whether the decision of acceptance is made in due time); secondly, informing the report-maker of the result of the handling of the report (whether the business is punished, how and when is it punished); thirdly, giving rewards to the report-maker for making a report (whether rewards should be given, how should it be given and how much should be given). The MSA has the duty to inform the report-maker of the result of the investigation. The professional complainant may, for example, exhaust all the above procedures for one report, and this means that he can at least bring the MSA to the court six times (three times for the first trial, three times for appeals), and to the administrative reviews three times for each stage, for the handling of one report. What is more, MSA officers complain that the professionals set up communication and similar barriers in order to make sure a case would not proceed – for example, they cannot be reached so as to be informed of the results of the handling of the reports; they do not come to the first court hearing in person but wait instead until there is a second summons compelling them to attend court lest their case is regarded by the judge as having been withdrawn by the plaintiff;[15] they raise concerns about the way officials are handling the matter to the local Commission for Discipline Inspection or the Procuratorate, which may affect the performance appraisal of the officials.[16]

Thirdly, the professionals may ask for 'disclosure of government information' (*zhengfu xinxi gongkai*), as a way to put pressure on the MSA. A citizen can request the government to disclose relevant information by means of the Regulations on the Disclosure of Government Information (*Zhengfu Xinxi Gongkai Tiaoli*).[17] The professional complainants have made good use of this mechanism, in particular to ask for the government to disclose the result of a case report to them.

This is regarded as a new approach to consumer protection, and I will discuss it in detail in chapter seven below. Suppose that the professional complainants initiate 100 reports against one retail store, they may later ask for 100 decisions of case acceptance, 100 replies of case handling and 100 requests of disclosure of government information (of the case result) from the MSA. The amount of paperwork necessary for preparing decisions, replies and disclosure offered by the MSA is enormous, and most of the MSA officers (as I learned) genuinely feel annoyed by the reports filed by the professional complainants.

[15] See Art 48 of the Administrative Procedure Law.

[16] The Commission for Discipline Inspection (*jilü jiancha weiyuanhui*) is the internal-control institution of the Communist Party of China, tasked with enforcing internal rules and regulations and combating corruption and malfeasance in the Party. There are local commissions at each level of government. Government officials are under the supervision and inspection of the Commission.

[17] The Regulations on the Disclosure of Government Information were issued on 4 May 2007 by the State Council, and in effect on 1 May 2007 (and in 2019 revised after completion of this manuscript). Art 1 states: 'This Regulation is formulated for the purpose of safeguarding the legal access to government information by citizens, legal persons and other organizations, improving the transparency of government work, promoting the administration according to law and giving full play to the role of government information of serving the people's production, living and social and economic activities.' Art 9 states: 'An administrative organ shall voluntarily disclose the government information satisfying any of the following basic requirements: (1) Information concerning the vital interests of citizens, legal persons or other organizations; (2) Information that should be widely known by the general public or concerns the participation of the general public; (3) Information reflecting the structural establishment, duties, procedures for handling affairs and other situation of the administrative organ; (4) Other information that shall be voluntarily disclosed by the administrative organ as prescribed by laws, regulations and the relevant state provisions.' These provisions have been amended slightly in the latest 2019 revision of the Regulations.

Here is an example showing the number of reports that are made. Some official data reveals that on a single day in December, 2013, one of the local MSA offices received 82 reports against the Ren Ren Le retail store located in the Pinghu shopping mall. It later received another 762 reports against the Vanguard and nine other local retail stores from 2–6 January 2014, and 91 reports against the Rainbow retail store on 8 January. All the above mentioned reports concerned the same issue on the same product – the label claiming that the product offered 'the most authentic flavour' to be found on packages of 'Zheng Lin's Salt Peanuts'. This claim was suspected of violating the Food Safety Law and the Advertising Law. Also, it was discovered that the reports were made by 93 different people. In addition to Shenzhen, the addresses of the report-makers were also from Beijing, Shanghai, Shandong and other 15 provinces and cities. What is more, later, the local MSA office received almost 200 requests for disclosing the information of the result of the investigation on the reported cases, and the requests were all made by citizens from many places other than Shenzhen.

As we have mentioned above, the 'complaint channel' and the 'report channel' are indeed different. It seems that the different styles the professionals choose, to complain or to report or to use both, largely depend on two factors: the attitude of local officers towards complaints and reports, and their own negotiation skills and beliefs in their own ability. In general, it does not make much difference to them, whether it is a complaint or a report that they file. However, this practice does make a difference to the administration (MSA) with regard to the workload it creates for the officials, especially when both complaints and reports are lodged on the same matter instead of just one or the other. On the other hand, there are some professionals who are less in favour of the complaint channel. Instead, they stick to the report channel, as the report channel is associated with rewards. According to the rules of the MSA, the MSA should offer rewards to people who file a report that in fact leads the MSA to awareness of a business's malpractices.[18] For example, for someone like Mr Chen, much of his time was spent on reporting and getting rewards from the MSA. Mr Chen enjoys the process of claiming rewards, and he seems very confident in getting such prizes. If he fails to get the rewards that he deserves, he may sue the MSA in the administrative court (or request an administrative review), or raise the procedural errors that the MSA officers make when they handle his report and rewards.

Some professionals told me that, in their view, the report system is indeed a more powerful scheme than the complaint system, as it results in an administrative fine of which the business is afraid. By observing the professionals' practice, I also found that the report system tends to help them to get 'bigger' deals with the business – such as those that are over 10,000RMB instead of a couple of thousand RMBs. Also, the report system does not necessarily require the purchase of goods – so the professionals can create hundreds of reports easily, as a way to put pressure on the MSA so that the MSA facilitates their negotiation with the business concerned. As mentioned earlier in this chapter, one professional complainant on one occasion filed reports against all the chain stores in the Shenzhen area by copying

[18] See Shenzhen Detailed Rules for the Implementation of Reward Methods for Reports on Food Safety Issues (*Shenzhen MSA Bureau*, 2012) www.sz.gov.cn/zfgb/2012_1/gb792/201206/t20120619_1925945.htm. The professionals are usually very familiar with these Rules.

a list of all the branch stores from the company's official website, pasting it into his report form, and claiming that the problematic product is sold in every store of the company in Shenzhen.

C. Who and What Are the 'Professionals'?

A significant part of the pressure that the professionals exert on the officials comes from their innovation and imagination: they are clever at opening up new areas, doing in-depth research and discovering new issues in any angle of consumption where they think they have a chance to successfully assert a claim. Some of my informants, especially the more 'senior' of the professionals, make a point of studying new regulations, digging out new problems on a regular basis, and are very proud of themselves.[19] They explained to me that they always try to think ahead so as to discover new issues and problems which have not yet been researched and exposed by their competitive peers (that is, other professionals). The issues they have brought up are by no means confined to food products even though, as I have pointed out, the Food Safety Law 2009 (revised 2015) has given the professionals much ammunition. I have seen that they deal with issues such as train tickets, doubtful receipts, mobile phone contracts, and even in respect of some more public-orientated and non-consumer related issues, such as reporting dirty public toilets (to get the public bodies to improve their condition). In addition to being very 'on the ball' in uncovering new and important issues in which to assert claims, they develop their negotiation skills to a high level and have innovative complaint and reporting techniques in the interests of securing a favourable settlement agreement, as I discuss further below.

The professionals are informally stratified. Some are at the 'lower end', focusing more on immediate profits and expect to earn relatively small amounts of money through routine complaints and reports; some others are at the 'higher end', and try to get very favourable outcomes through buying large quantities of doubtful products, and even take on 'apprentices' and hire assistants.[20] Those latter, 'seniors', are more likely to explore new issues, expand the complaint and reporting field and develop their negotiation skills. The less experienced professionals usually imitate the way that is done by the senior professionals – they tend to buy products that have been reported as having problems by other professionals, and try to keep an eye on the re-appearance of these products on the shop shelf after the business has been fined. This is mainly because many of the existing problems normally do not disappear in a short time, even after a case has been lost or settled on terms unfavourable to the seller or manufacturer. For example, the accreditation of the product on packaging claims that it is a 'first-class quality' product, but it is in fact not so, and the accreditation is proved to be a fake one by the professionals. Change of the packaging after a case has been lost requires expenditure, and it often takes time for the business (eg, a supermarket) to remove all the incorrectly labelled products from the shelf. It is highly likely that the product will still be on

[19] Mr Li and Mr Chen in the case study below are such figures.

[20] My main informant, Mr Chen – whose work is described in the text below – is reputed to train more apprentices than any other of the professionals, as indicated by the comments of both MSA officials and other professionals.

sale with its old packaging even after the seller or manufacturer has been punished or forced into an unfavourable settlement.

It also seems that those at the lower end of the hierarchy are more focused on profits, and may perpetrate some 'misconduct' in order to achieve their moneymaking goals. For example, one technique used is that some professionals deliberately hide yogurt pots at the very back corner of the refrigerator (or in other covert places), so that the shop assistants cannot see the yogurt pot when they refill the shelf in the refrigerated section. The professionals then come to the shop after a few days, find the hidden product and bring it to the till, and claim that it is expired according to the expiry date printed on the product – pretending that they have just found the expired product on the shelf and then asking for the ten-time punitive damages.[21]

The working style of the professionals also varies. Some professionals like corporations, with a team of workers, while some others simply prefer to work alone. Among the professionals that I have developed closest relations with when in the field, Mr Chen clearly is willing to form strategic alliances and cooperative work techniques with other professional complainants. With one such 'brother' the arrangement is that they share responsibilities and profits – Mr Chen is in charge of analysing the legal issues relating to the suspect product, uncovering the legally-recognised evidence for infringement, developing the strategies for negotiation and making complaints, and advising on how best to buy the suspect product or products (when to buy them and how many). His cooperating 'partner' is in charge of checking the problem 'on the spot' (often a supermarket), buying the suspect products at the right time, drafting the online complaint or report, and so on. On the whole, however, most professionals that I came across mainly work on their own – they design their own strategies, and some of them do not wish to share what they regard as their 'commercial secret' – that is, their particular strategy – with other professionals in case the others copy it in an effort to get a share of the 'pie' of a favourable outcome.

What is more, as described by some local MSA officers, it seems to be the case that in general many of the founding fathers in the ranks of the professionals, and some others who got going in the consumer complaining work in the early days, like to work on their own. They tried to keep a harmonious relationship with the administrative department (the MSA), so they do not claim too much – usually a relatively modest sum of money which the business is more willing to pay, such as several thousand RMB. However, since Mr Chen's rise to a high status, the rules that his predecessors, including the founding father in Shenzhen, Mr Zhao, maintained were disrupted. Mr Chen likes to buy large quantities of goods, file hundreds of complaints in one go, and is not afraid of fighting against the administrative department (even if this means going to court). He started to take on and nurture

[21] This strategy is also revealed in the advertisement discussed below that was posted by the professional complainants. This practice is found in many other cities besides Shenzhen. See news about anti-counterfeit professionals setting 'traps' (hiding food) in supermarkets in Nanjing; Y Chen, 'Nanjing: Nanzi ba Shangpin Cang Chaoshi Huojia, Guoqi Hou Goumai Yaoqiu Suopei' (Nanjing: Man Hid Products behind the Shelf, Waited until It Expired and Bought it) (*Yangtsz Evening Post*, 1 July 2015) js.ifeng.com/news/city/detail_2015_07/01/4061797_0.shtml; Another news item shows that hiding products on top of shelves has become a phenomenon among the profession, 'Dajia Mingren jie Hangye Luanxiang: Shipin Cang Huojiading deng Guoqi Suopei' (Scandals Exposed by Famous Anti-Counterfeit Professionals: Expired Food Hidden on the Shelf for Claiming Compensation) (*China News*, 22 October 2015) www.chinanews.com/sh/2015/10-22/7582587.shtml.

'apprentices', either instructing them to work for him, or to cooperate with him on specific cases in a rather more aggressive manner. Some of his 'apprentices' now make among the highest number of complaints and reports each month, and may later become independent, going out to work for themselves.

During my fieldwork, I found that the professionals have been given various names, often depending on the person who is describing them. The first and most widely used name is perhaps one that arises from the early history of consumer claims in post-Mao China, namely, the anti-counterfeit professional (*zhiye dajiaren*), indicating that this activity is 'inherited' from the 'Wang Hai' practices. The next most popular one is probably the 'hotspot complainant' (*redian tousu ren*), which is also the name that I first come across in the Consumer Council, though later on I found out that these complainants have moved their business mainly to the complaint and report platform provided by the MSA. Names like 'professional complainants', 'professional reporters', and 'professional litigants' are less popular, but are used by officials in different bodies, and they reveal the process that the professionals have initiated. The most official name that is in use within the MSA now is the name called 'concentrated complainants and reports initiators' (*jizhong shensu* and *jubao ren*), which is regarded by the MSA officials as a rather neutral term. This term, as explained by one officer, reveals the most distinctive feature of the professionals in the current days in Shenzhen – to file a large number of complaints or reports in one go, or repeatedly file complaints or reports on different matters.[22] They developed this new designation also in part because of pressure from the professionals themselves, some of whom complained that the previous characterisations – that is 'hotspot complainants' and 'anti-counterfeit professionals' – have carried unnecessarily negative connotations. The professionals themselves, on the other hand, declare that they are mere 'warmhearted complainant/reporters'.[23] Some, like Mr Chen, particularly emphasise that he is a 'citizen' or even a 'warmhearted citizen' who identifies malpractices in the consumer market and is a laudable advocate for consumers' rights and interests. He even suggested that the true '*dajiaren*' (the anti-counterfeit professional) should be the administrative departments, whose job is to investigate and negatively sanction the malpractices of the businesses. But since they do not do their job properly, he has to do it for them as well as for the public whom the officials should be serving.

One may also wonder, how these professionals start their 'trade'. Is what they are doing really something akin to a 'profession'? To what extent do they do this consumer rights claiming as a full-time occupation? I have talked to a number of these professionals, and they offer differing answers. One professional told me that he was qualified as a lawyer, but he chose to spend most of his time on working as a professional complainant because it gave him a certain kind of autonomy. In his words, 'if you are a lawyer, you have to serve your clients; but if you are a professional complainant, you don't have to serve [or work for] anyone … Lawyers often need to ask people for help [with the case] to get a good outcome,

[22] Ordinary consumers tend not to make a complaint, unless their grievances are so unbearable that they cannot be lumped together easily. Therefore there is a good reason to believe that a person who makes a large number of complaints against every single branch of a supermarket, or who makes complaints on a regular basis, is a 'professional'.

[23] Usually senior professionals make these declarations, as they care more about how people regard them.

but professional complainants can get people to work for them'.[24] He also pointed out that he enjoyed the pride that this 'profession' has brought to him – an equal or higher negotiating position with the defendant business because of the help by the official. His lawyer identity has brought him some convenience in his practice as a professional complainant, such as a better understanding of law and access to some documents in litigation, but he did not receive cases regularly, neither did he talk about his 'law career'. He is indeed a rare example, as the majority of professional complainants do not hold any formal legal qualifications.[25] Another, however, started working as a professional complainant for several years, and later he passed the judicial exam and became a lawyer. After qualifying as a lawyer, he concentrates on lawyer's work, so has no longer shown up in the MSA on a regular basis.

Another professional with whom I discussed matters at some length is a full-time university student. He was then a second-year postgraduate majoring in biological studies, and was considering doing a PhD. He told me that he learned about the 'professionals' from friends and that they were making good money. He hoped to earn some income to cover living expenses because he is not from a wealthy family. He did not reside in Shenzhen, but only came to Shenzhen during term breaks, did some work, and then went back to the university for his studies before the new term started. Like the lawyer noted above, he differs from most of the professionals working in Shenzhen, as they do not hold higher educational qualifications such as a degree.[26]

Another informant professional advised me that he used to be an employee in a company. He is well informed about business practices, the relevant regulations in the market, and has built up a strong interpersonal network within the consumer complaint and reporting area in which he specialises. I first came to know him from the ranking list created by the MSA.[27] However, no one among the officials knew much about him. When I asked around about him and his work, I initially did not get much response, but later he was introduced to me by one of my informants (Mr Chen, a senior) during a meeting they held for collaboration on a specific case. At that time, his name was relatively new on the ranking list, but it had shown up suddenly and he had occupied the top three ranking for several months prior to that meeting. During the collaboration conference, he introduced himself humbly to Mr Chen as a 'beginner' in this profession, with some past experience in the same field (as an employee of the company). However, he picked up the new profession very quickly and did well over a period of a few months, earning some 200,000RMB for several months' work, which prompted Mr Chen to observe that this was a rather good income for a rookie. He was seeking advice from Mr Chen, as he came across some difficult legal problems when he was studying new laws and establishing an argument with which to bring a complaint.

It is perhaps not surprising that there is active recruitment for this 'profession'. From what I have learned, the professional complainants have created their own online chat

[24] I suspect that here he refers to the work done by the official who has facilitated negotiations between the business and the professionals.

[25] This person was introduced by one of my informants because my informant thought that he and I could discuss legal issues and therefore he could help me with the development of my research.

[26] Even those 'seniors', like Mr Chen and Mr Li, are not well educated.

[27] The professionals' names are listed according to the number of complaints brought by them in descending order.

group, and there are advertisements posted asking for people to join the 'profession'. Some advertisements are even posted in the online chat group of the retailer. One advertisement, as it reads, requires 'people who are ruthless (*xinhen shoula*), thick-skinned (*hou lianpi*: literally, thick-skinned face), and gutsy (*danzi da*)' and adds that 'there will be professionals to teach you throughout the whole [learning] process'. The advertisement also gives an outline of the job specification, as it says:

> The content of the job is to go to large supermarkets and buy expired products. If the products are not expired, you can hide them first [for example, at the back of the shelf], and then buy them when they are expired (you will need to take a photo of it). Another task is to buy products of which the label has some error of characters, marks or logos, and then seek compensation for the error from the department stores. The department stores take into account their face (*mianzi*), so they pay very high compensation. Otherwise, you can seek compensation from the manufacturers or wholesale distributors. If these [methods] do not work, you can use other methods including threats and blackmail, to ask for compensation, and thus this job requires those who are ruthless, thick-skinned and gutsy. The current [official] policy does not support this activity, neither does it oppose this activity, so this is the right time to develop such a career.

This 'advert' also points to the fact that the professional complainants try to recruit insiders from within the business, because this advertisement is posted in the online chat group of the retailer.

The professional complainants work in groups from time to time, both on a temporary basis and sometimes on a much longer-term basis. The above-mentioned 'advert' was in fact posted by a coalition of two professional complainants, and they were recruiting assistants to help with their work. In a broader context, some very successful professionals, such as Wang Hai (the anti-counterfeit hero) whose practice can be found in many developed cities in China, have established companies in various cities (typically, Beijing, Tianjin, Nanjing and Shenzhen), and I am told that through this broader coverage he made an annual 'profit' of over 4 million RMB (£400,000) in 2014.[28] One figure, Liu Dianlin, has also scaled up his 'trade' by establishing a company in Guangzhou, and (like Wang Hai) he has extended his practice so he not only has cases for himself but also identifies counterfeit products for well-known companies.[29] Both Wang Hai and Liu Dianlin admit that they are making good money from their various efforts, and their paramount status is reflected in the fact that in many everyday situations they are addressed as 'boss' (*lao ban*) among their friends and others.

The Internet has become a very important resource for the professional complainants. The main way in which they file a complaint or a report is through the Internet – they often submit their complaint or report form, with detailed explanation on the issue and their inquiries, to the MSA through its online complaint and report portal.[30] They do sometimes

[28] F Pu, 'Zhiye Dajiaren Wanghai: Jukuan Mai Jiahuo 1nian Zuan 400wan' ('Anti-Counterfeit Professional Wang Hai: Spent Huge Money on Buying Counterfeit Products and Earned 4 Million One Year') (*The Beijing News*, 23 March 2015) finance.people.com.cn/n/2015/0323/c1004-26732619.html.

[29] F Ruo, 'Liu Dianlin: Dang "Dajia" Chengwei Yizhong Zhiye' ('Liu Dianlin: When 'Anti-Counterfeit' Activity Becomes a Profession') (*Guang Ming Daily*, 4, 15 March 2014) epaper.gmw.cn/gmrb/html/2014-03/15/nw.D110000gmrb_20140315_6-04.htm.

[30] As I mentioned earlier, this has become one of the features for the MSA official to tell whether a complainant is a professional or not.

use hard copy letters, but the internet is a much faster process. Unlike many of the 'ordinary' complainants, the professionals do not favour phone calls, and this is because they feel that a phone call does not give them enough time to fully articulate their opinions. What is more, the internet is also a good platform for them to meet new people, exchange ideas and skills, and even call for help when they have problems. As we shall see in the section below, they often seek other people's assistance in filing reports and complainants, so as to increase the number of cases and thereby create pressure for the MSA. Their net-friends can easily file complaints and reports through the online system, even when – as is sometimes the case – they are thousands of miles away.[31]

D. Why Does Their Strategy Work?

Due to the differences between the complaint process and the reporting process, in theory, only a complaint may be withdrawn (*che su*). If it is a report that has been made, then that report has to be followed up, and a preliminary investigation has to be initiated by the MSA, such as paying a visit to the supermarket and taking some samples of the product in question. However, in reality, things are a little different. First, in practice, the local MSA officers may not necessarily distinguish between the complaint process and reporting process initiated by the professional complainants – and indeed, it is commonly assumed by the officers that both processes do in fact serve to help the professional complainants to get a good settlement agreement with the defendant business. Secondly, in practice, the defendant business, which is often a large supermarket, often removes all the problematic products off the shelf before the MSA comes and checks them. Because no item is actually selling when the check is made, the business can easily claim that the product is not being sold, and the MSA fail to obtain any evidence – say, a sample of the product that it is claimed has the problem – in order to carry on with the investigation against the business.[32] In some situations, the business are informed by the professional complainants that they have bought the problematic products, and are preparing to file complaints or reports. With such information, the business removes all the problematic products from the shelf so as to avoid the spot-check and the administrative sanction that follows. The businesses, however, learn as they fight against the professionals; they sometimes even recognise the professionals' faces. When the shop assistants spot the professionals in the retail store (when the professionals are buying the product), they will quickly check with the cashier, or look at the surveillance monitor in the store, to see what the professionals have bought, so as to ascertain if there is any problem with the product, especially in the case of senior professionals. One retail store manager, seeing me in the store with a professional, confessed that he had been very nervous when he saw us together, as he feared trouble – but in reality the professional, Mr Chen, just went to the store to buy a gift for his friend.

If a settlement agreement is reached (either in a complaint process or report process), the professionals will return the problematic products to the business, and will inform the

[31] There is no limitation in the rules saying that only citizens in Shenzhen can file a report to the Shenzhen MSA.

[32] According to the official, the check done by the MSA is a one-shot one – it only checks the product when it is on the shelf. MSA staff visit the supermarkets on a regular basis and give a spot-check each time.

MSA that they have reached a settlement agreement. If the deal is not done, the professional complainants will continue the complaint or report process. So, in practice there is a great deal of strategic overlap between the complaint and the report in the hands of the professional complainant, especially the more skilful and experienced ones.

When the two parties reached a settlement, the local MSA officers may or may not agree to close the case. This is because, as I have noted, in theory, if the case comes in as a report, the MSA has the duty to start an investigation, no matter whether the parties reach an agreement or not. However, the most common practice is that the local MSA officers will abandon the case, if they know that the two parties have settled. One of the most important reasons for this practice, as the MSA officers often complain, is that they do not have the time to carry on with such a report (as this will mean going deeper into the matter and starting investigation) because of the increased workload they receive from these professional complainants. Also, since the MSA officers assume that the purpose for the professionals to make a complaint (when they have conversations in the office) is to get a settlement deal with the business, it is much easier to close a case by pretending that they cannot find evidence for investigation, since the products are off the shelf now and the only remaining products in question will be returned to the business by the professionals under the terms of the settlement. In this way, the local MSA officers help the professionals to get the settlement deal by putting pressure on the business, and promise that if this case is settled outside of the report system, they will not continue any investigation nor impose any fines.

The business, on the other hand, tends to accept the deal, if the price of settlement is not too high. This is because the administrative fines that the business may get (if the settlement is failed) are usually much higher than the price they pay to the professional complainants. As explained by one retail store manager, for example, if for one single item a business is going to be fined 2,000, and the product is sold in 20 branches of the chain store, the fine for one product will be 2,000 times 20, totalling 40,000RMB. Usually there is far more than one problematic product spotted by the professionals in one shop at a time, so this is surely a large amount of money when compared to the size of the deal that the professionals seek. Another reason is that the businesses that the professional complainants fight against are often large companies, some of which are listed companies on the stock exchange, and therefore likely to have 'deep pockets'. These companies, such as Walmart, Carrefour, China Vanguard Group and the Rainbow Department Store, need to take a great deal of care about protecting their commercial reputation and commercial credit. According to the MSA staff, once the company is fined, it also gets a stigmatic mark on its record in the MSA system. Particularly, for listed companies, there are duties which require the companies to inform their shareholders about these aspects of their performance. From this perspective, it may cost the company thousands of thousands of RMB, and certainly much more than the small sum of money paid to the professional complainants as part of a settlement to end the case.

E. Income v Risks

The professionals often earn a fairly good income through their consumer complaint activities. Some of the more successful, such as Mr Chen for example, are known to settle cases on very favourable terms. I regularly heard from him that he had settled cases with compensation in excess of 10,000RMB. From the time that he devoted himself into 'making money' as a professional complainant, he has been receiving an average 300,000 to 400,000RMB each year, and since the 'income' is regarded as compensation, it is not taxed.[33] One informant reported in an interview with me that he earned over 200,000 in the first seven months of 2014. I have also seen settlement agreements with compensation of 10,000RMB, 11,000RMB and 9,500RMB respectively for each complaint brought by the particular professional complainant. What is more, in the job advertisement mentioned earlier, the salary for a 'job' as an assistant to the leading professionals includes a basic remuneration of 6000RMB per month, food and lodging, plus a commission of 25 per cent of the total revenue of the particular cases handled by the appointee, and this likely brings up a total monthly income package of 18,000RMB or more. This sum is in excess of the salary of many full Professors in the PRC. The professionals' income is also sufficiently impressive for MSA officers to take note, sometimes with a touch of jealousy, of their 'conspicuously consumed' rewards. One officer, for example, pointed out that Mr X was now driving a brand-new Land Rover when he came to the MSA offices.

However, there are also those who are not earning much. For example, one professional, who sought the help of Mr Chen on how best to develop his 'consumer complaint' skill set, complained to Mr Chen that he was only making on average a couple of hundred RMB for each case, and that his income was not stable, in the sense that he could not rely on a regular income for each month. As Mr Chen explained to him, this was because he lacked Mr Chen's negotiation and complaint skills, and that his skills would remain rather elementary unless he improved his strategy. He buys one single item at a time, and files one complaint about that product. He also lacked the 'boldness' of other more senior professionals claiming a lot less than the thousands and ten thousands the seniors did, largely because of his limited knowledge about the goods in question and his limited command of the relevant regulations.

I also discovered that while a number of professionals may enjoy a good income from their activities, the work they do also carries risks and danger. Some professionals complained to me that they sometimes receive oral threats from the businesses whose products or services they challenge. Often they are regarded by the defendant businesses as 'not having a proper job', but instead using crooked ways to earn money. One of my informants reported that a business against which he won several cases put pressure on him by advising him: 'I have a good personal network in this local area. If you continue to do this, I can ask some guys to give you a bad time (*gao ni*).' Another informant, a university student, reported his experience of how the local SAIC (in his city) informed his university of what he was doing (earning money by filing complaints against certain businesses), and the university official 'talked' to him, and put pressure on him to abandon his 'improper' conduct. He further told me that he was afraid of some kind of revenge attack from the business, so he tried to stay in the university accommodation so as to be with more people and more visible, rather than renting a flat outside the university with a couple of friends,

[33] Mr Chen did not start to 'make money' until recently (in 2011). The officials comment that most professionals do not set up a company (for example, like Wang Hai) to do their 'trade', because the company has to pay tax, while this income is regarded as compensation (based on a contractual agreement) which does not fall within the taxable categories.

therefore being more vulnerable. One more significant detail is that he dressed up in a very mature manner and combed his hair in a 'smart' fashion, which made him look like a 'businessman' and older than he really was. He later explained to me that this was also his protection from revenge attacks, since a more mature look tended to give him more confidence in what he was doing and some toughness and strength in the negotiation with the business, and the other side would therefore be wary of intimidating him if he secured a successful outcome.

Most of the professional complainants are positive about their 'work' and its future prospects – they believe that at least in the coming 10 to 20 years, they will still be able to earn a good, stable income from buying counterfeit products and then claiming compensation. In fact they tend to talk about their work as a kind of 'profession'. However, at the same time, some worry that their profession will not last for a long time, as this might just be a temporary problem in China in the sense that it will vanish as the economy develops and issues like IP infringement are sorted out. What is more, as the administrative departments learn about their complaint and report strategies, and the relevant laws and regulations (especially on procedural matters) are reformed, the professionals may not be in such an advantageous position in their negotiations with defendant businesses.

III. Mixed Motives

The purposes, or motives, of the professionals' practice are frequently called into question by many officials dealing with consumer issues and also from time to time by the general public. It has been argued, especially by the doubting officials, that what the professional complainants have been doing is merely trying to make money – this consumer complaining is their job, and they 'go to work' in order to earn 'compensation' from the defendant businesses as their 'salary'. Back in the early days of this form of 'consumer activism', the man discussed above, Mr Wang Hai, used to enjoy a good reputation for his consumer rights protection activities. However, he was later attacked by some members of the public and by officials. The accusation levelled against him was that he was merely interested in securing an income through compensation awards and settlements. Several informants told me that in the early years, the court also occasionally took the view that these professionals could not be considered as 'real consumers', because they do not fit into the criterion of 'purchasing for the purposes of daily consumption'.[34] In more recent times, as the group of 'anti-counterfeit professionals' has become more numerous, their strategies become diversified, their deals with the businesses become larger, and their motivation continues to be widely called into question. They are characterised as profit-driven and they have become controversial figures in the eyes of many members of the public. The officials too continue to believe that the professionals' main purpose is to earn money, and some take a rather antagonistic stance as they feel that they are being used by the professionals (especially at the municipal level).[35] On the other hand, the courts have gradually given support to the

[34] See Art 2 of the Consumer Protection Law 2013.

[35] Details of the officials' view on the professional complainants are revealed in the section below on Official Attitudes.

professionals in according them more clearly the status of a genuine 'consumer', without giving much regard to their motives for making a purchase. In particular, in 2013, the Supreme People's Court published a judicial review concerning the handling of cases of food products which pointed out that 'the courts do not support a defence that the retailers [often] use to suggest that those who know food products are problematic but still purchase them are not consumers'.[36] In Shenzhen, the attitude of the courts is much clearer and the support is even more obvious: on 28 May 2014, the Shenzhen Intermediate People's Court revised the Guiding Notes on Adjudicating Cases Concerning Consumer Rights and Interests, of which the first article clearly states that 'any citizens, legal persons and other associations who make consumption for the purpose of "*dajia*" (anti-counterfeit purposes), are regarded as consumers under the Consumer Protection Law'.[37]

Indeed, in my view, the picture is more complicated than the stereotypical critiques suggest. We need to take a closer look at what makes a professional complainant continue with his work, and what ends these people pursue in their practice, particularly in terms of how they themselves understand their role. In my discussions with the Shenzhen professionals, I conclude that it is perhaps best to characterise them as possessing 'mixed motives' for carrying out their work. It is very obvious to me that profit-making is one of their most important motives. For most, their priority is getting a good settlement, and at times they do use inappropriate methods such as threatening conduct or 'blackmail' to secure their financial goals. They favour negotiated settlements, and are not very keen on the court and its more formal procedures for the handling of their cases. When they bring a lawsuit, it is primarily a strategic step intended to pressure the MSA into facilitating a settlement outcome. Thus, for example, they might file an administrative case against the MSA on grounds of procedural error when the MSA does not in their view do enough to help them get a good deal from the defendant business.

It also seems that some professionals nevertheless also have a genuine concern for the public interest. They consider themselves to be facilitators for the improvements for consumer rights protection in the long term. This is particularly so of the more senior figures, who often enjoy some degree of fame in the mass media. For example, the Shenzhen 'founding father', Mr Zhao, who started off as a profit-driven professional, who earns a very good income. He has developed concerns more about the public interests since he became 'successful', and he does make thoughtful reform suggestions to the authorities. For example, he proposed to the MSA the idea that it could establish an 'inspector system' in which the professional complainants would be authorised to spot commercial malpractices of sellers on behalf of the MSA, as 'inspectors'. Another senior professional, Mr Chen has given an enormous amount of advice to the officials on the workings and redesign of their system, and has regularly published his consumer redress experiences and knowledge in the mass media so as to enhance consumer awareness. What is more, for some professionals it was

[36] See Art 3 of Supreme People's Court Provisions on Several Issues Concerning the Application of Law in the Trial of Cases Involving Food and Drug Disputes, passed by the 1599th meeting of the Adjudication Committee of the Supreme People's Court on 9 December 2013, and in effect on 15 March 2014.

[37] Shenzhen Shi Zhongji Renmin Fayuan guanyu Xiaofeizhe Quanyi Jiufen Anjian de Caipan Zhiyin (The Guiding Notes of the Shenzhen Intermediate People's Court on Adjudicating Cases Concerning Consumer Rights and Interests), first published on 1 July 2007, last revised on 28 May 2018.

their own unhappy experience as an ordinary consumer with the complaint and redress system that triggered their decision to become a 'professional'. For example, one of the professionals, Mr Z, stated that he had purchased a defective product and attempted to obtain compensation from the business. But he failed, and became very frustrated with the consumer complaint and redress processes. Later, he got to know one of the professional complainants, and asked him for advice on the case. Through this experience with his own case, Mr Z gradually learned about 'professional complainants' and the techniques that they use. Even when his case was resolved, he continued to employ these techniques in other disputes. He had become 'converted' into a professional complainant.

I provide below two examples of two individual professionals, who have different priorities in their practices, and thus their approaches to securing compensation are different.

A. Pursuit of Personal Interest: The Case of Mr Li

Mr Li is constantly among the top names of the list created by the local officials, on the number of cases brought by the professionals. During the interview, he confessed to me that his only purpose for doing this 'job' is to make money. He treated this practice as his own profession, employing knowledge and techniques to enhance his practice, always updating his knowledge, calculating the benefits and losses of particular lines of action, and very focussed on work that brings him money. His approach to the issues is to stay at the negotiation level – a settlement agreement with the business is what he pursues. He has been using the strategy that I noted above: to spot a potential issue with one (or more) of the products in a retail store, study the laws and regulations about that product, file a report (or a report and a complaint at the same time) against the defendant business to the MSA, and then seek a settlement agreement with the business. When asked about why he does not bring cases to the court, he replied that the court often does not see it as a public interest matter, which may cause him some 'difficulty', and the compensation he can get from a successful court action is much less (capped at double the price of the money he spent on the item in question) than he would likely secure from a settlement. Instead, he prefers negotiating directly with the manufacturers for compensation, even if that means sometimes he has to travel to other cities since the manufacturers are not located in Shenzhen.[38]

Mr Li is very proud of what he sees as his 'professionalism'. He describes some of his successful cases with delight. For example, he decided to focus on the issue of the use of the name 'almond' on the food products, which is a common mistake that has been found on the labels of various food products that contain this ingredient. One particular product label

[38] Shenzhen is a city which does not have a large manufacturing base itself. Many of the products on sale in Shenzhen are not produced locally. The reason why Mr Li often goes to the manufacturers directly lies in the fact that often in Shenzhen (as elsewhere in the world) the retail store refuses to accept any responsibility for the presented problem and kicks the ball to the manufacturers, and it is often the manufacturers who pay the price of a settlement deal. In some situations, the retail store may even call the manufacturers to attend the negotiation (or mediation) meeting, so that they (the manufacturers) can make a deal with the professionals directly. Mr Li is aware of the relationship that often exists between the manufacturer and the retail store, so he knows it is better to not negotiate with the retail store and not be able to get compensation from it.

has used the term '*meiguo da xinren*' (literally translated as 'American Big Almond'), and this is very misleading. The product is indeed 'amygdalus communis', namely, 'almond' as the term is often used outside China. However, in Chinese, it should be called *bian taoren*, or 'Badanmu nuts', a very different food from what is considered as *xingren* (literally translated as 'almond') within China. The Chinese *xingren* (Chinese almond) has very different nutritional qualities that differ from those of the *bian taoren*. The ingredient 'amygdalus communis' (*biantao ren*) is also found in various other products such as 'almond milk' (*xingren niunai*), of which the ingredient is not Chinese *xingren* either.[39]

Although Mr Li does not consider himself as primarily working for the public interest, it seems that what he was doing has significantly helped with consumer protection in a number of ways. He has a sense of professionalism of which he is proud employing his knowledge to spot the problems in products, and making money out of his efforts (indicating that he is good at what he does). He considers the MSA as not having been very helpful to his efforts:

> I don't really expect that they [the MSA official] can help me earn much money … The main function that they have now, is simply to notify and to pass on the message [to the defendant business] … Well, [I suppose that is helpful because] at least we need to know against whom the complaint has been made.

He considers that the MSA officers are often 'too arrogant', and the fact that he earns more than they do makes him feel more confident than he otherwise might when he is present in the court with them. What is more, he observes:

> Many of my cases are targeted at foreign companies, such as Starbucks, like the case I showed you just now.[40] These foreign companies want the Chinese law to adapt to their practices, rather than changing their practices to fit the law in China … The MSA bureau, however, thinks that as long as there are no people who have died, these are not problems … Once there was a case I worked on, in which the final decision that the MSA reached, was to punish the company by a fine of 12.5 yuan. Only 12.5 yuan! This could not even cover the administrative costs spent on this case. Nevertheless, the official claimed that their punishment was in accordance with the law (*yifa chufa*).

B. Balance of Public Service and Personal Interest: The Case of Mr Chen

Mr Chen is a more complex figure. He emphasises that he is a 'citizen', particularly, a 'warm-hearted citizen' (*rexin gongmin*) who constantly reports issues to the officials, rather than seeing himself as an 'anti-counterfeit professional' whose only purpose is to make

[39] As a result, almost all the products using the ingredient *biantao ren* have stopped using the name *xingren* ('almond') on their packaging. The name 'ba dan mu', a transliteration of the term 'Badanmu nut' is now used.

[40] The case is about the quality of the receipt paper provided by Starbucks. Mr Li argues that the receipt paper is made of low quality heat-sensitive paper, on which the information fades away very quickly. Regarding some products sold in Starbucks, such as biscuits, which are not consumed right away, Mr Li has found out that information on the receipt may not last long enough to cover the shelf life of the food.

money. His title of 'citizen' is printed in his name card, as 'Citizen Chen Shu Wei'. Mr Chen has been a 'fighter' for consumer protection for more than a decade. He has devoted himself to the field of telecommunication services, where his efforts have promoted the changing of many rules, such as the cancellation of high price 'network access charge' for mobile phones in the early days of mobile phone usage.[41] As he described his history to me, he was not making any money in the early years from his consumer advocacy activities. Instead, he had spent all the savings which he earned by running a 'factory' on his consumer advocate activities, and he also collected donations from his online supporters in order to fund protests and boycotts.

According to Mr Chen, it was not until 2011 that he started the practice of being a 'professional complainant' in a real sense. However, even before this, he had already enjoyed widespread fame for his consumer activist practices. He established online chatting groups where he called for support for his activities, and where he disseminated his consumer knowledge and experience to his supporters; he distributed document templates of statement of claims, settlement agreements, request letters for disclosure of government information, and so on. In this way, he taught people in the online group how to deal with consumer disputes, not just to win a case in court, but also various skills needed in dealing with disputes such as making complaints and reports to the MSA officials, and the negotiation skills required for dealing with defendant business operators. He even, with the help of some friends, published a series of books on consumer laws and regulations, called the '*Liang Jian*' (Brave Sword) series.[42] He gradually nurtured many 'apprentices' who now possess good negotiation skills and professional knowledge on consumer issues. Some of his pupils, including the post-graduate student described above, now earn money by regularly spotting problematic products and claiming compensation. However, Mr Chen does not see himself as 'profit-driven' in that way. He explained that his purpose for establishing such a group and empowering people with consumer knowledge was to get allies and supporters in his fights against bad business practices and reluctant officials. He hopes to teach people to resolve disputes on favourable terms, so that more of them can, like him, fight effectively against business operators, and thereby force business operators to improve their consumer standards. He has a fascinating store of 'war stories' telling of his fights with big business, especially the telecommunication giants, such as China Mobile and China Telecom. Because these two giants are state-owned enterprises, with good 'connections', he had many struggles with the local government departments as well. But because of his efforts, he is a regular troublemaker in the eyes of the local police, and he described how he had played 'escape games' with the police – for example, after he successfully arranged an effective protest in one of the most commercialised areas in Shenzhen against one of the telecom giants.

Mr Chen is of course aware of the 'work' of the 'professional complainant', but he does not see himself as being in such a 'profession'. He dislikes to be called an 'anti-counterfeit

[41] As I noticed in the field, Mr Chen's efforts in the telecommunication consumption area were recognised by most officials.

[42] The title is taken from a famous Chinese spy drama.

professional' (*dajiaren*) in the sense that this term indicates a profit-driven motive. He also stressed that he was not of the same circle as some other successful professionals, such as Wang Hai, who has set up companies and commercialised his practices. He sees himself as one of those of the 'democratic circle' (*minzhu quan*) – who fought for public interests on various issues, including most distinctively human rights issues, and were even arrested and detained for many times because of their inappropriate speeches, protests and boycotts.[43] On the other hand, many of his 'pupils'[44] have made great money out of what he taught them, and in his view some of them have become arrogant and no longer show sufficient respect to him. He later abandoned his online chat groups, partly because of the attitude of his pupils. On the other hand, he has himself started to worry about his finances. As he explained to me:

> I have spent years of time fighting for consumers' interests. I used up all my savings, and at times, I even had to sleep in my friends' homes and asked them to support me. My sister also has given me a lot of monetary support for what I was doing. I am very grateful for her, but my parents were growing old, and I am the only son of the family. I didn't do much for parents because I wasn't living a good life. My sister has been supporting my parents for so long, and I should now take the main responsibility for caring for my parents too … My focus for this year [2014] is to earn money. I need money to support my family and live a proper life.

Mr Chen thus insists both that he is not so keen on earning money, but that unavoidably money is important to him. In fact, it is also evident that what he said was contradictory. Compared to his pupils, he had earned less than most of the more successful ones, because he did not start the professional complaining work with the same full-time intensity as they did. But once he started his more commercial approach, he earned well – the deals he secured from defendant business operators often exceeded 10,000RMB on average. He had earned more than 200,000RMB in the first half year of 2014. Because he is such a high-profile activist figure, with his experience suing the commercial giants in court, and his clever strategies in buying doubtful products, he continues to secure good settlement deals with the defendant businesses. Unlike some other professionals, Mr Chen often purchases a large quantities of products – several hundreds of items at any one time. Indeed, he has to rent a place to store his goods, and hire an assistant to work for him. Also, in contrast to Mr Li, whose focus is often on negotiating a settlement deal with the business, Mr Chen spends much time on getting rewards for making useful reports. This brings him a modest income, perhaps not as much as what he can get from negotiating with the businesses, but he enjoys the process. He dislikes many of the local consumer protection officials intensely and he constantly criticises them for not doing their job properly. He also explained to me that he developed various strategies (including one that is to file massive reports and complaints) to 'beat' the local MSA offices, so as to 'establish an authority' (*shuli weiyan*). He recounts how he at one time focused his fire on one local MSA office, employed his clever strategies to good effect in a number of cases, and fought

[43] Mr Chen said he had quit the democratic circle because he was let down by some of his friends there. I did not get the details of this event, but this could be another reason why he has focused on earning income since 2011.

[44] Mr Chen did not call those people 'pupils', but he taught them the professional complainants' skills through an online chat group.

the office until the cases went to the court (the Administrative Chamber). After several rounds of 'fights' on such cases, the officials in that particular MSA office started to take a less antagonist stance against him, gradually accepted his opinions, began to offer him awards in proper ways, and indeed became more willing to help him get settlement deals with the business.

IV. Official Attitudes

The professional complainants (and reporters) have been heavily criticised by a number of local officials, particularly by those working in the MSA bureau, to the effect that in pursuing their 'personal interests' they manipulate the MSA so as to use it as a 'gun' to attack and to blackmail defendant business operators. That is, it is assumed that there is little or no public interest motive in what they do. This point of view seems to be the mainstream opinion shared by MSA officers, both at the municipal level and at the district level. Indeed, in terms of some of the specific practices that the professionals use, the municipal MSA bureau holds very antagonistic views against what the professionals do. The officials strongly believe that making money is the only goal that the professionals pursue, and this makes them reluctant to facilitate negotiations between the professionals and defendant business operators. In the early days of my fieldwork, when I was interviewing a municipal MSA officer, I mentioned that I hoped to talk to the professionals for the purposes of my research. His first reaction was that 'well, you can try to contact them, but once they have found out you were nothing to do with their money-making (*zheng qian*) [activities], they won't cooperate with you'. The general attitude of local officials, and the 'guiding opinions' that the MSA produces in order to inform the work of the local officers are formalistic – to strictly follow the laws and regulations, do their job properly, sanction those that are supposed to be sanctioned, and try not to be afraid of being sued in the court.

Nevertheless, I found that the reality is that at the local level, officers do in fact hold a variety of differing attitudes towards the professionals. They may be quite active also in showing 'mercy' to the defendant business operators, and be quite sympathetic to the plight the defendants sometimes find themselves in. Also, they may be willing to facilitate negotiations between a professional and a defendant business operator, instead of conducting investigations and imposing sanctions, because they feel entangled and even confused by the numerous reports and complaints that come in. Another variable is the collectively held attitudes that emerge from the experiences of particular offices: the actions officials take may vary greatly depending on the general attitude that is shared by the local office in which they serve.

A. Municipal Level

At the municipal level, the clashes between the professionals and the bureau can become very fierce. In 2012, the municipal MSA bureau called together six officers with strong legal backgrounds, and formed a 'six-person' group to handle the cases brought by the professionals. After the group was set up, cases filed by the professional complainants, especially cross-jurisdictional cases stretching over several parts of Shenzhen municipality, have in general been forwarded to the Regulations Department of the MSA where the 'six-person' group is housed. The officers of this group analyse the issue, and then produce a guiding opinion on the issue in terms of the legal position, whether and what sanctions should be imposed, and whether any awards should be given to the professionals (who have made a report), and so on. The guiding opinion will then be sent back to the local offices for informing them in handling the case.

One of the most important purposes of forming such a group was to gather together officers to work on the legal aspects of the issues, and pass down their legal analysis to the local officers, so as to empower them in their work on the professional complainants. Also, the guiding opinion may to some extent unify the practices in different local offices. Due to limited knowledge on the issues spotted by the professionals, the local officers may hold different understandings of the issues, and this may result in a variety of responses. As a result, even in one local office, different professionals who have filed reports on the same issue may get different results. This may, again, become another potential procedure error that can be spotted and used by the professionals. The municipal MSA bureau hopes that the local officers will learn better the laws and regulations on the issue through the guiding opinion, so that they will reduce the mistakes in their work, as well as not be in a position of passively listening to the demands of the professionals. However, on the other hand, I have observed that while local officers may well read the guiding opinions, they do not necessarily follow what the opinion suggests in handling cases. The local offices are supposed to follow the instructions given by their superior, the municipal MSA bureau, but in reality, since the local offices have a degree of autonomy and are not strictly bound by the guiding opinions, individual officers still have the space to manoeuvre in their practice.

The MSA also sees the professionals as poorly educated, impolite and prepared to exhaust all means, legal or illegal, to pursue their profit goals. In one of the MSA's reports, the professionals are characterised in the following negative terms:

> The 'anti-counterfeit professionals' have publicly claimed that they are not really concerned with the results of investigation of reports and results of administrative suits. Their purpose is to increase our workload by a hundred or thousand times, so that our bureau will succumb to their demands, and we become a tool for them to extract their benefits and interests … They have abused their right to file reports and have exploited litigation possibilities for their personal interests … They ruthlessly insult our officers, often using malicious language, such as cursing the officers with the words that they hope that their 'family will all die', and they do this in public, in their statements of complaint, their report emails, and so on … Unfurling banners and holding up signs in front of the MSA offices with critical comments are also the "anti-counterfeit professionals" favourite tricks.

Also, some issues are considered by the MSA as 'trivia' that do not warrant the enormous time and labour that would be incurred in a comprehensive investigation, such as 'fake accreditation', unclear labelling, food additives, especially if compared with more serious issues, such as poisonous foodstuff which will more likely cause important health problems ('obvious damage' in the words of MSA officials). These are such 'common' problems in the case of food products, but not many of the manufacturers have noticed them until the professionals point them out.

Dealing with a report requires a certain workload to prepare materials to set up a case, go through internal procedurals of getting an approval for investigation, respond to those who make reports, offer rewards, and so on. Thus, it is generally regarded as very troublesome by the local MSA officers given the large amount of reports they receive from the professionals.

B. Local Level

At the local level, the picture is more diverse. As some officers in the local office described the matter to me, the municipal bureau's opinions usually come to them late, because the number of cases is really large and the specialist legal analysts are under great case load pressure as well. So for most of the matters they handle, they feel the need to adopt a more 'settlement'-oriented approach, rather than an 'adversarial' approach suggested and encouraged by the municipal bureau. As a result, sometimes a case has been settled even before an opinion is handed down to the local officers. When the work pressure gets to the local officers, what they aim at mainly is to just get the case resolved, by helping the professional to get the compensation so that he withdraws the report (and it seems as if it never occurred), and there is no need for the officers concerned to follow up the case anymore. One officer complained to me:

> Once I spent a long time searching for the judicial opinions (documents) that are mentioned by the professionals, but I just couldn't find them … The professionals have delivered a really deep analysis of the issue, and even drawn upon the experience and judicial practices from other cities and provinces, so settlement is easier for me.

In looking at local practice, it can be seen that different local offices take slightly different approaches to the handling of professionals' cases. As one officer told me:[45]

> Local office A's attitude is to go against the professionals (*dui zhe gan*). Their problem is that they have done their job on the procedural side [making sure that there is no mistake that can be spotted by the professionals], but they don't [are unwilling to] mediate for the professionals. They tell the defendant business operators too that they are not going to mediate the case, so you [the business] have to take punishment (*ren fa*). As for local office B, where most of the staff are senior people, their attitude is gentler. Their approach is softer, and they try to solve the problems raised by the professionals as far as they can. Therefore, in most situations, the professionals don't give them a bad time (*gao*), and there are very few lawsuits or administrative reviews brought by the professionals against this local office. The officers in this office consider that working on a case is troublesome, and they don't want to work on the case [just as that the professionals often don't really want to go on with the case], so they get the business to compensate the professionals, and then they can say that the problematic products were now off shelf … In the case of another office, local office C, their approach is perhaps somewhere in the middle [of the above two offices]. They have done their procedure job to the fullest. Unlike local office A, [who says no to mediations], if the professionals ask for a mediation, they will arrange one [but they don't take the responsibility of making sure that it will necessarily succeed and result in a settlement]. But after the mediation, if [they think] the business needs to be fined [for its misconduct], they will still fine it.

He considers that the MSA's opinion is perhaps too idealistic, in other words, they consider their people (the local officers) as nicer than they really are. What he sees at the local level

[45] This officer comes from a district MSA bureau, which is one level above that of the local offices, and therefore, he receives information about the work of local offices in the district.

is that things are very messy. There is a tight connection between the local stores and some administrative officials – their interests are intertwined, but each side has its own different interests as well, so it is often very complicated.[46]

Another officer advised me in frank terms about problems at the local level. He points out that before these professionals appeared on the scene, the MSA officers basically had the freedom to do whatever they wanted to do. If they wished to, they could carry out a spot check on the products sold in the local area, but if they do not feel like doing this, then they do not have to go out and check. There was (and still is) no scheme which can effectively monitor their performance. In addition, most of the local officers know the businesses in their local jurisdiction very well. The business has often made a point of creating and maintaining a good relationship (*guanxi*) with them. They do not want to impair such a good relationship by doing things like an unannounced spot check, which in Chinese culture even today would be seen not as 'doing the job properly' but rather as being 'overzealous' to the detriment of the established good relationship. He states:

> So basically, they can choose which shop to visit and check, and which shop not to. No one can really challenge what they do. However, after the professionals come along, the officers are forced to do more spot-check investigations because of the reports made by the professionals. But in fact, [they feel that] this spot-checking is not really necessary as it only serves the professionals' money-making purposes … and they simply don't feel as powerful and autonomous as before.

The local officer also suggests that:

> We should try to blur the concept of the 'anti-counterfeit professionals', or whatever names given to them [anti-counterfeit professional, hotspot complainants, concentrated report makers, etc.] … All these names are labels. We [the MSA bureau] have changed the way to call them for several times, as some of them objected to the way they are called … But why should we label them? Is it for the sake of 'dealing with' (*ying dui*) them better? What is 'dealing with' (*ying dui*)? It gives us the feeling that we regard them as our enemy, a group of people whom we should attack, and in this way, we distinguish them from the normal consumers. At least in my local office, we are trying to blur these distinctions. But this does not mean that we abandon labelling them completely. We still label them, but this labelling only means that we will be more cautious when handling their cases. This is because the laws have become stricter in recent times, and place more requirements on us. If we treat all the cases as carefully as we do in the professionals' cases, employ the same skills to handle them, there will be enormous amount of work for us to do.

He continues that the office he works for has proposed the idea of establishing an 'open cooperation [scheme]' (*kaifangxing hezuo*). In this scheme, there would be publication of company registration information and information on a good's production permit, and dissemination of the knowledge of how to identify fake products, and so on, so that 'normal' consumers, whose motive is not necessarily profit-driven, can join in the 'anti-counterfeit' activities. He implies that his leader, the head of the office, now goes far to suggest that the officials should be able to hire the services of the professionals, or give them anti-counterfeit projects to work on, especially those who have set up companies to 'professionalise' (broaden)

[46] It was once seen by one of my professional complainant informants that some officials, as he spotted them, carried bags of selected items out of the supermarket, without going to the till and paying for them. They were let out of the supermarket by the shop assistant of the supermarket via a special lane.

their practice. However, he explains that this suggestion, and indeed, many other innovative ideas shared by the office in which he works are not sufficiently mainstream to be supported by the MSA bureau in Shenzhen.[47] The municipal MSA bureau instructs them not to support the professionals in getting compensation, and to try not to punish the business when their malpractices are only very 'minor',[48] as according to the administrative laws, they can be exempted from punishment.[49]

V. Conclusion: Professional Legal Culture and the Consumer Citizen

This chapter has focused on a new type of actor – the consumer professional-activist – who is hitherto only known about a little through the activities of Wang Hai, but who has never been researched in depth before, and who is a very important part of China's slowly emerging civil society – the nearest thing China has to the 'consumer citizen' concept discussed earlier in this study (chapters one and two).

It has been shown how these actors often have mixed motives – profit and social reform – and how these motives are intertwined. Some, such as the founding father Mr Zhao, started off with financial gain as a main goal but gradually came to be also a kind of reform activist. On the other hand, there are others, such as Mr Chen, who only really started to consider financial gains after years of activist practice. It has also been demonstrated that these professionals operate in their own distinctive and fairly uniform 'socio-legal culture', including styles of transmission of knowledge and skills to their 'apprentices', which develops through their social practice of bringing claims and making reports, and is diffused through cooperation and competition ('competition' because they often try to guess what the others are doing so as to get one step ahead, and that makes them reflective about aspects of their legal culture). Their socio-legal culture also includes a kind of symbiotic relationship with the Shenzhen consumer protection officials, as they contribute (and can be seen to contribute) to consumer protection on the one hand but their motives are not necessarily 'pure' on the other. So the officials have a kind of 'love-hate' relationship with them. That is why they can discuss things with each other in an informal, relaxed manner on the one hand, but then on other occasions officialdom will be fiercely critical, especially of the motives of the professionals, and develop 'hidden rules' or practices as countermeasures, and all this happens in the shadow of the Consumer Protection Law and relevant local regulations.

[47] As far as I know, there is no such buying-service practice in any of the governmental offices across the country. Wang Hai and Liu Dianlin may work for some companies, but do not work for the officials in any sense.

[48] In the view of the MSA bureau, these refer to the issues on the packaging and labelling of food products, the type of issue most frequently raised by the professionals. This shows that the municipal MSA bureau is very much against the idea of helping the professionals to get compensation, especially given that the issues brought by the professionals seem so 'minor' to them.

[49] See the Administrative Penalty Law, promulgated on 27 August 2009, Art 27, 'A party shall be given a lighter or mitigated administrative penalty in accordance with law, if … Where a person commits a minor illegal act, promptly puts it right and causes no harmful consequences, no administrative penalty shall be imposed on him.'

However, at the same time, this chapter has shown that there are a number of differing ways or styles of being a 'consumer professional-activist', and has offered a typology of the different types.

What is more, it seems that the professional complainants have been utilising hybrid forms of dispute processes in their practice, which we might usefully call 'negotiating in the shadow of mediation', that is, negotiating in the context of 'if negotiation fails then the dispute will be resolved through mediation'; and 'negotiating in the shadow of what are essentially administrative processes or avenues of justice', that is, negotiating in the context of 'if negotiation fails then the dispute will be resolved through administrative mediation'.[50] They do of course also use the hybrid process of 'litigotiation' in some circumstances. We can also see that the issues of 'power imbalances' have run through the process in the professionals' practice, and the professional complainants have dealt with these imbalances by employing a variety of innovative strategies at different stages of the consumer complaint and reporting processes.

[50] The concept of 'medi-gotiation' or 'admini-gotiation' is proposed here based on Mark Galanter's concept of 'litigotiation' – see M Galanter, 'Worlds of Deals: Using Negotiation to Teach about Legal Process' (1984) 34 *Journal of Legal Education* 268, especially at 268 where he writes: 'On the contemporary American legal scene the negotiation of disputes is not an alternative to litigation. It is only a slight exaggeration to say that it is litigation. There are not two distinct processes, negotiation and litigation; there is a single process of disputing in the vicinity of official tribunals that we might call *litigotiation*, that is, the strategic pursuit of a settlement through mobilising the court process.'

6

Consuming Litigation: Going to Court

I. Introduction

This chapter explores the role that the local court plays in consumer grievance redress in Shenzhen. As noted in chapter three, a large number of consumer cases go to the Consumer Council in Shenzhen, far more than those that end up in court. Compared to making a telephone call to the Consumer Council, going to the court incurs more time and cost, and this is perhaps the biggest reason that many consumers do not do so. On the other hand, the professionals, mentioned in chapter five, have been quite adept at using the court to pursue their goals of redress for their claims, both directly in the sense of using their claim to secure judgment and indirectly in the sense of using the track of litigation for their negotiations with defendant businesses. These professionals possess extensive knowledge of consumer laws and regulations, industry standards, and a good understanding of procedural rules, not only those rules which apply in administrative complaining and reporting, but also the rules and procedures of the court. They are repeat players in the court, and tend to be much more skilful than the ordinary consumer.

At the legislative level, the civil procedure laws and consumer protection laws allow for several forms of action through which a consumer may bring a suit. The 2012 revision of the Civil Procedure Law has, for the first time, called for the establishment of schemes of public interest litigation by different courts, which would be helpful for combating group litigation. One year later (2013), the Consumer Protection Law (CPL) was revised in a number of ways, including the provision in Article 47, which empowers consumer associations at the provincial level to represent consumers in court.[1] This enhances the possibilities of access to public interest litigation for consumers.[2] What is more, Article 23 of the CPL has been revised to switch the burden of proof from consumers to business operators on the issue of defective 'durable products' – to some extent, too, this reversal of the burden of proof lessens the barriers for consumers who pursue a case in the court.[3]

[1] Art 47 of the Consumer Protection Law states that: 'For infringement upon the lawful rights and interests of vast consumers, the China Consumers' Association and the consumer associations formed in provinces, autonomous regions, and municipalities directly under the Central Government may file lawsuits in the People's Courts.'

[2] New developments of consumer public interest litigation are provided in ch 7 of the book.

[3] Item 3 of Art 23 states that: 'For durable commodities such as motor vehicles, computers, televisions, refrigerators, air conditioners, and washing machines and services such as decoration and remodelling services provided by business operators, if consumers discover any defects within six months of receiving commodities or services and disputes arise therefrom, business operators shall bear the burden of proof regarding the defects.'

The PRC's legal system provides several court-focussed schemes for tackling consumer issues. But, in reality, this potential for the court to serve as an avenue for access to consumer justice is not easily realised. Indeed, in many cases, Chinese courts are unable to deliver on their promise to provide consumers with access to justice, in particular, with adequate compensation, and we shall see this in this chapter below.

II. The People's Courts in China

The People's Courts in China are stratified into four levels: the Supreme People' Court is situated at the top and is the court of first instance for only the most important cases in China and more usually the appellate court for cases heard on appeal from the higher or provincial courts. However, many of its functions are in fact administrative and it also has quasi-legislative power in that it is authorised to issue judicial interpretations (*sifa jieshi*) and other normative documents which are interpretations of the law binding on courts. The Higher People's Court lies at the provincial level, and handles cases so important that they are characterised as affecting the whole province. Appeals from the Higher People's Court go to the Supreme People's Court, which also a court of first instance for cases affecting 'the whole country'. The Higher People's Court also serves as an appellate court for the Intermediate People's Courts, which are located at the municipal level. These handle important cases as courts of first instance locally, including those with a significant 'foreign' element (*shewai*) and as appellate courts, cases on appeal from the Basic People's Courts at the district level. According to Articles 18, 19 and 20 of the Civil Procedure Law, the Basic People's Court handles most of the first instance civil cases, except for those with a significant 'foreign' element or of such importance that they should be handled by the Intermediate People's Court or the Higher People's Court.

In looking at the handling of consumer cases by the courts, my fieldwork was mainly focussed on the situation in the lowest level of court, the Basic People's Courts, in the local districts of Shenzhen. The local courts in Shenzhen share the distinctive features of people's courts throughout China. First, courts handling civil cases are mediatory in nature, in the sense that the judges aim at resolving the disputes that come before them by 'mediation' (*tiaojie*) rather than by adjudication. There are several layers of mediatory intervention, including at the case filing stage, even before a case comes before the trial judge. If the case has not already been resolved, ordinarily the judge will himself or herself conduct the mediation, an unusual feature of court focussed mediation in comparative terms. A judge is empowered – indeed is encouraged – by the civil procedure rules to stop trial proceedings and to attempt mediation at any point in a trial prior to judgment, and in appellate hearings mediation is also given a similarly strong emphasis.

It is not surprising that judges are often praised for their performance in achieving a certain rate of withdrawn cases, as well as a rate of cases resolved by mediation. A withdrawal of a case by the plaintiff means that the parties outside of the court have reached a mutual agreement, and it is likely that the agreement has already been enforced (in the case of the professionals, this means that they have received compensation money). The mediation implies a similar scenario: the parties are happy, relationships are maintained, and most importantly, that the plaintiff is likely to receive compensation. The emphasis on these withdrawal and mediation rates is an indication of the fact that the judges' primary role is seen officially as one of maintaining social stability, and therefore, as reflecting the success of the court in the task of 'soothing away' antagonism between the parties – who may well be residents of the same local neighbourhood. The mediation approach is also particularly prevalent in consumer disputes, as these cases are generally considered as 'small matters' by the judges and not even worthy of being adjudicated. In this sense, it is unlikely that individual consumers can alter the unfair business practices which they have experienced by bringing their grievance in the form of a case heard by the court.

Secondly, there are some other organisational features of the courts which support the use of mediation in civil cases. For example, the appraisal system of Chinese judges. The mediation and withdrawal rate is one important factor in the official assessment of a judge's performance. In addition, judges tend to consider the moral aspects of a case rather than the law alone when deciding cases, and judgment by the higher courts does not have binding (or reference) effects on similar cases handled by lower courts. A judge is likely to worry that a simple consumer case will be revealed as not so simple, and a routine handling of the case will become instead something that attracts the attention of the Adjudication Committee.[4] Also there is the worrying (especially from the courts' point of view) possibility of collective actions (*jituan susong*; *gongtong susong*), which are likely to attract media attention and make the courthouse more open than it otherwise would be to the public gaze. These are likely to be factors lurking in the mind of a judge when handling consumer cases.[5]

Thirdly, as much of the English language literature on Chinese courts has pointed out, the people's courts are well connected to, and indeed dominated by, the CCP and have to conduct themselves and their business under Party guidance. Another lies in the fact that most judges are themselves CCP members. A distinctive feature of the organisational aspect of the Chinese courts is a Communist Party committee which implements the Party's policies so that they are followed by both the courts and their judges. More generally, Chinese legal culture does not encourage judicial autonomy, and does not even embrace the idea of separation of powers. So, in reality the work of courts and their judges is dominated by the CCP and by government. Lack of judicial independence is, not surprisingly, a well-discussed feature of Chinese courts.[6]

[4] See eg He Xin's observations: 'China's unique Adjudication Committees are the highest decision-making body in any court, and operate at each level of the Chinese court system, wielding enormous influence. By analysing the minutes of the Adjudication Committee from a basic-level court, several patterns can be found regarding their operational and decision-making processes. First, almost all of the criminal cases (96.8 per cent) were reviewed by the court's Committee, as a result of jurisdictional rules. Second, and more importantly, the Committee modified almost 41 per cent of the adjudicating judges' suggested opinions in criminal cases – a much higher proportion than in civil cases. Third, the Committee tended to increase the penalty given to defendants, especially when the penalty was a fine. Overall, the data suggests that among the criminal cases reviewed by the Committee, legally speaking, very few were difficult or significant, but a relatively high percentage of the adjudicating judges' opinions were modified. In contrast, many of the civil cases reviewed were legally complex, but the Committee was less willing to intervene.' X He, 'China and its Adjudication Committees' (2011) *East Asia Forum*, 3 December, www.eastasiaforum.org/2011/12/03/china-and-its-adjudication-committees/.

[5] M Palmer and C Xi, 'China' (2009) 662 *The Annuals of the American Academy of Political and Social Science* 270 at 273. For an interesting discussion of the relationship between courts and the media see RX Liu, *The Media, the Public and the Courts under Chinese Governmentality: Case Study of a Highly Publicized Trial in a Transitional Society* (Master of Arts thesis, University of Iowa, 2015) ir.uiowa.edu/etd/1874.

[6] For a general discussion see eg R Peerenboom, 'Judicial Independence in China: Common Myths and Unfounded Assumptions' (2008) *La Trobe Law School Legal Studies Research Paper No. 2008/11* ssrn.com/abstract=1283179.

Fourthly, for the consumer, administrative suits may be a relevant avenue for securing justice. Consumer cases are by nature civil cases but, as mentioned earlier, the professionals also from time to time bring administrative suits against a government department, as a strategy to obtain a settlement for the other party in a consumer case. The Administrative Chambers in People's Courts deal with suits that are brought by citizens against wrongdoings by the public agencies and their officials. What is worth noting here is the importance of the mediatory nature of judicial case management in administrative cases. During the administrative procedures, judges hold several 'mediation' meetings with government officials and plaintiffs, despite the important fact that there is an explicit ban in the Administrative Procedure Law for mediation to be used in determining the outcome of administrative suits.[7] As a result, the cases often conclude in the form of what is called a settlement (*hejie*), rather than mediation (*tiaojie*), in order to avoid using the term 'mediation', as this is literally against the law.

In practice, this settlement approach is a facilitative type of mediation where the court extensively promotes the negotiation between the parties and persuades the plaintiff to withdraw the suit.[8] Similar to the situation regarding judges in the Civil Chambers, the mediation and case withdrawal rate is part of the judges' appraisal scheme in the Administrative Chamber. The higher the rates, the better the annual appraisal evaluation is likely to be for a judge.

Another obvious issue is that funding for the court comes from the local government's budget. This results in the fact that the court has to consider the interests of the local government when handling an administrative suit, especially if it seems that a judgment is a likely outcome. My lawyer informants joked with me about the fact that the public body sends its people to '*gong guan*' the court, that is, to network and communicate with the court on certain issues, lobbying in this way so as to get an outcome that is in their favour, and at the very least does not result in a loss (and 'loss of face'). In many situations, a case is closed by an informal 'indoor' settlement (a mediation meeting) and withdrawal of the case, sometimes with a promise by the defendant government department to alter some of its acts, rather than by an open process of adjudication and judgment, particularly when politically sensitive issues are involved.

[7] Art 50 of Administrative Procedure Law 1989 states that 'A people's court shall not apply mediation in handling an administrative case.' The position is slightly relaxed in the equivalent position in the 2014 revised version of the Law where the first paragraph of Art 60 now provides: 'A people's court shall not apply mediation in handling an administrative case. However, a case involving administrative compensation or indemnity or the exercise by an administrative organ of the right of discretion by prescribed laws or regulations can be mediated'.

[8] The *hejie* process has been discussed in ch 3 of the book. Suffice it to say here that the term *hejie* carries the same meaning in the court context as we found in our discussion of administrative dispute resolution of consumer disputes in ch 3. It is commonly translated as 'settlement' or 'reconciliation' in English-language accounts of Chinese dispute resolution. But as a dispute process, I see that *hejie* is essentially a facilitative type of mediation, while *tiaojie*, a term which literally means 'mediation' in Chinese and is often rendered as 'mediation' in English language accounts of Chinese dispute resolution, is best characterised as an evaluative type of Chinese mediation. The outcome of *hejie* is often associated with a withdrawal of case by the plaintiff in the litigation context (and in the Consumer Council and the MSA, it is also linked to a withdrawal of complaint by the complainant).

III. Consumer Disputes in the Shenzhen Court

A. Dispute Resolution by Ordinary Consumers

As discussed previously, a majority of consumer disputes are resolved through the complaint and redress system provided by the Consumer Council or the MSA. Particularly, in the Consumer Council, complainants who go through the quasi-official complaint processes are mostly 'ordinary' consumers[9] who happen to buy faulty goods and make complaints for the first time, and they have hardly ever taken further steps to the court when the settlement fails. This is consistent with the figures from the court, that each year, a Basic People's Court only receives an average 300–400 consumer cases out of some 3,000 to 4,000 registered cases in the First Civil Chamber of that court,[10] which is far less than the many thousands of complaints received by the Consumer Council. Among these consumer-related court cases, it seems that only about 1 out of 100 is brought by ordinary consumers who are one-shot players and have only exceptionally gone to the court to seek redress. This figure is an only an estimate on my part, but based on the views of officials in the Consumer Council, judges and the professionals, and my search in the court's case archives.

It is therefore not easy to seek out consumer cases brought to the courts by ordinary consumers. Going through the electronic archives of cases (roughly from 2010–13), most of the cases where plaintiffs are ordinary consumers are in the end, mediated (or settled), and often followed by a withdrawal of the case, so that no verdict is rendered. Instead, such cases are closed by the Civil Ruling in Writing (*Minshi Caiding Shu*) rather than a formal judgment, and the details of the deal made are not open to access by the public. Also, it is not always easy to dig out and clearly identify the cases that have a consumer element. Cases in the court system are categorised by the cause of action. As noted by court clerks, consumer cases are more likely to be found in the following categories of causes of action: disputes over contract for sale and purchase, disputes over the right of life, health and body and disputes over tortious liability.[11] As a judge experienced in dealing with consumer cases

[9] The term 'ordinary consumer' is used in this chapter, in order to distinguish consumers who do not possess extensive knowledge and skills of consumer litigation from those who are 'professionals' in using the consumer litigation process. The 'professionals' in this chapter are the same group of 'professionals' who can be found in the extra-judicial consumer complaint processes, as particularly discussed in ch 5. The 'professional complainants' are regarded as 'professional litigants' when they are involved in the litigation process.

[10] In the PRC, courts have several trial chambers and administrative divisions. Trial chambers are divided into Criminal, Civil and Administrative Chambers, and there are usually several kinds of Civil Chamber or Division. The First Chamber handles cases involving marriage, family and inheritance, labour disputes, property rights, rights of personality, and contract and tort cases in which one of the parties is a natural (rather than a legal) person. The Second Civil Chamber (formerly called the 'Economic Chamber') deals important tort and contract cases in which the parties are legal persons, and larger commercial cases involving such issues as securities, company law, financial instruments (cheques and other payment bills), futures trading and so on. In many courts now there is a Third Civil Chamber which deals with intellectual property, technology contracts, and unfair competition. Finally, there is often a Fourth Chamber, responsible for handling foreign-related cases (civil and commercial), maritime cases, and recognition of foreign judgements and arbitral awards. Other substantive divisions within the court deal with the filing of cases, enforcement of court orders and judgments, trial supervision of trials and legal research. The courts also have an administrative division which contains a general administrative affairs office, a personnel office and a judicial administrative apparatus office (*sifa xingzheng zhuangbeichu*: an office which manages permanent assets, court vehicles, court police facilities and so on).

[11] Causes of action also include: disputes over private lending, disputes over divorce, etc.

patiently explained to me, very few cases over personal injuries caused by purchased products are brought to the court, and the reason is simple: claiming damages over personal injuries is time-consuming and costly, because this normally requires an identification and analysis of the offending product from experts.

What is more, for ordinary consumers, it tends to be only issues that have an immediate and clear negative impact on their lives that will encourage them to think about bringing their grievance to the court. As discussed earlier, these only occupy a very small proportion of cases in the court (my estimate, is 1 out of every 100 consumer cases brought to the court). Indeed, the monetary damages that can be obtained from a court judgment award, in most situations, are very limited. The burden of proof (until the recent change in law noted above) lies heavily on the plaintiff, and there is a high risk of not getting adequate compensation for the plaintiff's losses, which include transportation fees, taking a day off from work, etc. Unlike the professionals, most aggrieved consumers, who are involved in less immediately pressing and severe matters, turn to the Consumer Council and the MSA, rather than spending time and money on pressing a claim in court in which the harm is difficult to prove. They also know that it is highly likely that the plaintiff will be persuaded into mediation under the auspices of the court.[12] The outcome, therefore, is not so very different from the outcome that a consumer would be likely to achieve by means of the complaint process of the Consumer Council or the MSA. All these bodies, the Consumer Council, the MSA, and the court, are using the same set of skills for the dispute process – mediation that is evaluative and largely persuasive. On the other hand, it might also be that the consumer can get a better outcome through mediation outside of the court rather than bringing a suit in the local court – especially as the defendant business is often more willing to pay in cases that have not gone to court, because it is less troubled by the trial preparation and trial procedures and its reputation is largely retained.

Consumer cases, particularly those brought by individuals, are generally relatively small in value, and therefore the cost for going through the court process is always a concern for the plaintiff. The 2012 amendment to the Civil Procedure Law has introduced small claims court procedures that, inter alia, may be used to handle small consumer claims.[13] As part of the civil procedure reforms, local courts in Shenzhen have in recent years established various types of simplified procedure, such as 'fast-track' procedures (*sucai chengxu*) and the 'small claims' litigation (*xiaoe susong*). These innovative procedures seem to have brought in the possibility of lower costs of the parties and so consumers might be reasonably expected to favour these procedures and opt for their cases to be handled by them. However, this is not the situation in practice. Most consumer cases have directly gone to the summary procedure, which is a standard procedure in civil cases, because the parties' views on the facts and over the disputed issues are so wide apart, and the simplified procedures cannot accommodate these arguments. As court officials have explained the situation to me, the fast-track trial, a pilot scheme established in recent times, applies to cases where the parties

[12] A case study below shows how the judge persuaded the parties to agree to 'mediation'.

[13] Art 162 stipulates: 'When the basic people's court or its dispatched tribunal tries simple civil cases specified in the first paragraph of Art. 157, and the amount of the target in a case is less than 30% of the annual average wage of the employed in the last year in a province, autonomous region or municipality directly under the Central Government, the judgment of first instance shall be final.'

have agreed on most of the facts and do not have significant disagreements over potential compensation. The small-claim court is also a type of fast-track process, as different local courts may have different practices or policies for handling cases (some have a policy of fast-tracking the cases, some tend to rely on small-claims court, in order to handle cases more efficiently). These simplified procedures are designed for cases covering simple and determined facts, while consumer cases are often more complicated than what their values seem to be. This process is seemingly not very attractive to aggrieved consumers who seek redress in the court, and it may also be because of the ready availability of Consumer Council dispute resolution.

On the other hand, the procedure of public interest litigation, which has been nationally promoted as an innovative method for protecting consumer rights and interests, is not in much use. The 2013 revision of the Consumer Protection Law has specified the organisations that may have standing for consumers who wish to bring a suit in court. However, as will be discussed in chapter seven, this practice is still rather embryonic and has many limitations, such as that many civil society organisations who it was anticipated would play a role in public interest litigation, often do not have the standing, and the 'professionals', who possess the knowledge and practice experience to effectively fight for consumer rights, do not have either the inclination or the status to lead public interest litigation. Up to the latest development in this area (March 2017), there are no public interest cases handled by the courts in Shenzhen.

The reality is that mediation is still the dominant type of resolution for consumer disputes. On the surface, this echoes the tendency in European jurisdictions in which alternative dispute resolution schemes are encouraged for dealing with consumer issues.[14] However, in the China case, the context is very different. While drawing on well-entrenched traditions in Chinese legal culture, the Chinese emphasis on mediation is also motivated by a desire to prevent consumer cases being 'publicised' in open court trials, and for even cases which raise public interest issues to be 'privatised' in informal processes.

B. Dispute Resolution by the Professionals

In contrast to the approach often taken by ordinary consumers, the court processes have been constantly used by the professionals – who, in general, are much more skilful in arguing consumer issues in court. Judges remark that over 90 per cent of the consumer cases are indeed brought by the repeat players – the professionals who buy goods strategically and seek compensation mainly to make a profit. Although the professionals bring most consumer cases, it is the non-professionals – the ordinary consumers – who have a better chance to win their cases. As one judge notes in his report on consumer disputes in the years 2010 and 2011, the success rate of the professionals was in fact less than 10 per cent. According to the report, the low success rate is attributed to the fact that the court did not support most of the claims made by the professionals for the ten-times punitive damages for problematic food items. The cases brought by the professionals – who are in effect 'litigants

[14] C Hodges, I Benöhr and N Creutzfeldt-Banda, *Consumer ADR in Europe* (Oxford, Hart Publishing, 2012) 1.

in person' – are mostly about the issues of unclear and incomplete food product labels (or packaging), and in the judges' eyes, these cases do not fulfil the requirements laid down by the Food Safety law for securing the ten-fold punitive damages. Before 2014, it was generally understood by judges that there are three specific conditions for supporting the punitive damages in a food dispute: first, the case must be related to a food safety issue. Secondly, the aggrieved consumer (the plaintiff) in the case must have received actual personal injury or property damage. Thirdly, the aggrieved consumer (the plaintiff) can only ask for punitive damages from the seller. Most of the cases brought by the professionals are not considered by judges to meet the requirement for claiming punitive damages, because they do not cause the plaintiff any personal injury or property damage.[15] This understanding, however, has been overturned by the Supreme People's Court's provisions published in 2013: The Supreme People's Court's Provisions on Several Issues Concerning the Application of Law in the Trial of Cases Involving Food and Drug Disputes, in which the requirement that 'the aggrieved consumer must have received personal injury or property damage' has been cancelled. As a result, the professionals' cases, most of which concern non-pressing issues such as labelling and packaging errors, are regarded as having met the requirements for claiming punitive damages. The success rate of their cases, thus, is likely to increase.

Cases closed in the form of decisive judgments are mostly those brought by the professionals as plaintiffs, and are relatively simple cases concerning sales of products and services. Among the various causes of action, the cause of action of 'dispute over contract for sale and purchase' is what most consumer cases that have come to the court are about, and are in fact, mostly brought by the professionals. It is not surprising that professionals favour cases with relatively limited technical elements. In a case of faulty goods, the process to get the product examined is much more time-consuming, and only a few organisations and experts are qualified to do such work. The professionals, who are the main 'plaintiffs' in the court in terms of consumer cases, try to avoid the identification and analysis process, as a way to eliminate some of the costs they incur in bringing suits. They are skilful in raising issues based on purchase contracts such as fraudulent product prices, unclear and incorrect product information on packages, labels, brand names, and so on – problems that can be easily observed by the litigant himself (and, indeed, by many others), so that arguments can be made and conclusions can be drawn on the basis of these facts and the relevant laws and regulation instead of by expert reports.

What is more, the claims of their cases on average are very small – from just a few RMB to a couple of hundred RMB in value. Judges explain that these small claims are brought in part because it costs very little for the professionals to bring cases in the court – literally they just need to pay 25RMB for courtroom fees for a case. As I have indicated, in most situations, the professionals litigate in person. In some situations, however, the plaintiff may be somebody else 'on paper' – he or she can be a relative or a friend of the professional, or an assistant that the professional has hired, but in practice it is the professional who spots the issue and handles the case.

[15] Some professionals argue that the issues they brought up may cause long-term personal injury or property damage that cannot be seen immediately, because unclear messages on the label can mislead consumers on their purchases and confuse consumers. So, the label issues should be considered as causing potential problems to the consumer.

C. Lawyers and the Courtroom: Ms Wang's Online-Shopping Case

Despite the political sensitivity of conducting research in the courtrooms of the PRC, and the relatively paucity of court cases on consumer complaints, I was able to observe several cases during my fieldwork. One of the most interesting was a case brought by a Ms Wang against the famous e-commerce platform (Suning.com), whose parent company is one of the largest retailers in China, Suning Commerce Group Co Ltd. Ms Wang bought a Joyoung brand food processing machine from Suning.com in November 2013. However, soon after she received the machine, she discovered that the machine did not work when it was plugged in. She had made complaints to the company, as well as to the Consumer Council in Guangzhou (where Suning.com is located), and later, to the Consumer Council in Shenzhen (where she lives), but all to no avail. As a last resort, she took her case to the court and her claim was presented by a lawyer to the court.

The court accepted her case on June 2014, and a court hearing was scheduled one month later. I was with the lawyer who handled Ms Wang's case and observed the court proceedings. The summary form of procedure was applied to the case, and there was one judge and a clerk in the hearing. The plaintiff, Ms Wang was not present. Instead, her lawyer represented her in the hearing. Both of the defendant businesses were present, and represented by their employees. The first defendant was the e-commerce platform, Suning.com, and the second defendant was its parent company, the Suning Commerce Group Co Ltd.

I gained the distinct impression that from the point of the judge this was an 'unnecessary' hearing. The judge, who was a female in her thirties, was very impatient during the hearing. When she arrived and sat down, her first words were, 'Are you [the plaintiff] willing to mediate?' This was asked robustly before the court hearing started – before the judge read the courtroom rules and rapped her gavel to start the hearing. It was also clear to me that the plaintiff, Ms Wang, was the party who did not agree to mediate before the court hearing, because Ms Wang was not satisfied with the terms offered by the business. Indeed, it may have been that she stayed away from the hearing precisely as a way of resisting judicial pressure to have her claim mediated rather than adjudicated.

Nevertheless, in the hearing, the judge spent quite some time in pushing the parties, particularly, the plaintiff, to mediate. In so doing, she exerted some pressure by questioning the 'basis' upon which Ms Wang was asking for compensation of 10,000RMB – the sum she had proposed in previous mediation meetings. The judge advised, 'If you ask for return of the goods, the business can accept that … but the 10,000RMB loss is yours.' Ms Wang's lawyer answered: 'There is no [justified legal] basis for claiming such compensation, and nor is there a basis [for making this claim] in mediation, but then added: 'however, my client has spent much time in dealing with this matter'. The judge responded, 'But there are no objective losses. What shows that you have [objective] losses?' The lawyer answered, 'well, first, my client needs to hire a lawyer; second she needs to [take out time to] talk about her business [with me]; third, she needs to … Her salary is rather high … In fact, we did not claim for any particular losses, but if you do want us to mediate, we …' But the judge interrupted before the lawyer could finish his reply, and corrected him on the point of voluntariness of any mediation – she claimed that it was not herself who wanted the parties to mediate. The judge nevertheless then continued to 'persuade' the parties in precisely that direction: 'This is such a small matter, and it is supposed to be mediated.

It does not become a big matter because the plaintiff hires a lawyer.' The lawyer argued that the reasons that the client wanted to pursue the case in the court were more than just getting compensation. More importantly, the plaintiff wanted to have the industry's unreasonable practices be corrected by the court. As in Ms Wang's case, he added, it is unfortunately the situation that typically it is the practice for the consumer to be asked to pay the court fees and to have the faulty goods examined by accreditation bodies, before he or she can get compensation.

The judge, however, kept trying to create doubt in the plaintiff lawyer's mind by asking again 'well, just how big a matter is this complaint?' And 'what if the practices [of the company] were unreasonable, does this really matter?' She pointed out that there were no personal injury or other serious aspects in the case, so it should not be characterised as 'a big matter', and it could be resolved by mediation. The lawyer, on the other hand, emphasised that it was the client's goal to quash the unreasonable industry practices (which are against the law) in the court. He explained:

> Honorable Judge, you can see that in cases like this, clients normally do not hire lawyers, largely because of the high litigation costs for their cases. So in these situations, the result of having bought faulty goods is regarded as the plaintiffs' own fault and they are expected to put up with it. This happens so often and we want to correct this practice.

However, the judge retorted by questioning the significance of any change in the practice (or rule), and emphasised that even speaking as a citizen herself, this was really not a big matter.

After several rounds of questioning and answering, the judge finally accepted the lawyer's request to proceed with the court hearing. However, it seemed that she was trying to speed up the pace of the court hearing by speaking fast, asking questions impatiently, and interrupting the parties if they spoke for too long (as she saw the situation). The primary goal of Ms Wang, as her lawyer explained, was to nullify the standard term in the business's practice, as she was told by the business that 'the consumer needed to provide the accreditation of the faulty product by a qualified organisation, in order to have the product returned to the business'. Ms Wang's lawyer argued that his client discovered the problem of the product immediately, and raised the issue with the business. However, this claim was not discussed much in the court. The judge, on the other hand, focused her attention on the compensation part of the plaintiff's claims. She had heard the defendants' counter-statement to the plaintiff's claims, watched a demonstration of the product's working status (the product, indeed, did not appear to be working) and explored the defendants' willingness to compensate the plaintiff. The judge, to a large extent, was trying to 'resolve' the dispute of the particular case, rather than to have the issue fully discussed, and have the business' unlawful practices changed, as the outcome of the case.

In subsequent interviews with Ms Wang's lawyer, I further discovered that he was helping her pro bono to bring about changes in the practice of imposing unfair terms by the business. He took Ms Wang's case on as a kind of 'public interest' case, hoping that the unfair business practices could be changed through a judgment made by the court. He did not charge Ms Wang any fees to cover his costs incurred on the case, including transport fees, time and effort. As he pointed out in the court, the cost for bringing a case in the court with the aid of a lawyer is relatively high, especially when compared to the money spent on buying the product. Also, even if he won a case, the practice in the court is that the judge will not support the plaintiff's non-direct, non-obvious losses. For example, the losing party does not pay the lawyers' fees of the winning party, neither does it pay any transport fees. This aligns with my findings on other judgments in the archive that only the amount of money spent on the product is ordered as compensation, as the judges hold that no other losses should be counted. This outcome is indeed not very different from what a consumer can get from mediation in the Consumer Council or the MSA.

From the account of this case, my experience with other cases, and detailed research into electronic archives of cases, I conclude that in Shenzhen the local court serves mainly as a forum for resolving single disputes by persuading parties on agreeing to mediation terms, rather than rendering judgments that deal with the correctness of business practices and have a broader impact on the citizen's life. Because Ms Wang refused to mediate throughout the court process, the case closed in the form of a judgment. In the judgment, she was able to secure compensation for her expenditure on the faulty product, but no further compensation. The judgment did not support Ms Wang's primary aim to stop the business' practice of setting an accreditation barrier for consumers who wished to return a faulty product. Finally, Ms Wang returned the product to Suning.com, and got back her money from the company – the 79RMB she spent on the product. As Ms Wang and her lawyer explained their disappointment to me, even though she 'won' the case in the end, this outcome was unreasonable (*buheli*), and the compensation awarded was so unexpectedly small that it could not cover any of the expenses that Ms Wang spent on litigation. The result was no different from, and the compensation awarded even much less than, what Ms Wang might have secured from an out-of-court mediation and settlement.

IV. The Professionals and the Court

The professionals, as explained above, are the main consumer case actors who take their cases to the court. In the previous chapter (chapter five), I have discussed the professionals' practices in extra-judicial dispute processes. In this chapter, the professional 'complainants' have become professional 'litigants', and they employ a different set of strategies to handle court cases to maximise their returns.

Judges explained to me that the professionals are likely to spot the same problematic product again and again, and bring the same issue to the court every now and then. The way they do it is like this: professional A has spotted a problematic product and has won a case regarding it. The case is closed and the professional has secured compensation. The next day, professional B who is informed of his peer's success, goes out and finds those problematic products which are still on the shelf and buys them. By bringing up the same issue on the same problematic product, professional B's claims are supported by the court for sure. It is not just B, but A may also bring a second case on the same product in a period of time (say, one month), and with no doubt, his claims in the second case will succeed in the court too. In this way, the professional obtains compensation.

The Shenzhen Intermediate People's Court has issued a document which forbids the repeated buying of the same problematic products and claiming compensation in the court. This document, as a judge explained it to me, states that it is only the first time the professionals buy the problematic products and ask for compensation that they are considered as consumers. From the second time, the professionals are not regarded as consumers, because this is what the court describes as 'deliberately buying fake products for making profits' (*zhi jia mai jia*, literally, 'knowing the fake (still) buying the fake'). In this way, when the same professional buys the same problematic product for the second time, his claims are not to be supported.

The professionals, however, have developed another strategy to bypass this court practice – they ask friends or relatives to appear to be the ones who buy the problematic product, and whose rights are infringed. They themselves, instead, represent the friend or relative in the court, as it is not necessary to be legally qualified to present a case in court. As one judge complained to me,

> The professional becomes the agent of the plaintiff. So, today, they argue about the issue on behalf of A; tomorrow, they argue about the same issue as found on the same product, on behalf of B … Before the revision of the Civil Procedure Law in 2012, a citizen's representation in the court was a very easy matter. You only needed to explain to the court the relationship between the plaintiff and yourself. Now, it is much more difficult, as the new Procedure Law requires that citizens (non-lawyers) can only represent those who are their relatives, or if they are recommended by the company the party works for, or by the local street committee … However, these people [the professionals] somehow can get a proof of ties of kinship, or a recommendation letter from the company that the plaintiff works for, or from the local street council … In most cases the plaintiff is not present. I ask for the plaintiff's ID card for a check, and it is unlikely that the plaintiff is a relative of his, since the plaintiff is too old.

Another technique used is that the professionals use an old ID card, which shows the address of their hometown (a very remote village or somewhere not in Shenzhen) rather than their current residence. Here the motive is different however: the professionals want to protect themselves as they worry about being harmed by revenge from the business. The professionals indeed are reluctant to disclose their real home address in the court papers, especially in their statement of claim.

The professionals are strategically adept at utilising court procedures, and thereby cause trouble to the other party. One of the strategies they use, for example, is to request the judge to recuse (*huibi*) himself or herself from the case.[16] It is often the case that the professionals recognise the judges who have appeared and dealt with their cases in the past. If the professionals have lost cases before a particular judge, the next time they meet the same judge on another case, they are likely to request the judge to recuse himself or herself at the beginning of the court hearing, giving as the reason that the judge made them lose the previous case or cases without proper reasoning. This request, in the eyes of the judge, is not acceptable according to the Civil Procedure Law, and the request is invariably rejected

[16] Art 45 of the Civil Procedure Law (2012) states that: 'Any member of the adjudicating personnel in any of the following circumstances shall be disqualified, and the litigation parties shall also have the right to request, orally or in writing, such an adjudicator to be withdrawn from this case. The relevant circumstances are: (1) He is a party or a near relative of a party or a near relative of a litigation representative to the case; (2) He has a personal interest in the case; or (3) He has some other relationship with a party to the case, which could influence the impartial adjudication.' The above provisions shall also apply to clerks, interpreters, expert witnesses, and examiners.

by the judge. But after this, the professional may then request a review of the decision. As a judge complained to me,

> These people [the professionals] use recusal (*huibi*) every day. They deliberately create procedural troubles for the judge and the other party, so that the court hearing cannot be carried on. The defendant party, the business, came to the court, only to find that the hearing was interrupted or postponed by the requests made by the professionals, so they came in vain, and had to return again. If the defendant business is a big company, it may not care that much, since it has money to employ in-house lawyers to deal with such issues. But in some situations, the defendant business is not a chain-store or a big company, and these business usually litigate in person, so it increases much of their cost.

The professionals may bring up other procedural issues, such as those governing the rules of exchange of evidence. For example, normally, when the judge asks the defendant business to submit evidence in the course of the trial, the professional may argue that this is against relevant laws which require that evidence be submitted before the court hearing. In practice, particularly when judges are faced with a plaintiff (and his or her lawyer) who is focused more on the substance of the trial, the procedure is not necessarily strictly followed. The judge is not too concerned with procedural matters, and the court hearing is indeed mediatory in nature. The professionals on the other hand are so sharp and strict with procedure and its technicalities, and they do not hesitate to point out that the defendant is in fact submitting 'surprise evidence' (in their words, *zhengju tuxi*), and they cannot ratify the correctness of the evidence in the hearing. As a result, they request the judge to adjourn the case to a later date. As one judge described the problem to me:

> The professionals have done a thorough study on laws and regulations … They now have the money to buy [a good] computer, and so in the court hearing, they open the legal documents in their computer, and show them to us [the judge and the defendant business] … Their command of laws and regulations is even better than qualified lawyers, who spent at least four years in the law school … They always wear suits and leather shoes, and dress up formally, like lawyers [but they are not], but the real lawyers, on the other hand, dress rather casually now.

So, we might say that at least as far as this judge is concerned, the professionals are, in terms of both substance and style, now rather more professional than the professional lawyers who also appear in court.

The professionals may also adjust their strategies in order to be consistent with the courts' practices. One example is asking for the ten-times punitive damages. In a case concerning the packaging of a product, the professional (the plaintiff) claimed for the 'ten-times' punitive damages on the grounds of defective wording on packaging, and the court of first instance, the district court, supported his claim. The court made an award in his favour. However, when the case came to the appellate court – the Shenzhen Intermediate People's Court – the judgment of the district court was overruled by the appellate court. The latter took the view that as long as there was no 'actual damage' to personal health, an award of 'ten-times' damages should not be supported. The professionals, who often exchange information about court practice with each other, came to know the court's ruling that it would not support the 'ten-times' claim for punitive damages for minor issues, such as packaging, label, accreditation of products, and so on. They developed a collective sense that the courts in Shenzhen had become 'more strictly controlled and have higher standards' in dealing with cases for punitive damages. So, later, the professionals who buy products with relatively minor defects or problems, changed their style, dropping any claims for the 'ten-times' punitive damages in the court. Instead, they decided only to ask for one or two-times the price of the product in compensation, based on the punitive damages article (Article 49) in the Consumer Protection Law 1993, so as to increase their chances of winning the case and getting their compensation claims fully supported by the court. Also, they may draw on cases adjudicated by courts in other cities, print out the judgments, and give them to the presiding judge of their own case for their reference in order to strengthen their argument and put pressure on the judge in the trial of their own case. Once a case is decided within the Shenzhen courts, and a new 'judicial norm' (such as that on the award of punitive damages in cases involving packaging problems) is 'created', other judges handling similar cases will tend to be guided by the decided case, once they have come to learn about the decided case.

What we see emerging here is a system of informal 'precedent setting' in the specialised world of consumer litigation in Shenzhen. Although the Supreme People's Court, as noted above, has the authority to issue judicial interpretations (*sifa jieshi*) and other normative documents which are interpretations of the law binding on courts (including the new Guiding Case system), the PRC, as a civil law system, does not have a formal system of binding judicial precedent. However, in the relatively small world of consumer protection in Shenzhen, it seems that the courts do take into account each other's decisions, and are persuaded by the evidence of court judgments elsewhere in China that the professionals present to the court. Judges in Shenzhen are known to be under some of the greatest work loads of judges in any part of China, and each judge often handles more than 400 cases a year. In these circumstances, they often do not have an immediate command of the specific area of the law that the professional brings to court. They look to other judge's decisions, and to the sometimes superior knowledge of the professional to help them in their decision-making. Like judges nearly everywhere, they want to make a good decision that does not get appealed.

As mentioned earlier in this chapter, the professionals may also file administrative suits against governmental departments, particularly against the MSA bureau, as a way to put pressure on the administrative department to help them to get a favourable outcome in a settlement with the business. In the 2014 Work Report of Administrative Adjudication in Shenzhen, published by the Shenzhen Intermediate People's Court, the MSA bureau was ranked first for the number of administrative suits received by public bodies, as well as ranking first for the number of administrative cases it lost in a twelve month period from 2013 to 2014.[17] The professionals spot the procedural mistakes made by officials in the administrative complaint processes, such as failure to issue a reply within a required seven day period to inform the complainant of the result of the investigation in the form of a report that has been made, or failure to ensure that the 'stamp' on the reply is the 'chop' of a superior bureaucrat in the local MSA office, and so on. They may bring administrative suits against the MSA's doubtful practices at virtually any step of the complaint or report process. This, as discussed in chapter five above, increases – sometime significantly – the MSA's workload, and the professionals are for the most part disliked by the MSA officials for this added pressure. Some professionals, such as Mr Chen, like to bring administrative suits against the MSA in order to chase the awards that the MSA is supposed to give him

[17] The report is available at sz.people.com.cn/n/2015/0701/c202846-25421246.html.

for his public-spirited good conduct in reporting to the MSA unlawful business practices in the market.[18]

To some extent, the administrative suits might seem to work for the professionals in terms of helping them secure their personal interests, but from a more general perspective there are still many limitations in the system. From my interviews with judges, I know for example that there are worries among judges that an administrative suit is not that helpful in pressuring an administrative department to improve its actions. In adjudicating an administrative case, the judge has to take into account the feelings and interests of the government (and its public bodies). 'How can we oversee the government?' as one judge put it:

> You do not dare to give a judgment … so that you have to mediate, which is what we called a 'settlement' … It is of the most difficulty to file administrative suit. If the government [bodies] lost a case, first, the leader may feel that they 'lost their face' (*mian zi guo bu qu*), and secondly, he [the government leader] will find ways to send people to put pressure on the court … so in fact, [in handling these cases], the Administrative Chamber of the Court receives much more pressure than the pressure on the Civil Chamber of the Court.

So, it seems, many cases are withdrawn (*chesu*) under pressure from the judge. The withdrawal rate of administrative cases was high, as the judges have suggested to me. My analysis of court statistics indicates, indeed, that in 2014 it was more than 70 per cent.

A. Types of Issue Brought by the Professionals

The professionals are not only 'professional'. They are also 'expert' in the sense that they focus their efforts on certain specific areas, and the judges often know that the professionals possess this expertise. One professional, for example, is known to be very good at spotting problematic issues in the field of luxury goods, such as fake watches, bags, mobile phones, and so on. This professional is in his fifties, and was a civil engineer who designed machine tools. The mobile phones he bought all cost more than several thousand RMB. The brands he brought suits against are not those that can often be seen on the market. One judge described his skills and knowledge to me in terms that clearly reflected a degree of both admiration and concern:

> That professional who bought luxury goods … his techniques are really difficult and challenging. He focuses on finding problems with imported goods, for example, mistakes on the year-dating of Japanese products which use a Japanese way of numbering the years (such as Showa, Heisei)[19] … I do not understand any of these details … problematic details that are identified by him [the professional] … He really knows his area and is very good at it.

[18] Mr Chen once filed 60 administrative suits against the MSA in one go in 2014. He sued the MSA for their act of omission in not imposing administrative sanctions on the businesses for their unlawful practices that he reported, and for not awarding him for making those reports. Mr Chen claimed that he was persuaded by the court to abandon some of the suits, because the number was so large and the court was under pressure. However, he resisted this pressure. In the end, the MSA lost all 60 cases in the court. See the news report on Mr Chen filing 60 administrative suits against the MSA in a local District Court in Shenzhen, M Gao, '7ge Gongzuori Weihuifu Jubao, Shenzhen Shijianju Huoyou jin Qiandan Baisu' (Failed to Reply within 7 Days: Shenzhen MSA May Lose Near A Thousand Cases) (*21CN Jutousu*, 31 October 2014). Copy on file with the author and available upon request.

[19] eg Showa 62 is the year 1987. Heisei 18 is the year 2005.

Others are IP 'experts'. They file suits on Intellectual Property cases in the Third Civil Chamber of the district court. Usually, the professional will sign an agreement with the plaintiff company (which holds the IP rights), in which they agree on the shares of compensation to be given to them by the defendant business upon the winning of a case. The professionals go to the retail stores to search for fake or copied products, which illegally use the well-known brands (eg, Louis Vuitton), and buy hundreds of items of the product and then store them in their own (secret) storage sites. Then, they sue the business that is misusing the famous brand name, in the name of the plaintiff company. The plaintiff wins the case (or secures a very favourable settlement), and the compensation awarded is then shared with the professionals, as previously agreed.

Another professional, Mr Ma, is a frequent user of Article 25 of the 1993 Consumer Protection Law, seeking 'mental damages' (*jingshen sunhai*).[20] His strategy is to create a situation in which he can protest that retail store staff have searched his belongings – and his body – unlawfully, for the 'spurious' and 'unfounded' reason that the staff suspected that he had stolen some items from the shop. Mr Ma does, in reality, set a 'trap' for the retail stores. Thus, he may well go into supermarket A with a bottle of shampoo that was bought from supermarket B in his bag. While he is in supermarket A, he takes a bottle of shampoo (from supermarket A's shelf) and put it into his bag. After a while, he takes out the bottle of shampoo (from supermarket A) he just put into his bag, and secretly leaves it somewhere in supermarket A. Later, he walks out of supermarket A, without going through the till to pay for the shampoo. Staff in the supermarket A who saw him putting a bottle of shampoo into his bag, but then noting he is not paying for it before leaving the supermarket, stop him at the entrance of the supermarket, and search his belongings for the shampoo. They find a shampoo in Mr Ma's bag, but it is proven to be not from supermarket A (but from supermarket B). Mr Ma then claims that this is against the law, and the supermarket should not have searched him, and therefore he is entitled to ask for mental damages. Because such cases are invariably handled on the spot in an informal manner, Mr Ma is able to make something of a periodic habit of this practice.

Mr Ma has also brought several cases upon the same grounds, seeking compensation, to the courts. In one case, the judge was able to have a careful check of the CCTV footage from the supermarket, and discovered Mr Ma had deliberately set out to confuse the staff in the supermarket. The judge deemed that the search carried out on Mr Ma by the staff was not offending Mr Ma's personal rights, and thus, in his judgment did not support Mr Ma's claims.

V. Conclusions

One of the most important findings of this chapter is that the court shares the broader mediatory culture for dealing with consumer cases. The relatively closed nature of the court, and

[20] Art 25 provides that 'Business operators may not insult or slander consumers, may not search the body of consumers or the articles they carry with them, and may not violate the personal freedom of consumers.' It is now Art 27 in the revised 2013 Consumer Protection Law.

the court's passive role in consumer protection are intended to help individual consumers to settle individual disputes, but not more than that. The more public schemes, such as collective action and public interest litigation, are not really much used in practice. Judges focus on resolving single cases, where it is hoped the outcome does not impact on business practices. Also, the range of compensation for the plaintiff's losses is narrow, as the judge will support only direct and obvious losses. However, costs for bringing a consumer case are high.

Consumer cases are regarded as 'small matters' by the court, and therefore, a mediatory approach is used throughout the court hearing wherever possible. Nevertheless, the court is a place for achieving some changes, particularly through cases brought by the professionals. Such cases have raised the public's attention on certain consumer issues, unlike the many disputes and complaints that are normally settled through government-led compensatory schemes outside of the court.

Also, I have indicated that court decisions do have an informal precedential effect, through the networks of information that exit in the judiciary on the one hand and amongst Shenzhen's consumer protection professionals on the other. It is through the court cases in particular that these two 'conversational networks' in turn speak to each other.

On the other hand, the court's function is still limited, even with the 'help' of the professionals. The professionals mainly bring cases to the court that do not need expert reports. This clearly saves much time and money and is preferred by the professionals. Some are personal injury cases, but still, it is hard to establish the causation connection between consuming the products and resulting damage to the body, and expert reports on such matters takes time and money. The compensation rules in the law are such that if consumption of the product does not cause obvious damage to the body, then it is hard to get compensation. Because many defective consumer products cause gradual damage to the body rather than an obvious and immediate problem, it is hard to prove the damage that has been caused by the defendants' product or service in the court.

Finally, it should be pointed out that whereas a number of jurisdictions elsewhere in the world have been developing a consumer protection ombudsman system (in large part as an alternative to the courts), there is as yet no such avenue available in China. This is because China has yet to introduce any kind of ombudsman system, making it one of the few jurisdictions anywhere to lack this form of access to justice.

7

Going 'Public': New Approaches in Resolving Consumer Disputes

I. Introduction

In earlier chapters, I have discussed the manner in which consumers in Shenzhen use public schemes, including non-judicial mechanisms – such as the Consumer Council mediation system, and the MSA mediation and report system – as well as the courts, to seek redress for their grievances. In China, as in other parts of the world, there are also various modes of pursuing a grievance that open the problem to a wider gaze and put pressure on those thought to have created a problem. In Shenzhen, these include drawing in the mass media, using the online complaint channels, and seeking information through 'open government' type regulations.

This chapter introduces some of these methods. They are less routinely used by aggrieved consumers, but may nevertheless serve as effective avenues for assisting unhappy customers in obtaining compensation and other remedies. The distinctive feature of these new methods is that consumers open the dispute to the wider public gaze, and in China this means drawing on – or at least potentially drawing on – the power of public supervision (or social supervision, *shehui jiandu*).

II. Consumer Redress and the Media

Consumer redress and the media have a very close relationship in many parts of the world,[1] and although the media is closely controlled by the party-state in the PRC, there is nevertheless also a strong linkage here too. TV shows, for example, have taken a strong interest over the past two decades or so in consumer issues. At the top, there is a national TV gala (*wanhui*) on the International Consumer Day (15 March) each year, where various consumer-related issues are examined in general terms, such as national data on consumer complaints, investigative reports on product safety, influential consumer infringement

[1] eg in Australia, consumers resort to the highly popular television consumer programme, *The Investigators*, to publicise their individual grievances. See J Goldring et al, *Consumer Protection Law* (Leichhardt, NSW, The Federation Press, 1998) ch 10 on consumer remedies at 387. Also, see research in Turkey on social network and consumer complaints. N Creutzfeldt et al, 'Consumer Protection in Turkey: Law, Informality and the Role of the Media' Melbourne, Australia (2016) *Department of Business Law and Taxation, Monash University: Working Paper* 21.

cases, ill-behaved companies, and so on.[2] The gala has been run on station CCTV One – China's most authoritative TV channel – since 1991, and is usually co-planned by the CCTV, consumer related government departments and, most importantly, the China Consumers Association (CCA). From 2009 onwards, there has been a new slogan for each year's gala, adding to the programme's dramatic impact. The gala is intended to educate consumers with knowledge and information, arousing rights awareness and popularising consumer laws – which are indeed, part of the important function of Consumer Association staff in their everyday work. An official website is established for each year's gala, in which consumers can comment on and review reported issues.[3]

At the local level, such as in Shenzhen, consumer infringement cases are often reported in popular TV programmes. One such Shenzhen programme is the 'First-hand Report' (*diyi xianchang*), a news programme broadcast from 6:30pm to 8pm each evening.[4] Livelihood problem stories, such as residential areas polluted by an illegal rubbish burning factory, citizens' reactions to the city's new rules on fees for parking on the road, and consumers buying unbranded cosmetic products causing damage to their skin, are the kinds of issue that feature in the programme's public-interest stories. The programme has a 'spill-it hotline' (*baoliao rexian*) through which consumers dial the special number and inform the media of the problematic issues affecting their daily lives. The hotline has now become the most important news sources for the 'First-hand Report' programme.

Another popular programme is called 'City No. 1' (*LuLu Tong*). This is a local news programme with a specific focus on citizen's daily lives, which is broadcast on Shenzhen television in the late afternoon, immediately before the First-hand Report. In 'City No. 1', news reports on consumer issues and infringement cases occupy most of the programme, and special sections are shown every now and then. For example, a section on introducing the new features of the revised Consumer Protection Law was broadcast soon after the promulgation of the revised law, and this section was on air for months.

Reporting to print newspapers is very popular too. In Shenzhen there is quite a range of Chinese-language newspapers locally published, as well as, of course, many national and provincial newspapers locally available. Among the former are *Shenzhen Dushi News* (*City News*), *Shenzhen Economic Daily*, *Shenzhen Evening News*, *Shenzhen Special Zone Daily*, *Shenzhen Youth News*, and even several English language daily newspapers such as the *Shenzhen Daily*. These all carry consumer issue stories. The *Southern Weekly* – one of China's most outspoken newspapers published in Guangzhou but widely read in Shenzhen – has many reports on matters of consumer interest. Consumer news is officially categorised as a matter of '*minsheng*', meaning 'people's livelihood', and relates to the daily life and well-being of ordinary persons. It is also therefore connected, albeit indirectly, to social and political stability – a central concern of the party-state leadership of the PRC over the past 15 years or so. This is because in general terms, the legitimacy of the party-state is seen in China as being dependent on continuing material well-being, as this, rather than, say,

[2] For an example in an English-language news report on the account of the 2016 gala, see www.bloomberg.com/news/articles/2016-03-14/china-state-tv-to-name-and-shame-in-gala-for-consumer-protection.
[3] The website of the gala is available at: 315.cntv.cn/special/2016/index.shtml.
[4] Ranking No 1 in the audience ratings in Shenzhen.

political reform, is seen as a benefit that the post-Mao economic reforms have delivered.[5] Accordingly, in addition to its role in consumer disputing, the newspaper media takes on a responsibility for enhancing consumer awareness – that is, an educational function.

One of the most popular *minsheng* columns was called '*Xiaofei Guangchang*' ('Consumer Square'), a consumer-specific column published in *Southern Weekly*. The Consumer Square was a hot section of the paper during its existence from 1996 to 2002, and at that time was regarded as a consumer protection 'frontline' (*qianxian*) by the general public. It offered and encouraged full and robust discussion of 'hot' consumer issues, such as the poor quality of telecommunication services and excessive charges, medical disputes between the patient and the hospital, and the controversial concept of who is a 'consumer' in the law – whether or not people who knowingly buying fake products are to be regarded as true consumers (as discussed in chapter two).[6] Unlike many other newspapers – which mainly rely on one-off reports – the *Southern Weekly* developed its Consumer Square column with continuous and sometimes serialised reports on consumer-related issues and stories, as well as cases dealt with by consumer professionals. I talked to these professionals, and they suggested to me that the Consumer Square was very influential in its heyday – so much so that some local governments even tried to stop the newspapers being sold in the area under their jurisdiction, after they found out that the Consumer Square had published investigative reports about consumer issues in their territory.

After playing an active role for some six years in consumer protection, the Consumer Square column was abolished in 2002. The former chief editor of the column suggested to me that the reason for the abolition of the Consumer Square was largely because of the development of online media and mobile media, and that the traditional medium for the media, newspapers, was diminishing. I discovered in the course of fieldwork that the chief editor has not left the field of consumer infringement issues, but rather, now heads a team working on a web-based consumer dispute resolution platform which indeed helps aggrieved consumers to resolve their dispute by using the social media.[7] In my view, it is also likely that using social media freed him and his team from some of the political controls that are typically found in the Chinese print media.

A. Role of Media in Consumer Disputes

During fieldwork in the Consumer Council, and as noted in chapter four above, I observed that in the final stages of negotiating a settlement – in particular, in the bargaining phase in Gulliver's model of negotiating – many aggrieved consumers tended to 'threaten' the defending business by asserting that if the defendant business did not compensate them for their loss, they would expose the issue to the media so as to let the public know 'all about' the

[5] See eg BG Guo, *China's Quest for Political Legitimacy: The New Equity-Enhancing Politics* (Lanham, Lexington Books, 2010) ch 1, which explains the 'unique' Chinese cognitive model of political legitimation.

[6] A former chief editor stressed these points to me during interviews with him. A book on mass media and public policy based on the stories published in the Consumer Column has been produced: see FS Xiao, *Gonggongxing Shijiao xia de Dazhong Chuanmei yu Gonggong Zhengce Yanjiu* (*Study on Mass Media and Public Policy from the Angle of the Public*) (Beijing, China Social Sciences Press, 2013).

[7] The platform here is the *Jutousu* website which is introduced below.

dispute and the misconduct of the business. In this sense, it seems that consumers' decision to use the media to go public is a last resort but nevertheless also a powerful negotiating tool. Most consumers, as I learned from follow-up interviews in the Consumer Council with aggrieved consumers, do not wish to proceed with their disputes all the way to the court. In other words, the court is not seen as the last resort in their eyes, and instead, the threat of media intervention, rather than court involvement, is what they tend to look for when they want to apply external pressures to defendant businesses. In this sense, we may think of the negotiations intended to settle consumer disputes as sometimes taking place in the shadow of media exposure rather than the shadow of the court.[8]

B. A Successful Example: The Meten English Course Dispute

In some cases, media exposure seems to be more effective than consumer redress and complaint for resolving consumer disputes. The Meten English course dispute, as mentioned in chapter four, is one such example.[9]

The basic facts of this dispute were as follows. Ms She was a young lady and an ordinary working class person. In order to improve her English language skills, she went to the language school calling itself 'Meten English' and signed up for an English-language course. According to her agreement with the school, the course would last for 12 months, include 360 classes, and cost around 19,800RMB in total (which was a discount on the original price of 25,800RMB). As a down payment, Ms She paid 4,800RMB at the start of the course. As Ms She recalled the matter in an interview with me, the course consultant of Meten suggested that she should apply for a credit card with which to pay the remaining fees by instalments, and this process would not incur any interest. She did this and signed the agreement with the consultant. However, after three days of classes, Ms She felt they were not nearly as good as she has been led to believe by the encouraging words of the course consultant. At the same time, Ms She was shocked when she received messages from her bank about problems with her account. She discovered that she was locked into a loan-contract, meaning that without realising it, she had borrowed the rest of the tuition fees from a small-loans company. With this loan agreement, she was already in debt for 15,000RMB and had to repay 888RMB each month for 18 months.

This came as a surprise to Ms She as she had not noticed – nor had her attention been drawn to – the fact is that she had signed an agreement with a small-loan company and was indeed in debt for what for her was a very large sum of money (Ms She's monthly income was only 4,000RMB). Ms She admitted that she signed the contracts in a rush on the day she paid for the course, and was not careful enough to read all the documents in detail (including the loan contract which she indeed signed). However, she claimed that the course consultant did not explain to her clearly that the instalments plan was in fact a type of financial product provided by the loan company. This product had the effect of

[8] cf RH Mnookin and L Kornhauser, 'Bargaining in the Shadow of the Law: The Case of Divorce' (1979) 88 *The Yale Law Journal* 950. Also see M Galanter, 'Worlds of Deals: Using Negotiation to Teach about Legal Process' (1984) 34 *Journal of Legal Education* 268 on the concept of 'liti-negotiation' ('litigotiation') as explained in ch 5.

[9] The language course case is discussed for the first time in ch 4, where it is used as an example for explaining consumers' multi-channel approach to address their grievances.

trapping her in the English course and forcing her to continue with the programme and the payments. In one article (written in bold letters) in the course-learning contract, it is said that customers could terminate the course within 10 days of the start of the course, and get a full refund except for 1,500RMB handling fees. Therefore, Ms She contacted Meten as soon as she decided to stop the course, and asked for a refund of her money.

However, Meten's course consultant took the view that since she paid for the course at a discounted rate, she could not terminate the contract in the way stated in that contract. The Meten staff member showed Ms She that in the supplementary contract, it was clearly stated that the refund policy in the course-learning contract would not be applicable to those who enjoyed discounted tuition fees.

Ms She felt hurt and aggrieved after hearing the explanation given by the course consultant. When she happily accepted a discount on her fees, she was not thinking about the exemption of a refund policy and had not even noticed the potential problem. Her attention at the time had not been drawn to it by the Meten salesperson. The day after Ms She had gone to Meten to complain, she visited the Shenzhen Consumer Council (SZCC), and filed a complaint in person. She was so worried about the loan that the very next day, she also dialled the 'spill-it hotline' for 'First-hand Report' and related her sorry experience to the media. The staff of 'First-hand Report', although they initially seemed uninterested, in fact replied even before she heard anything from the SZCC. On the evening of the next day, her case was broadcast on the 'First-hand Report' show. Her case was introduced as an example of unfair contract clauses as well as a new trap in private education services, of which consumers should be wary. The non-refund clause in the supplementary contract was clearly unfair to consumers and exempted Meten from accepting liability – for example, for failing to provide good enough teachers for the courses. The payment for education fees through instalments looks like a good method on paper, but in practice, it may become a way to force consumers to continue with courses that they wish to abandon.

In the TV programme, the journalist pointed out an important detail in the loan agreement: the signature of the handler of the loan was not that of a staff member from the small loan company, but that of Meten's course consultant. Obviously, Meten was neither qualified nor authorised to provide financial services. What is more, Ms She recalled from her memory of events that the course consultant had prepared a document that stated that Ms She was a department manager of her company and her salary was 80,000RMB per month. The consultant asked her to get it signed by her employer. As the journalist pointed out, based on Ms She's actual financial status, she was not even eligible for such a loan. Meten's handling of the loan, including providing advice to Ms She on the loan, and checking Ms She's documents, had indeed violated administrative regulations (*weigui*) for the financial sector.

Later, Ms She and the journalist, together with a cameraman, arrived at the Meten office. The staff member at the reception in Meten was very reluctant to accept the media's queries about Ms She's case. Under the pressure of the journalist's continuous requests, the staff member finally agreed to get the manager to address them. In front of the camera, the manager was rather aggressive towards Ms She when she asked about possible solutions for her fees problem. She insisted that Meten did not hold any responsibility for Ms She's contract, and the course could not be cancelled and refunded since she was given a discounted price. The journalist, however, was very helpful to Ms She with her negotiations by telling the manager that some of the terms in the contract were unfair and in fact violated the Consumer Protection Law.[10] However, the manager maintained a firm position and was unwilling to make any compromises.

During the investigative TV programme visit, the shots in Meten's premises were filmed apparently unnoticed by Meten staff (a line of text stating 'special filming' was shown at the corner of the screen when the programme was broadcast). The programme focused on the clashes between Ms She (with the media team) and Meten's manager at the office. The programme emphasised that these two parties disagreed with each other, and the fact was that Ms She was being denied justice by the business in her search for a refund. The programme did not show the ending of the case, but in a private interview with Ms She, I discovered that a few days after the show, she received a promise from the business that her loan contract would be cancelled, and except for a sum of 1,500RMB deducted as 'handling fees', she would get the rest of her money (3,300RMB) refunded. Ms She gave much credit to the investigative media team who had helped her in the negotiations with the business. When asked about how she felt about her experience, she answered:

> I never tried spilling anything (*baoliao*) to the media. I viewed it as 'treating a dead horse as if it's still alive' [Clutching at the final straw when in desperation] (*si ma dang huo ma yi*), and made three calls on that day to the media. Each time I was very anxious … It was not until the third time I called that the guy called back and agreed to help me … I was not satisfied with Meten, but as for the First-hand Report, I think the programme did a good job considering what it helped me get back [at least some of my losses].

Ms She was not very sure about precisely how her case was resolved – nor why Meten became willing to compromise – but as she understood it, what was crucial was the media's influence. In a later interview with the journalist, I learned that besides the impact of media exposure, the success of Ms She's case was also down to the help of an individual staff member of the media team. He happened to know the director of the Meten branch. With such a personal connection, it was easier for the media team to negotiate with Meten for Ms She's refund – Meten agreed to solve Ms She's problems if the media stopped reporting Ms She's case. The journalist suggested that during the negotiation with Meten, some staff members turned out to be very tough to handle, such as the aggressive staff member broadcast in the news report, while some others were 'softer', and so easier to talk to. At a later stage, the director at Meten went to his contact in the programme team and asked this journalist not to report the case anymore, and in return he agreed to refund Ms She.

As the case shows, media exposure on a consumer issue may help a consumer complainant in obtaining compensation, especially when the consumer is allied with influential local media such as the First-hand Report. However, Ms She may have been rather lucky in her case being picked up by the media, because it contained a timely 'newsworthy angle' for a report. As the journalist explained to me, Ms She's 'spill-it' call came in at a right time – the media team was planning a feature news report on disputes against unfair clauses in a contract, and Ms She's case – in which the supplementary contract invalidates the refund policy – was an example of an unfair clause which fitted squarely with the concerns of

[10] The journalist refers to Art 24 of the 1993 Consumer Protection Law on standard form contracts: 'Business operators may not, through standard form contracts, notices, announcements, entrance hall bulletins and so on, impose unfair or unreasonable rules on consumers or reduce or escape their civil liability for their infringement of the legitimate rights and interests of consumers.'

the feature. Also, as it is a relatively new phenomenon in China that consumers get a loan to pay their tuition fees for private educational services, the ordinary 'person in the street' may not know how to spot the hidden traps in the new type of consumer service. The media team was hoping to attract citizens' attention on such issues and make them more prepared for such tricks. The filming of Ms She's case was done very quickly, and took less than two hours to finish. This gave Ms She more time to negotiate effectively with the business. What is more, the inter-personal connection between the Meten Director and the member of the media team significantly facilitated the successful bargaining between Ms She and the business. My informants in this case did indicate, however, that not all complainants are so lucky. The fact is that in many cases, a grievance may sink into a sea of complaining calls and 'tip-offs' and the aggrieved consumer cannot be sure that there will be a positive response from the media.

Even so, it is true that cases that do get reported by the media seem to enjoy a high success rate. As some journalists reported to me, in around 9 out of every 10 cases where the media is brought in, consumers will get a favourable result and are satisfactorily compensated. The situation may vary slightly as between different businesses. Normally, media impact works well with small 'street' businesses on the one hand and with large companies on the other. As for small businesses, the money spent on a product for which there is a complaint is usually quite small, so after a show is broadcast, in most cases the business will be willing to compensate the customer the small sum involved, simply to make the trouble go away. In the case of large companies, such as shops for famous brand names or chain-store supermarkets, there is also a willingness to be cooperative in compensating consumers, in order to stop negative media reports which threaten potential damage to their business reputation. The medium size companies, on the other hand, are often the most difficult to handle, as they care least about media pressure. Thus, in the Meten dispute with Ms She's case, the staff were very unfriendly towards her and the media team during their first visit. It was only after a while that Meten did consider the impact on them of the media exposure and become willing (albeit reluctantly) to compromise, and one important factor in facilitating dispute closure was the personal connection between the media team and Meten's director.

In general, the influence of media exposure not only assists in the settlement of consumer disputes, but also creates a positive image of the media in the eyes of the public: the media is seen as a deliverer of justice. Aggrieved consumers regard media exposure as a 'short-cut' (*zou jie jing*) – one which is useful for getting their disputes resolved, and likely to be faster and more effective than the procedures they have to go through using institutional dispute processes. They particularly like the fact that settlement aided by the media is fast – a strategy by means of which consumers actually get the compensation money in their hands quicker than many other ways.

From the media's point of view, it is not necessarily their wish to take on the role of a dispute-resolver – a role that is supposed to be played by consumer bodies such as the SZCC and the MSA. Several journalists confided to me that they do not consider it to be the media's duty to help individual consumers to get compensation. The media in their view should be neutral in its reporting and analysis of unfolding stories, and consumers should rely on the formal dispute processes, such as those provided by the Consumer Council and the MSA, for claiming compensation. However, the effects of the investigative reporting shows send a signal to the audience that having their consumer grievances reported by the media can change the disadvantaged position of the consumer in the negotiating process, and make it more likely to get compensation. Other journalists are more positively involved in consumer cases – besides exposing a case of consumer injustice, they might also make a report to relevant regulators by themselves on the business' malpractice, especially when a business has committed what they see as a clear violation of the law. With the media's intervention, the investigation of businesses' practices by the regulator is put under the public gaze. It largely facilitates the handling of the report and pressures the regulator to work efficiently. As one journalist pointed out to me, by being a 'supervisor' for the regulator's acts, 'the media has performed and stimulated some of the functions that would otherwise rest with the governmental department'.

III. Web-Based Consumer Complaint Platform

As the Internet has become increasingly important in modern Chinese society, especially with a robust development of online shopping, dispute resolution channels have been put online as well. Worldwide, we can easily detect some famous ODR (online dispute resolution) platforms that provide services to parties over various kinds of dispute.[11] ODR platforms are also favoured by many consumers given that more and more disputes now arise over purchases made electronically, over a distance, and having disputes settled online may well save time and costs compared to face-to-face settlements. What is more, the development of the Internet has also brought a surge in the use of social media – consumer information and consumer complaints are circulated faster than ever before on social media. This has a significant social impact and puts businesses under great pressure to take responsibility for their misbehaviour.

This section examines two web-based Chinese consumer complaint platforms. Although both of them are Internet-based, they rely on very different powers and are shaped by different models: the first, the *Jutousu* platform, is a website that gathers similar consumer grievances and utilises the power of social media to facilitate negotiations between consumers and businesses. The second is the complaint handling platform of Taobao, the biggest online shopping website in China, established by the now globally well-known e-commerce company, the Alibaba Group. These processes are not specific to Shenzhen, but there is no doubt that Shenzhen online consumers are increasingly drawn into these new forms of dispute resolution, and electronic goods sellers in Shenzhen cause a number of consumer problems for online shoppers not only in Shenzhen, but also in other parts of China.

A. The *Jutousu* Platform

Jutousu, or the 21CN *Jutousu*, is a consumer complaint platform based on one of the top ten biggest news portals in China, 21CN. com. The name *Jutousu*, meaning 'concentrated complaints' in English, suggests its main feature, namely, collecting consumer complaints of

[11] eg Square-Trade, Smart-Settle and ICANN.

the same kind (and against the same defendant business upon the same issue), and assisting these complaining consumers in seeking collective compensatory redress from the defendant business. As the base for *Jutousu* platform, 21CN.com is a wholly owned subsidiary of China Telecom, a state-owned telecommunication company. It is one of the few websites to have obtained a permit issued by the Cyber Affairs Leading Group (of the Communist Party), allowing holders to provide Internet news information services. In other words, the website is considered as a news providing service that runs 'within the system' (*tizhi nei*) – meaning it is seen as carrying out functions similar to public sector organisations and is regulated by governmental administrative rules. I talked to staff members working in *Jutousu* and they inform me that the *Jutousu* platform is regarded as part of China Telecom's corporate social responsibility initiatives. With the special permit that it holds by being part of 21CN.com, *Jutousu* is also considered as a platform that operates 'within the system'. One staff commented on the nature of *Jutousu* as follows:

> As a web-based media run within the bureaucratic system, people often feel that the media is in an embarrassing position when it comes to speaking for the public voice [because the media is not neutral] … However, to run a web-based platform [like *Jutousu*] that helps people to solve their problems is always welcomed [by the people]. If you really want to do something, it is easier to have it done within the system, and you are more likely to succeed … The problem is, however, that many of the government officials don't do anything [even though they are within the bureaucratic system].

This comment echoes the problems I have noted: the difficulties for establishing an NGO in China, and the findings in this research that most consumer organisations are publicly funded. By the end of my field research, I got the impression that the CCP is trying to limit the role and growth of civil society as a bearer of consumer rights consciousness whenever it can, and the *Jutousu* platform is one of the many ways used to achieve this.

Complaints received on the platform's complaint portal will be collected by the backstage system of the website where staff of *Jutousu* can see the content and contact details of the consumer complainants. The complaints will be posted on the *Jutousu* website where registered users can comment on and indicate whether or not they like them. As for each individual complaint, staff will normally add to the website post the symbol @ followed by the names of those who they wish to communicate with, so that in particular the business is informed of the complaint. The business, which has seen the complaint, will normally give priority to dealing with those who publish their complaints on *Jutousu*. This is not only because the business is concerned with the negative impact caused by the publicity of the complaint, but also because *Jutousu* has made efforts in getting collaboration with some large businesses in the process of complaint handling. However, as a media-run platform, *Jutousu* is not equipped with enough staff to handle each individual complaint, and thus many posts do not get an immediate reply (unlike at the Shenzhen Consumer Council, where generally speaking full-time staff invariably pick up the phone promptly when a call comes in). Its main focus still lies in creating web-impact for large scale collective redress.

At *Jutousu*, all message exchanges are posted on the website. There is a progress bar in the web-post where the complainant, as well as all the website visitors are able to view the progress in the handling of the complaint. As staff members explained their involvement in the process to me, in some circumstances, he or she may contact the business and the complainant offline to seek their consent on a settlement and its terms, but nevertheless they try to show everything on the website for normal site visitors to view the details of the case and make comments. Also, when a staff member notices that there are a certain number of complaints against a same party on a same issue, he or she will establish a feature report (post) on the *Jutousu* website, with a short description of the story on top of the page, and a list of the complaint posts of the same kind. Visitors to the website can view the total number of complaints posts that each feature report contains (ie, the total number of complaints made against the same business for the same issue).

In addition to the service delivered by the *Jutousu* website itself, the *Jutousu* platform works in a particular way that is best characterised as 'three plus one'. As staff members have explained to me, the 'one' here refers to making complaints or reports to the regulators, that is the SAIC at different levels. Staff of *Jutousu* will contact the consumer complainant, and provide guidance to them on how best to proceed with their grievance – this is normally done by telling the aggrieved consumers to turn to authoritative complaint channels, such as SAIC. Staff may sometimes do a little homework for the consumer complainant, so as to assist them in making effective complaints. For example, they will help search for the registered company name of the exact subsidiary (usually of a multi-national enterprise) in China that should be responsible for the issue, or in searching for laws and regulations in support of the complaint.

The 'three' refer to three tools they use on the web to expand the coverage of the issue and create an impact. The first tool is the feature report on *Jutousu* website, as mentioned above, which collects similar complaints against one company. Staff members actively seek out aggrieved consumers who have suffered from the same problem – they may make a phone call to the complainant, for example, and ask if there are any other people the complainant knows of who have also suffered the same problem. If so, then the staff member might well encourage the complainant to ask them to post their complaints on *Jutousu*, and then the staff member creates a feature report based on the complaints.

The second tool is to use chat-room software, such as the most popular one in China, Tencent QQ, as a way to communicate. *Jutousu* staff will help to create a QQ group, and invite all the complainants of the collective complaint to join the group. Through invitation by complainants in the QQ group, the group gathers more and more complainants together in a sort of 'on-line grievance community' and it becomes a useful place for members' discussion and sharing of experiences.

The third tool is to use a microblogging website, that is the Sina *weibo*, for spreading information about the issue.[12] This is perhaps the most important part of the *Jutousu*'s strategy in pressuring the businesses into making compromises. *Jutousu* has an official account on *weibo*, and has a 'fan base' (followers) of around 370,000 people. Staff members of *Jutousu* will post the issue reported by aggrieved consumers on *Jutousu*'s *weibo* page, while at the same time, notifying the defendant businesses, as well as relevant regulatory organisations. Nowadays, most of the businesses and regulatory organisations have a *weibo* official account, so it is not difficult to tag their names in the post. In this way, the tagged organisations and businesses will be notified about the post (the issue), and be able to see the comments on the post made by web visitors. This is an initiative proposed by *Jutousu* in

[12] The Sina *weibo* is one of the most popular websites in China, and is rather like a hybrid of Twitter and Facebook. It is used by over 30% of Internet users. Subscribers of *weibo* can post their own stories, share others' posts and give comments on the posts. One can raise points or talk to other people (or organisations) by using '@UserName' formatting to tag them in the posts.

an effort to make more consumers (and indeed other citizens) aware of the issue, so as to create an impact about the emerging case on the web. With a large fan group and the media influence of *Jutousu*, the posts created by *Jutousu* almost certainly will attract more attention on the web than those created by individual consumers or other citizens. *Jutousu*, with all the tags, speaks to the businesses and the regulatory organisation on behalf of the aggrieved consumers, so that the response from the tagged organisation is faster and more effective.

As *Jutousu* is a relatively new website, it is not yet an especially well-known complaint channel among consumers and other citizens. To a web-user, when he or she comes across a problem, the first thing that he or she will do is to search the issue on the web. With the establishment of a QQ group as well as a *weibo* page, consumers can find *Jutousu* more easily – they can find its QQ group and *weibo* page for a collective complaint, even though they are not aware of the *Jutousu* website itself. Thus, *Jutousu* is becoming a new means of enhancing consumer rights awareness, and offers a web-based process by means of which aggrieved consumers can help each other to 'name, blame and claim'.[13]

i. The Nike Case

One example that illustrates well the *Jutousu* approach is the Nike case. In this dispute, consumers placed orders with Nike's official online store to purchase Air Jordan 6 retro 'Carmine', which is a limited edition of a particular style of basketball shoes. As the shoes are limited edition, the website required that payment should be made within 15 minutes of the order being made. Many customers adhered to the requirement, and the purchase was made successfully, with payment drawn from the consumers' bank account. However, after half an hour, many customers' orders were cancelled, on the basis that their payment for the shoes had not been made on time. The status of the orders remained cancelled after that, but no money was returned to their bank accounts. Several unhappy customers stated that they had contacted Nike's customer service, and were told that the issue would be resolved in couple of days. However, as the shoes were a limited edition, once a purchase was made online, a customer could not make a second purchase on the same item.

Consumers who bought the shoes strongly pressed Nike to revive their order, so that they would not miss the chance to purchase the prestigious, limited edition, shoes. However, the email replies from Nike did not acknowledge the consumers' payments (and indeed kept asking for a payment to be made by consumers), and the order remained cancelled. This was not an isolated case, and unreasonable termination of online orders by Nike happened throughout the month – specifically on 3, 24 and 29 May 2014 – on purchases on the same item. Many customers tried contacting Nike a number of times, but none received any response. They suspected that the 'chopping-off' of orders was a deliberate act by Nike, as Nike had advertised the shoes, but in fact did not have enough stock for consumers to purchase. They felt that Nike had simply used the process as a kind of marketing ploy and its misconduct had robbed them of a chance to purchase the limited edition shoes.

Some consumers started to make complaints to *Jutousu*, and on 27 May, a collective complaint (a feature report) was formed on the web, with a QQ group and *weibo* posts

[13] W Felstiner, R Abel and A Sarat, 'The Emergence and Transformation of Disputes: Naming, Blaming, Claiming …' (1980) 15 *Law and Society Review* 631.

established. Consumers who came across the same issue were gathered together by the QQ group and *weibo* post, and experiences were shared. After that, consumer complainants started to disseminate the issue on the web. They re-posted the *weibo* post created by *Jutousu*'s official *weibo* account to various places, and each time, the tags in the post – Nike's official *weibo* page, the *Jutousu*'s feature report webpage, and the local SAIC – were also circulated. By 31 May 2014, the post had been viewed more than 1,293,000 times and was shared 257 times. At the same time, complainants were also advised by *Jutousu*'s staff to raise their grievances to their local SAIC. As it was not clear which local SAIC was in charge of a complaint to Nike, *Jutousu* staff had done some research on the registration place of the company's subsidiary in China.

As a result, all complainants were directed to make their complaints to the valid regulatory organisation, the SAIC, in Shanghai. On 29 May, two days after the web posts of Nike's dishonest acts were established and circulated, Nike, for the first time, agreed to refund all its customers, together with a voucher of 1249RMB (the same amount of money of the price of the shoes) as compensation.

However, on the evening of 29 May, again, Nike terminated a number of orders of the same shoes on limited edition. The excuse given by Nike this time was that their order system had a fault and that this error was due to a software update, which resulted in sold products still being listed for purchasing. Again, consumer complainants demanded that Nike continue performance of the purchase contract, or instead, compensate the unhappy customers for not being able to buy the shoes. This time, however, Nike only agreed to provide consumer complainants with a 25 per cent off code for next purchase as compensation. Not surprisingly, the aggrieved customers were not satisfied with this 'voucher' deal. The customer was able to present a winning first-trial decision against Amazon on the same issue. In the Amazon case, consumers placed orders on buying low-priced Changhong TVs which were listed at a really good bargain price on the Amazon website – the TVs were sold at 10 per cent of their original price and only cost 161.99RMB. However, after one day, some customers started receiving emails claiming that their orders (on a discounted price) were cancelled, and the TVs were sold out. On the other hand, many customers saw that the same type of TV was still on sale at its original price of 1489RMB on Amazon. In January 2014, three consumers successfully sued Amazon in Chaoyang District Court in Beijing at the first trial in April 2014. The judgment declared that Amazon must honour its sales contract with consumers, and pay all the court and lawyers' fees. By referring to the Amazon case, the Nike consumer complainants successfully argued for a return of the money that they had paid Nike plus a voucher for the same amount of money as compensation.[14]

The successful settlement of the Nike case reveals that a new type of consumer complaint mode has emerged – one which works effectively by using social media through the web. However, it is as yet by no means a universal or commonly used method. The success of the Nike case largely relied upon the active role played by the netizens – the consumer complainants in this case are mostly young adults who are relatively well-off, skilful at web browsing, and have enough time to spend on social media (those who bought limited edition shoes were mostly young active netizens). What is more, the company needs to have

[14] Amazon entered an appeal. In October 2014, however, the appellate court upheld the decision handed down by the court of first instance.

a *weibo* official account in the first place, so that the views, likes, shares, comments and tags on the post can work effectively. It does not matter that much if the company is large or small, but the minimum condition is that it has put itself online in the world of social media. If it has not done so, all the views, shares and responses that create the pressure on *weibo* have no specific target to affect.

B. The Online Dispute Resolution Platform of Taobao

The growth of the Internet and, in more recent years, the emergence of analysis of 'big data', have encouraged some companies and organisations to develop special online dispute resolution systems for relatively routine disputes: that is, for quarrels over items that are low in value, but enjoy a high volume of sales. The most impressive of these new systems is that offered by Taobao – where a form of e-adjudication characterised as 'crowd' (*dazhong*) decision-making is used to deal with buyer-seller disputes that occur on Taobao website. Taobao is China's primary online shopping website. Founded in 2003, it is operated in Hangzhou, Zhejiang by the Alibaba Group. Its function is to promote consumer retail by providing a platform for small businesses and individual entrepreneurs to open online outlets that mainly cater to consumers in the mainland and other Chinese-speaking areas in the region such as Hong Kong, Macau and Taiwan. Thus, in a large city such as Shenzhen, many consumers will increasingly not only think of making purchases from local stores but also over the Internet using a service such as Taobao. One of Taobao's most spectacular successes is its now annual autumnal 'single day' promotion, explicitly given the seal of approval by China's Premier, Li Keqiang, and characterised in a leading Hong Kong newspaper as a 'shopping orgy'.[15]

In 2004, shortly after it was set up, Taobao established its online payment system 'Alipay' (*Zhifubao*) in order to deal with payment problems in its basic transactions disputes. But there were still too many disputes arising, and a Customer Service Hotline called 'Taobao Assistant' (*Taobao Xiao'er*), manned by real human beings, was created so as to handle customer complaints and disputes with sellers. However, because the operators of the system were human, other problems arose. These included inconsistency, poor categorisation of disputes, employment costs (it was expensive to employ the many dispute resolving 'customer service representatives' that were needed to operate the system). Therefore further reforms were needed and in 2012, Taobao set up an online dispute resolution site for handling disputes: Taobao Panding Zhongxin – the Taobao Determination Centre.

In this new system, disputes are resolved by voting: votes are cast by randomly selected 'crowd' or 'public' adjudicators (*dazhong pingshenyuan*). Who can be a 'crowd adjudicator'? The qualifications are different as between those who have used Taobao for buying, and those who have used it for selling. For all adjudicators, the requirements are that they must have been registered with Taobao for one year or more and have a 'sesame credit'

[15] C Sun, 'Singles Day Sale Beats Spectre of 2014 by Delivering Record US$10bn for Alibaba, after Arch Bachelor James Bond Launches Event: Online Shopping Promotion Delivers for Jack Ma's Alibaba' (*South China Morning Post*, 11 November 2015) www.scmp.com/news/china/money-wealth/article/1877664/alibabas-jack-ma-counts-chinese-premier-li-keqiang-among-his.

score over 600.[16] For consumers, they must fulfil the following three requirements: reach level VIP 2 (have spent altogether 5,000RMB or more on Taobao), reach a three-heart credit rating (given good comments (*haoping*) on 41 or more occasions), and have not been involved in disputes for more than three times in the past 90 days. But for sellers the requirements are a little different: they must reach a one-diamond credit rating (given good comments (*haoping*) on 41 or more occasions), have a refund rate lower than the average refund rate among the industry in the past 30 days, and have not violated rules of Taobao in the present year. This threshold is not harsh, and most of Taobao's frequent users can fulfil the requirement to be a crowd adjudicator.

C. Process of Crowd Adjudication

At the current stage of development (as of 2014), there are mainly three types of dispute that are open for crowd adjudication: The first type of dispute arises when there is a seller's complaint that he or she has been unfairly punished by Taobao for putting the product for sale in a wrong category. The second type of case arises when there is a seller's complaint on being punished for failing to live up to advertised promises. These two types of case (complaint) will go to the Taobao Assistant (*Taobao Xiao'er*) in the first place. If the complainant (the seller) is not satisfied with Taobao Assistant's decision, the case will then be sent for crowd adjudication. The third type of dispute is one brought by the buyers during transactions between sellers and buyers, particularly the disputes that arise because there are problems regarding exchange or return of products. In this type of case, the plaintiff is the consumer – he or she can choose between the handling by the Taobao Assistant and the adjudication by the crowd adjudicator.[17] However, Taobao feels that two types of problem are not easily dealt with by 'crowd adjudication': first, where there have been fraudulent transactions, and secondly, where comments and criticisms against sellers have been made in bad faith.

Once the process is initiated, the parties will upload images of receipts, the item, chatting history, and so on, as evidence in support of their claims. They can also key in a short statement of the position regarding the dispute on the system. The crowd adjudicators can shop around in the Determination Centre and pick up cases they are interested in. Each case is given a trial period of 168 hours that is, just under seven days – and a party wins over the other side when it obtains 16 votes.[18] If none of the parties to a dispute has obtained

[16] The 'sesame credit' refers to a 'social credit' scoring system developed by Ant Financial Services Group (an affiliate of Alibaba). The company is one of the eight companies approved by the Chinese government to provide credit rating services. It uses Alibaba's database of consumer information to rate each citizen's trustworthiness in social life. A high score of sesame credit can bring a citizen benefits on access to loans, job offers, etc. However, the system has also been criticised as a mass surveillance tool by human rights organisations. See J Burke, 'The Social Credit System in China Is Another Way to Control Its Citizens' (*Vision Times*, 23 December 2015) www.visiontimes.com/2015/12/23/the-social-credit-system-in-china-is-another-way-to-control-its-citizens.html.

[17] See the protocol of Taobao Crowd Adjudication (for trial implementation) at: pan.taobao.com/ (access is only available through Taobao's mobile app).

[18] The number of winning votes is given in Art 11 of the protocol. Taobao limits the number of adjudicators at 30 for each dispute, so 16 votes mean a majority.

over 16 votes, and the trial period has passed, the adjudication is deemed to be void, and the Taobao Assistant will decide the trial outcome. An adjudicator cannot determine more than 40 cases per day.

In general, the adjudication work is pro bono, but some 'social status' rewards might still be given to the crowd members as incentives. Thus, for example, each crowd adjudicator will collect 10–20 'experience points' per decision, and they will in due course be awarded a 'title' based on the number of experience points they have earned (Foundation, Diploma, Bachelor, Masters or PhD holder). Another reward is that adjudicators now can choose to donate the points to various charities, and 'earn' a token gift – a toy – as a proof of their generosity.

In the first year (2013) that crowd adjudication was put online, over 820,000 Taobao members became crowd adjudicators – this group now consists of 480,000 consumer adjudicators and 330,000 seller adjudicators, and they together have adjudicated over 340,000 cases in the Determination Centre.[19] This has helped reduced Taobao Assistants' workload in a great deal. What is more, it is also suggested by the press that these crowd adjudicators have helped Taobao in improving over 140 rules on product sales management.[20] As for individual entrepreneurs – the sellers – they point out that they have learned the Taobao rules better through their experience as crowd adjudicators.[21]

D. Diffusion of Alibaba's Approach to the Local Courts in Zhejiang

The ever-growing importance of Taobao and its apparently successful innovations in online dispute resolution have been an important factor in encouraging the growth of online courts. In cities in Zhejiang Province – the same province as that in which Alibaba was set up and has its headquarters – some local courts have started to use 'e-courts' to handle disputes over e-shopping, commercial transactions disputes, copyright infringement and low value financial loans. As the plaintiff and defendant are often situated far apart, the courtroom is replaced by three-way video conferencing. All procedures are carried out online, including service of process, discovery and other evidentiary requirements, trial and delivery of judgment. The judgment on the online court is final and enforceable.[22] It is not yet clear that these developments do actually enhance access to justice for consumers and others. However, we can see that an e-court saves travelling costs for disputing parties and may well enhance case-handling efficiency. As mentioned in chapter three, Shenzhen is the centre for electronic appliances, and many small businesses that sell fraudulent products on Taobao are indeed based in Shenzhen. Going online for trial or hearing of reports handled by the MSA (the regulator) would likely be a good system for Shenzhen (especially its courts) as well, but as yet there have been no developments in this direction.

[19] See LH Zhang, 'Taobao Jiaoyi Yinru Dazhong Pingshenyuan Jizhi' (Taobao Introduced Crow Adjudicator System to its Transactions) (*Hangzhou Daily*, 31 December 2013) at B10.

[20] ibid.

[21] ibid.

[22] See news report 'Xinhua Insight: E-Courts Promise Online Justice for Chinese Shoppers' (*Xinhua Net*, 11 December 2015) china.chinadaily.com.cn/shizheng/2015-12/11/content_22697685.htm.

IV. Access to Knowledge: Disclosure of Government Information

In consumer complaint and redress, it has become increasingly popular for the consumer plaintiff – particularly the professionals, to ask for disclosure of government information in assisting with their consumer claims. The practice of making requests to the government for public information has gained national support since the promulgation of an important guideline – 'Regulations of the People's Republic of China on the Disclosure of Government Information' (herein after, the Regulations) – in January 2007, which came into force in May 2008. In a centrally controlled and paternalistically administered state like China, the opening-up of an avenue of access for the public to obtain government information is not an easy step, nor one taken lightly. As we have seen in chapter three, the handling processes of complaints by the Consumer Council and the MSA are so opaque that working guidance and rules are only circulated within the organisations. The 2007 Regulations are thus considered by scholars as a major event in the legal construction of good government, and were rated as 'one of the top ten constitutional law events' in 2007.[23]

This channel for securing information is not only liked by consumer professionals, but also favoured by NGOs and individual activists working on various issues, such as environmental protection, children's rights to education, corrupted officials, and so on. After the Regulations were introduced, local governments at different administrative counties have been required to establish a working system for disclosure of information, and appoint a specific government department to handle the daily work involved.[24] The disclosure of government information has become a duty of the government, and is one of the factors that have to be taken into account in the evaluation process of a local government's performance. According to the 2007 Regulations, certain kinds information must be freely disclosed to the public – these include information concerning the vital interests of citizens, information that should be widely known by the general public or which concerns the participation of the general public, and information that reflects the structural establishment, duties, procedures for handling affairs and other situation of the administrative organ.[25] Article 14 also states, however, that '[N]o administrative organ may disclose any government information involving state secrets, commercial secrets or individual privacy.' Nevertheless, other than these kinds of secret, the scope of information that can be disclosed is indeed very broad.

In practice, under the influence of these Regulations, local governments have been gradually setting up official webpages and putting on some of the information concerning their governance. However, the openness and transparency of the government's work varies in a great deal as between different places. In developed areas, such as provinces along the east coast (including Guangdong Province, where Shenzhen is located), significantly more information has been published online than provinces in less developed areas.

[23] YC Mo and HC Lin, 'A Research Report on the Enforcement Preparation of the "Government Information Disclosure Regulation"' ("Zhengfu Xinxi Gongkai Tiaoli" Shishi Zhunbei Diaoyan Baogao') (2008) 6 *Faxue (Law Science)* 113.

[24] Art 4 of the Regulations.

[25] Art 9 of the Regulations.

Still, information that local governments are in reality willing to allow to be published without some kind of specific pressure is limited. As we can see from its provisions, the 2007 Regulations are a general guideline for the practice of disclosure of information, and that allows a good deal of discretion to local authorities – to what extent the information can be disclosed is in fact largely decided by each local government. The reported experience of one NGO in submitting requests for the disclosure of the same information to different local governments is nevertheless encouraging. The NGO sent off 80 request letters in 2012 to the Environmental Departments in 80 different cities (requesting disclosure of the companies that are under intensive controls for their water and air pollution), and received 63 effective replies. This response rate of 78.75 per cent is considered very high by the NGO concerned.[26]

A. The Usage in Consumer Complaints

One of the consumer professionals, Mr Chen, as noted in chapter five, is very experienced and skilled in making requests to various administrative departments for disclosure of government information relevant to his 'disputing' work. The first time that Mr Chen used this resource in his 'dispute methodology' dates back to 2005, when the Futian District Court in Shenzhen declined to accept any of his suits against the telecommunication companies.[27] Mr Chen, indeed, sees himself as the pioneer in requesting disclosure of government information – not only in Shenzhen but in the whole of Guangdong Province. His requests for disclosure were made three years before the 2007 Regulations, the national law, were established. The legal justification Mr Chen used for his request was twofold in nature: first, there were newly introduced rules in the Guangdong Regulations on Disclosure of Government Affairs published in July 2005; secondly, in Shenzhen, a document published by the General Office of Municipal CCP (Chinese Communist Party) Committee, Shenzhen, had encouraged – perhaps ordered – all government officials to endeavour to construct a transparent government (called the 'sunshine project').[28] These two documents have formally given citizens' the right to ask for release of information about the government's administration.

At the time, Mr Chen tried this new approach, he was – he admits – really only thinking about bringing some 'trouble' to the government's doorstep, because he was bullied by the court and felt he was being denied justice. However, his act of pressuring the government

[26] See *Guidance on the Practice of Asking for Disclosure of Government Information* (*Zhengfu Xinxi Gongkai Shiwu Zhinan*) 16, at blog.sina.com.cn/s/blog_74d272900102v074.html. Copy on file with the author and available upon request.

[27] Mr Chen recalled that immediately after he won his first case against the telecommunication giant in 2004, he was unable to have any case accepted by the Futian District Court in Shenzhen. The court did not accept his case files, neither did it provide a written order on the decision of denial of the case to Mr Chen (who was only informed orally). This situation lasted from November 2004 to March 2006. See news report L Li, '"Zanghua" Shangsuzhuang Beihou de Zhenzheng Zhujiao' (The Real Antagonist behind the Rude Words Petition for Appeal) (*Legal Daily*, 21 May 2009) www.newsinfonet.com/view.php?d=252.

[28] The Guangdong Regulations on Disclosure of Government Affairs (2005) is available at www.gd.gov.cn/govpub/zfxxgkzdwj/szfwj/201610/t20161018_240969.htm. The document which enforces the 'sunshine project' in Shenzhen is available at www.sz.gov.cn/zfgb/2006/gb471/200810/t20081019_94567.htm.

by using the information demand weapon won him back his right to file cases at the court. Mr Chen sent off letters to all the main administrative departments in the Shenzhen government, and their bureaus at district level. The content of the request was simple – it asked for information, for example, who was the department head, what was the deputy head in charge of? What was the mailbox address for the official letters and visits system of complaints? How did the department spend its budget? Such information is mostly available online now, but in 2005, only one district bureau was able and willing to give a reply to Mr Chen. The government departments, as Mr Chen described the events, did not have an 'established habit' of replying to citizens' requests. Mr Chen later sued the 'no-reply' departments in different local courts (specifically in their Administrative Chambers) for their neglect in responding to requests for disclosing administrative information. He made similar attempts in more than 20 cities in Guangdong Province, and even sued the provincial government when it too did not reply to the requests. During those days, Mr Chen had been involved in more than 500 administrative reviews and suits. This impacted significantly on the Provincial bureaucratic system. The Guangdong Provincial government in the end came to see itself as violating the regulations it had created, and agreed that the 20 cities in the Province had not complied with the regulations because they did not reply to Mr Chen's requests for disclosing government information.

Given Mr Chen's impact on the local governments, it is perhaps not surprising that he was then invited by the a high-ranking official to an earnest talk (*kentan*) to chat about his then recent rights protection activities. It was during this talk that he mentioned the difficulty he had in filing consumer cases in local courts in Shenzhen. Subsequently, he found out that he had been given the green light on case acceptance in local courts on cases against telecommunication companies. His litigation rights were resumed, and the problem was somehow resolved. As he described events, he had for the first time tasted the 'sweetness' of the fruit gained from the process of requesting disclosure of government information.

In later years, he refined and disseminated the techniques of making information requests, and taught his trainees about them, including how to write a request letter, what administrative departments they should target, and how to present questions so as to get effective replies from the departments. In current times, these techniques are widely used in consumer complaints and reporting at various stages of the dispute process: some use it particularly for creating pressure on the complaint handling department, for example, asking for disclosure of information which is normally deemed as 'secret', but not necessarily relevant to the case (such as the internal disciplinary rules of the Shenzhen MSA). Some use it for obtaining and consolidating evidence that might be of use at later stages of the bargaining with the business. For example, the company needs to provide documents showing that the products are of standard quality, or that the label of the products is put on record, when the products are imported into the country. Through requesting disclosure of government information, the professionals are able to access details of information on the procedures that the company has gone through and documents it provides for clearance of import, which may indeed be good evidence to be used for negotiations with the business in the future.

As discussed in chapter five, the professionals are good at perceiving the procedural errors of the work of officials. Administrative lawsuits and reviews may follow if the administrative department does not give a reply, fails to provide a reply on time, gives a reply that is not in a proper format, and so on. To a large extent, this has increased the workload of many officials, and sometimes such pressures may assist the professionals in getting better settlement deals with the defendant business.

V. The Emerging Public Interest Litigation in Consumer Disputes

As Cappelletti has suggested, in the contemporary society of 'mass production-mass consumption', there is an increasing tendency for 'human actions and relationships [to] assume a collective, rather than a merely individual character; they refer to groups, categories, and classes of people, rather than to one or a few individuals alone'.[29] China is rapidly approaching this state of 'massification phenomena' that Cappelletti suggests, and it has indeed looked for a processual approach that has the potential to enable members of different social groupings with their particular collective interests to gain access to court, to secure their 'social rights' and obtain justice.[30] In 2012, for the first time, China formally introduced public interest litigation into the legal system. The revisions to the Civil Procedure Law included this procedure, so that Article 55 of the Law now provides that 'relevant organs and organisations prescribed by law may initiate lawsuit at competent courts against conduct jeopardising the public interests, such as causing environment pollution or damaging the interests of a large number of consumers'.[31] However, as many Chinese scholars have suggested, a major concern about China's version of PIL is that it only allows 'relevant organs and organisations' to represent the public interest in court, and excludes the representation of individuals for such collective interests. Article 54 of the revised Civil Procedure Law on representative group litigation has enabled a certain level of collective redress, but this representation is rather limited because representatives must come from individuals who have a *direct* interest in the case.[32]

The Consumer Protection Law revision in 2013 was for the first reform in two decades, and other changes were introduced which are relevant here: Article 47 of the 2013 Consumer Protection Law gives Consumer Associations at the provincial level standing to bring cases where rights of a large group of consumers have been infringed (which are often characterised as potential public interest cases). The law has clarified what organisations may bring a public interest lawsuit on behalf of the consumers. However, the range of qualified organisations is rather limited, and initially there were no detailed rules on how to handle the consumer-related public interest cases. However, there was further reform in May 2016, when the Supreme People's Court published its 'Interpretations on Certain Issues Concerning the Application of Law in the Trial of Consumer-Related Civil Public Interest Actions'. This deals with some detailed issues such as the jurisdiction over consumer-related public

[29] M Cappelletti, 'Vindicating the Public Interest through the Courts: A Comparativist's Contribution' (1975–76) 25 *Buffalo Law Review* 643, 646.

[30] ibid.

[31] Art 55 of the Civil Procedure Law (2012).

[32] Art 54 of Civil Procedure Law provides that '[I]f the persons comprising a party to a joint action is large in number, the party may elect representatives from among themselves to act for them in the litigation. The acts of such representatives in the litigation shall be valid for the party they represent.'

interest cases, the documents that the plaintiff should submit when filing a case, and the type of claims that the court will support, and so on. Also, the rights of standing of PIL have been further expanded to include the People's Procuracy through the revision of the 2012 Civil Procedure Law in 2017. A second paragraph is added to Article 55 that gives the People's Procuracy standing in the court for food and drug safety cases, '[to] file a lawsuit with the people's court if there is no authority or organisation prescribed in the preceding paragraph or the authority or organisation prescribed in the preceding paragraph does not file a lawsuit'.[33]

However, the judicial interpretation does not clearly identify the court's position regarding case acceptance of the plaintiffs' claims for damages. The Interpretation does indicate the requests that the court may uphold – these include, a request for the defendant to cease infringement of rights, remove obstacles, eliminate danger, offer an apology (Article 13), as well as any request for the defendant 'to bear the expenses incurred in adopting reasonable prevention or disposal measures in order to stop infringement, remove obstacles or eliminate dangers' (Article 17). However, these provisions nowhere indicate that the court will accept requests for suits seeking compensation for consumers. One commentator, Deng Juan, argues that omission is intentional, and reflects the Chinese authorities' worries that such litigation may be too complex for the court to handle easily: it is likely to be technically difficult for the court to decide on the standard for compensation for damages and on the burden of proof, and even if an award is made, difficult for the parties to then decide the allocation of the funds awarded in compensation.[34] Between March 2014 when the Consumer Protection Law 2013 came into force, and March 2017, there have been across the whole of China altogether only seven PIL cases in which Article 47 litigation has been used by the Consumer Associations on behalf of aggrieved consumers.[35] Of these seven cases, six were brought by the Consumer Association (or Consumer Council) at the provincial level, and one was brought by the relevant people's procuracy. None of the cases have involved claims for compensation for consumers' losses.[36]

There is an indication that perhaps the situation will become clearer in the not-too-distant future. The first case in which the court has dealt with a request for compensation under the Article 47 provisions seems to be one brought by the Guangzhou People's Procuracy on behalf of consumers against Mr Liu for manufacturing and selling fake salt. Unfortunately, to date it seems that there are only news reports on this case, and that the judgment has yet to be published. Prior to this suit, however, Mr Liu had already been sentenced to three years' imprisonment and a fine of 80,000RMB was imposed on him in a successful criminal prosecution for the same misconduct by the Baiyun District Court in Guangzhou.[37] The Guangzhou Intermediate People's Court adjudicated the civil case,

[33] This is the only revision made to the 2012 version of Civil Procedure Law in 2017.

[34] J Deng, 'Research on Type of Claim of Public Interest Litigation for Consumers' (*Xiaofei Gongyi Susong de Qingqiu Leixing Wenti Yanjiu*) (2017) 4 *Academic Search for Truth and Reality* (*Tan Qiu*) 59, 63. The author is an officer who works in the Civil and Administrative Procuratorial Department of the Guangzhou People's Procuracy.

[35] ibid at 60. Deng has also pointed out that from May 2015 until June 2016, there were altogether 93 PIL cases on environmental issues brought by various 'social organisations'. The number of consumer PIL cases is thus clearly much smaller than PIL actions involving environmental issues.

[36] ibid.

[37] ZL Wu, 'The Procuracy Filed Public Interest Litigation, Fake-Salt Manufacturer Was Ordered to Pay 1, 120,000RMB' (*Jianchayuan Tiqi Gongyi Susong, Jiayan Zhishouzhe Panpei 112wan yuan*) (*Southern Metropolis Daily*, 16 March 2018) GA01.

and rendered a judgment in which Mr Liu was ordered to pay an award of compensation of 'ten-times punitive damages' totalling 1,200,000RMB. However, since he had already been fined 80,000RMB in the criminal case, the award against him in the civil action was reduced to 1,120,000RMB. Because no consumers had apparently even noticed that they were consuming fake salt, no one lodged claims for a share of the damages. The compensation award is therefore to be turned over to the state treasury. It would seem, therefore, that the civil judgment against Mr Liu has at best only benefitted consumers indirectly, by warning producers who engage in such misconduct that the financial penalties that might be imposed on them may well be much heavier than they anticipate.

VI. Conclusions

This chapter has explored the methods by which consumers in Shenzhen may seek to pursue remedies for what they see as unfair treatment at the hands of sellers. Their use shows consumers to be skilled and flexible in their attempts to secure justice, and in using various channels other than the courts, including the effective use of new resources stemming from the growth of the web and the creation of new and quite radical approaches to consumer dispute resolution. One area where the latent 'consumer movement' has had a significant influence is in securing greater access to consumer-relevant information. Particularly, the skilled professional consumer litigants seize upon new legislation that perhaps was never intended to be rigorously enforced, and use it to pressure the local governments in many parts of Guangdong, including Shenzhen, to be more open and transparent in the way in which they handle public requests for greater information. This chapter has also noted the introduction of the process of public interest litigation for consumer cases. In such litigation, consumers seek redress for damages collectively. As I have observed, there is now a preliminary legal framework at the national level for consumer related public interest litigation. However, it is still at an early stage of development and to date it seems that the courts have yet to find in favour and to award damages for aggrieved consumers.

8

Conclusions

I. Dispute Resolution in China

In China, as elsewhere, aggrieved consumers look to a variety of available avenues when seeking access to justice. I have noted that governmental departments continue to offer extensive mediation services in a manner consistent with China's 'paternalistic' legal culture, and courts face a steady stream of cases, including cases arising out of the activities of what I have characterised in this book as 'consumer professionals'. Also, in the complicated situation of today, the media has become an important and favoured method for resolving consumer disputes, even though it continues to be under party-state control.

To elaborate, first, this book enhances our understanding about mediation in China. As I indicated in the Introduction of this book, the process of mediation is indeed central, rather than alternative, in China's civil dispute resolution mechanism. For many decades, observers of dispute resolution in China have used the term 'mediation' to translate the Chinese process of their party intervention in a dispute known as '*tiaojie*'. However, Chinese understandings of 'mediation' are, to a significant extent, culturally embedded. A more nuanced and accurate translation for *tiaojie*, I have suggested, would be 'evaluative mediation'. In China, this is the dominant approach to 'mediation' and it is often proactive, interventionist and judgmental in nature.

Literature on ADR in the 'western' context often suggests that mediation in an extra-judicial setting is a third-party intervention process primarily intended to facilitate negotiations. The mediator should adhere to the principle of 'impartiality' – being unbiased in the resolution of the disputed matter. There are other important principles which inform and assist the process – for example, what is disclosed in the mediation meeting is confidential and should not be further disclosed, especially in court proceedings, unless there are exceptional circumstances. Hodges' empirical study on consumer ADR (or CDR) bodies, also reveals that the kind of mediation that EU promotes for resolving consumer disputes is one in which principles of impartiality and confidentiality are generally adhered to in the mediation process.[1] He points out that confusion may arise in our understanding of consumer mediation if we fail to appreciate the difference between using mediation as a 'technique' and as a 'structure' – in fact, mediation is used mostly as a 'technique' in different procedures in the western context, such as in court and arbitration processes where parties can choose to mediate before or during formal procedures, and is also used by lawyers, professional mediators and ombuds in settlement negotiations and mediations, or in the

[1] C Hodges, 'The Private Sector Ombudsman', in M Hertogh and R Kirkham (eds), *Research Handbook on the Ombudsman* (Cheltenham, Edward Elgar Publishing, 2018) 54.

ombuds process.[2] Consumer mediators and mediation in China, on the other hand, lacks the professionalism as identified in Hodges' studies, and is more evaluative and results-focused.

As Leonard Riskin suggests, depending on the style of mediation, mediators may be characterised as either facilitative or evaluative in their approach to handling disputes, although the preferred model in many western jurisdictions is often 'facilitative'.[3] My observation of mediation meetings clearly shows, in contrast, that the favoured style of Chinese '*tiaojie*' is strongly interventionist and often quite judgmental (evaluative) about the conduct of the parties. In the Chinese context, 'mediation' (*tiaojie*) often takes the form of a paternalist style of third-party intervention, applying where considered appropriate non-legal rules – social norms and moral values – rather than legal norms to help resolve the dispute, a process far removed from dominant understandings found in 'western' contexts.

My experience in the Shenzhen Consumer Council is that (as Riskin has also suggested), where it seems appropriate to the mediator, he or she will sometimes also try to be facilitative during the mediation meeting. This largely depends on the type of complainant – the mediator can choose to be less evaluative, if the dispute is resolved and the consumer is satisfied, and no further effort is needed. However, if he or she has a more stubborn streak, 'persuasion' and 'education' will take over the mediation meeting, and there is little or no limit for how far the mediator can go in terms of providing evaluative judgments. The predominant style, therefore, is seen as a didactic process, offering much education and persuasion. Moreover, the process is not stringently regulated especially in terms of confidentiality. The mediation meetings in the Shenzhen Consumer Council show that in order to fully resolve the problem and develop mutual understanding between the parties, mediators are largely involved in deciding the 'rights' and 'wrongs' of the disputed matter, and they sometimes even actively 'educate' the parties to make compromises or to behave better in the future. The mediators' purpose is to prevent disputes from occurring, or at least, try to ensure that the disputants will not come back to the SZCC again with their grievance. Most mediators are not professionally trained, and there are no specific codes of practice to regulate their behaviour during the mediation meeting. Consumer Council mediation is not characterised as 'people's mediation', and therefore not regulated by the 2010 People's Mediation Law, which provides rules and guidelines for the work of people's mediators. For consumer dispute mediation, the processual intervention is more arbitrary, and the mediated outcome is not binding. By contrast, a decision of people's mediation (mainly dealing with civil matters and minor criminal offences) may be made binding through a process of court recognition, which means it has the same legal enforcement effect as a court judgment.[4]

[2] ibid.

[3] See also ch 3 above. Riskin's division of facilitative and evaluative mediation is widely cited (and accepted) by scholars and practitioners. See L Riskin, 'Understanding Mediators' Orientations, Strategies and Techniques: A Grid for the Perplexed' (1996) 1 *Harvard Negotiation Law Review* 7. He later replaces the 'facilitative-evaluative' dichotomy with 'elicitive-directive', and creates a new grid which is a far more complex system. However, this does not affect the discussion here in my book, as I use the terms only to single out the features of the Chinese mediation. See L Riskin, 'Decision Making in Mediation: The New Old Grid and the New New Grid System' (2003) 79 *Notre Dame Law Review* 1.

[4] The second paragraph of Art 33 of the People's Mediation Law (2010) provides that 'Where the People's Court confirms that the mediation agreement is valid, one party refuses to fulfil or has not completely fulfil, the other party may apply to the People's Court for mandatory execution.'

On the other hand, the mediation style often found in the common law world, namely, facilitative mediation is also common in China, but I would say that another term – *hejie* – is the Chinese label that is applied to this process. The mediators that I met in the field insist that in a *hejie* process, their job is to set up the meeting venue, act as a channel for parties to have dialogue, to initiate and facilitate the parties' negotiation, while it is the parties' job to determine the outcome by reaching their own agreement; if the parties fail to reach an agreement by themselves, the back-up plan is to initiate the *tiaojie* process. As a result, seeing *tiaojie* as evaluative mediation, and *hejie* as facilitative mediation is the best way to characterise the culturally appropriate modes of their party mediatory intervention in the Chinese context. To unlink '*tiaojie*' from 'mediation' will help us further understand the key features of Chinese *tiaojie*: with a judgemental and educational nature, the Chinese process of *tiaojie* uses a mix of techniques to keep a potential social problem within control,[5] to quickly resolve the underlying issues in the dispute, to prevent any re-occurrence of the dispute, and finally (as a generalised goal) to promote a more 'harmonious society' (*hexie shehui*). The unlinking of '*tiaojie*' with 'mediation' is also helpful in understanding Chinese dispute resolution processes in comparative terms. Scholars in the UK, who attended a presentation of my ongoing research work, found that referring the Chinese '*tiaojie*' in English as 'mediation' somewhat confusing, as the practices of Chinese '*tiaojie*' that I revealed to them are so different from what they understood as 'mediation' in the sense that is practiced in the common law world.

What is more, 'mediation' in the mainstream ADR discourse is concerned with securing parties' interests, and is a private and flexible process, but also expected to function within a legal framework that is the product of rule of law values and is often conducted in the 'shadow' of the court (which is not necessarily seen in positive terms).[6] The Chinese '*tiaojie*' process, on the other hand, often involves a flexibility that draws on morals, social norms and social compassion in its decision-making process.[7] Moreover, the consumer dispute processes are in fact carried out under 'the shadow of administrative power'. As Galanter has observed, negotiations in the common-law world are often conducted within the track of civil litigation preparation for trial and therefore take place in the shadow of the court. In China too there is negotiation in the shadow of the court, but this is not nearly so important as negotiation in the shadow of administrative bodies. In the authoritarian legal culture of the PRC, in fact in many consumer cases if negotiation between the parties fails, a public body, such as the Shenzhen Consumer Council and the MSA, rather than a court, will deal with the matter. In some situations, cases that have exhausted the court proceedings, but not been satisfactorily resolved by the consumers' standard, can show up again and are handled by the public bodies. Some of the professional litigants are very good at getting favourable outcomes because of their skill in this sort of negotiation, knowing just how far they can push the defendant business that is often anxious not to draw the attention of a public body to its customer discontent.

[5] Hence '*da tiaojie*', or 'grand mediation' in which local institutions, using these techniques, combine into a protective network to contain the dispute and keep it at the local level: see XC Zhang, 'Rethinking the Mediation Campaign' (2016) 10 *Journal of Comparative Law* 44.

[6] On this last point see eg RN Mnookin and L Kornhauser, 'Bargaining in the Shadow of the Law: The Case of Divorce' (1979) 88 *Yale Law Journal* 950.

[7] Perhaps in part reflecting the fact that law itself in China is often infused with moral concerns. See T Murphy, 'Durkheim in China' in M Freeman (ed), *Law and Sociology* (Oxford, Oxford University Press, 2006) 107.

Secondly, consumer dispute resolution is largely a public matter in China, and those with administrative powers are careful when handling consumer disputes. As Yu Xingzhong, whose writings often offer subtle insights into law and society issues in China today, has pointed out, while the post-Mao economic reforms in China have resulted in the creation of a private sector, the distinction between public and private law still does not work very well. Much that might be thought of at first glance as private, actually seems rather public in China, largely as a result of the willingness of the party-state to intervene in the economy.[8] As Yu suggests, consumer law also reflects this blurring, and is characterised in China as a social law that 'ha[s] both a public and private nature and ha[s] been developing in light of new social and economic changes in contemporary legal systems ... and such laws regulate the social behaviour of the citizens, which is necessary for constructing a harmonious society'. Processually, this blurring of the distinction between the public and the private is expressed in Shenzhen Consumer Council by the fact that on paper, the Shenzhen Consumer Council is a social organisation (*shehui tuanti*), which resembles in some respects non-governmental organisations found in western societies. However, when we examine its nature more closely, we find that it is run by the state, equipped with civil servant personnel and a shared working platform with the regulator (the MSA in Shenzhen). In this respect, the mediation that is offered by Shenzhen Consumer Council is essentially an 'administrative mediation' (*xingzheng tiaojie*), rather than a form of alternative dispute resolution operating in the private law sphere.

The public nature of the Shenzhen Consumer Council is not only shown by its own structure, but also in perceptions of the Council by user citizens, who tend to assume that the Shenzhen Consumer Council is the representative of the government on consumer matters. Yu suggests that there is a 'privatisation of public law' in which 'consumer protection, which was seen as the responsibility of the government, is now regulated by law on the basis of individual rights'.[9] However, in my view, this argument only holds true 'on the books'. It is correct to say that in the law, consumer rights are protected as individual rights. However, in practice, protection of the consumer is still treated largely as a responsibility of the government towards society – the dispute resolution bodies are publicly funded and staffed, and citizens treat it as the government's responsibility to give them a voice and thereby empower them when the opposing party is one of the business giants. Even the consumer professionals, whose activities are often looked upon negatively by officials, press the government to take actions on consumer matters. So in their minds, too, the government is responsible for consumer disputes, particularly when the consumer has a dispute with large, state-owned, enterprises such as China Mobile, even though they themselves make a living from pursuing consumer grievances and making complaints.

Consumer protection is generally considered as both a private and public matter, but it is still very difficult for consumers to seek redress through private law remedies, and this is not a China specific issue. As mentioned in chapter one, Ramsay identified two main difficulties in consumer redress: information shortcomings or failure[10] and the failure of

[8] XY Yu, 'State Legalism and the Public/Private Divide in Chinese Legal Development' (2014) 15 *Theoretical Inquiries in Law* 27 at 48–49.

[9] ibid at 49.

[10] That is to say, consumers are not given enough information when they choose to purchase products, so that competition pressures alone do not work to ensure protection for consumers, and therefore government has to intervene and regulate the businesses. See ch 1 in this book at 9.

private remedy schemes to protect consumers. Governmental intervention is thus called for in order to deal with these issues, and reforms and new dispute processes that can empower consumers in litigation have arisen.[11] However, mechanisms that are supposed to help consumers to litigate collectively, for example through 'class-type' actions, are not yet well developed in China. As a result, the practice of consumer protection continues to be a public matter in China, and one that relies a great deal on administrative pressures and mediatory processes to secure 'consumer' justice for an aggrieved individual. The Chinese public continues to feel that the government bears a heavy duty towards its citizens, and this is especially so when consumer issues concern the interests of a large number of people. In many other jurisdictions, it is more or less the case that the government will take action to handle large-scale damage to consumer interests, but is less interested in smaller cases. However, in China, because of the continuing involvement of the state in economic activities, the fact of the government's spirit of paternalist administration, and a strong sense in public consciousness that the government should take responsibility for consumer matters are much stronger. The position is more complicated, and the distinction between public and private is less obvious. What is more, this mixture of 'public and private' spheres has long been entrenched in Chinese political culture, because in the Confucian understanding, there was indeed no separation of public and private life. As Yu Xingzhong observes:

> What might be justifiable in family life was also considered to be true in public life. Standards for addressing family relations were also standards for public relations. Any separation of the two spheres of life, public and private, did not appeal to Confucian thinkers as a way of addressing the moral and practical dilemmas presented to them.[12]

In observing Shenzhen Consumer Council mediation, I felt that this understanding offered a very accurate characterisation of the attitudes of both mediators and the disputing parties.

The blurred division between the 'public' and 'private' also helps to explain why there is no consumer-protection-specific dimension to civil society in China. Given the emergence of NGO type organisations in the area of environmental welfare, and the Shenzhen government's relatively relaxed attitude towards civil society organisations, it is something of a surprise that in the course of my fieldwork, it became apparent that few NGOs are specifically aimed at helping consumers, especially the handling of their disputes. The paucity of consumer NGOs is perhaps because of the government's reluctance to allow registering a civil society for consumer welfare when the same government has a felt need to take good control of consumer matters through dispute handling. As staff in the Shenzhen Consumer Council suggest, the Council always tries to prevent consumer disputes from being brought to the Council again, and in my view, this is also a means of containing the social problem at the local level and avoiding its escalation into social instability. The situation may be characterised as the promotion of social harmony and containment of unrest at the expense of opportunities for rights assertion, a problem that Laura Nader and other critics of ADR have robustly argued to be the product of the imposition of a harmony ideology.[13]

[11] I Ramsay, *Rationales for Intervention in the Consumer Marketplace* (London, Office of Fair Trading, 1984) 15–24.

[12] ibid at 33.

[13] L Nader, 'Controlling Process of the Rule of Law: Hierarchy and Pacification in the Movement to Re-Form Dispute Ideology' (1993) 9 *Ohio State Journal on Dispute Resolution* 1.

Thirdly, one of the most successful experiences of handling consumer disputes elsewhere in the world – the consumer ombudsman – is missing in China. The ombudsman, which originates from the Swedish 'grievance man', has become an important consumer dispute resolution mechanism in the many jurisdictions (especially within Europe), as we pointed out in chapter one.[14] For example, in the UK, following the successful example of the financial ombudsman the idea of a 'consumer ombudsman' spread to many other consumption areas, such as telecommunication,[15] public transport (proposed),[16] energy,[17] and so on.[18] The Consumer Ombudsman may be characterised as generally offering the following features: first, it is an independent body (may be an individual or an organisation);[19] secondly, it is mostly publicly funded or industry funded[20] – in the UK, for example, the funding for the financial ombudsman comes from industry donations, but this is a compulsory requirement of membership in the scheme and is regulated by the law; thirdly, despite its original form of decision-making – a kind of quasi-adjudication with a non-binding ruling – the ombudsman in practice may well use facilitated negotiation and mediation as ways of settling the consumer dispute, and only if this informal intervention fails is a more robust from of decision-making used, such as a superior ombudsman's determination, or adjudication or arbitration by another body.

At first glance, it may seem that the Shenzhen Consumer Council shares some of the features of a consumer ombudsman as found in some jurisdictions in the west: they are both publicly funded, offer a service free of charge, provide advice for consumers and mediation services to disputants; and so on.[21] Hodges also suggests that ideally, there should be an umbrella ombuds scheme that handles all kinds of consumer dispute. The Consumer Council (or Consumer Association) in China indeed offers such an umbrella organisation for handling various types of consumer complaints. However, I would argue that the consumer ombuds in the west are very different mechanisms from those found in China, and the Consumer Council is not capable of functioning as, or even in the near future evolving into, an ombuds-type institution. The independence, and some other features, such as impartiality, transparency, liberty and legality,[22] that an ombudsman enjoys, is not a feature that may be enjoyed by a consumer body in China such as the SZCC Council.

[14] See examples in C Hodges, I Benöhr and N Creutzfeldt, *Consumer ADR in Europe* (Oxford, Hart Publishing 2012).

[15] Ombudsman Services, 'About Ombudsman Services: Communications' www.ombudsman-services.org/sectors/communications.

[16] Public Transport: Ombudsman, www.parliament.uk/business/publications/written-questions-answers-statements/written-question/Commons/2017-09-05/8896/.

[17] Ombudsman Services, 'About the Energy Ombudsman' www.ombudsman-services.org/sectors/energy.

[18] Financial Ombudsman Service, www.financial-ombudsman.org.uk.

[19] It is said that 'Independence is at the heart of Ombudsman Services and how we operate' on the website of Ombudsman Services, www.ombudsman-services.org/docs/default-source/website-content/independence-fact-sheet.pdf?sfvrsn=2.

[20] See C Hodges, I Benöhr and N Creutzfeldt, *Consumer ADR in Europe* (Oxford, Hart Publishing, 2012) for consumer ombudsman practices in different European countries.

[21] C Hodges, 'Consumer Ombudsmen: Better Regulation and Dispute Resolution' (2014) 15 *ERA Forum* 593; C Hodges, 'Consumer Redress: Implementing the Vision' in P Cortés (ed), *The New Regulatory Framework for Consumer Dispute Resolution* (Oxford, Oxford University Press, 2016) 351.

[22] These are the criterion set out for an ombuds in the EU Directive 2013/11 on alternative dispute resolution for consumer disputes. Art 32 of the Directive states that 'The independence and integrity of ADR entities is crucial in order to gain Union citizens' trust that ADR mechanisms will offer them a fair and independent outcome.'

In the People's Republic of China, there is no real socio-political basis for establishing a proper ombuds system, and nor are there any serious proposals for pushing it onto the legal reform agenda. Some Chinese scholars have suggested the importance of drawing on the ombudsman experience of the 'West', and using that experience selectively to build up ombudsman schemes, or their functional equivalents, in China.[23] However, such suggestions tend to overlook the important fact that in the process of legal transplantation, a transplanted scheme will often change its nature and purpose during the course of moving from one jurisdiction to another. Bearing in mind the culture of the government being a paternalist administrator of the society in China, an ombuds scheme transplanted into the PRC would likely suffer from a lack of independence and impartiality, seriously inhibiting its chances of success. Another key issue may also be, as I have suggested in earlier published work, that if any such transplant is attempted, the key questions will be: who is it that initiates and who controls the transplantation process. In China's current political climate, those in charge of any such transplantation of the ombudsman would be unlikely to allow significant independence.[24]

II. Consumers' Access to Justice

A. The China Case

As mentioned in chapter one, the China case has been largely ignored in the studies on consumers' access to justice, internationally and comparatively. This book has addressed this gap by offering an examination of the Chinese experience of consumers' access to justice. It is also the first in-depth research into the consumer dispute resolution system of a socialist country – albeit one which has seen rapid economic developments through market orientated reforms in recent years. So what does the China case tell us?

First, 'mediation' is the primary form of consumer dispute resolution in China, and it works well in some respects. In China, consumer mediation services are publicly funded, and for the user both free and convenient – a simple phone call will trigger the process, and the majority of cases are resolved by such phone calls. The public nature of the institution, and the fact that within the Chinese system, state owned enterprises play a key role in the economy, make it easier in some ways for the institutions to persuade defendant companies into making compromises to aggrieved consumers. However, sometimes institutions play a negotiation game of 'ping-pong', passing the consumer complaint back and forth

See C Hodges, 'The Private Sector Ombudsman' in M Hertogh and R Kirkham (eds), *Research Handbook on the Ombudsman* (Cheltenham, Edward Elgar Publishing, 2018) 53, 60–61.

[23] Much of the Chinese-language literature centres on borrowing the experience of the UK Financial Ombudsman to establish a similar institution in China. See eg D Yang, 'Research on the Categorization of the Financial Ombudsman Mechanisms' ('Jinrong Shensu Zhuanyuan Zhidu zhi Leixinghua Yanjiu') (2013) 4 *Faxue Pinglun* (*Law Review*) 77; J Ran, 'Constitute Financial Ombudsman Institution Suitable for Our National Situation' ('*Goujian Shehe Woguo Guoqing de Jinrong Shensu Zhuanyuan Zhidu*') (2016) 6 *Research on Finance and Education* 21.

[24] L Zhou, 'The Independent Director System and its Legal Transplant into China' (2012) 6 *Journal of Comparative Law* 262.

without actually resolving it. Moreover, Nader's criticism that mediation may become a tool to suppress rights should not be overlooked.[25] The China case is obvious in this perspective. There is the danger of rights suppression when mediation is used to resolve a consumer dispute. The Chinese government tries to promote a harmonious society, and endeavours to keep social conflicts under control so that disputes do not escalate into collective protests. As this book shows, this mentality is embedded in dispute handlers' consciousness and permeates into their dispute resolution practices. Above all else, they want the dispute to be shut down, and not to be persisted with, though that is not necessarily to the disadvantage of the aggrieved consumer. What is more, as discussed in chapter six, mediation is often merged with court procedures, so that a judge in handling a consumer case has to consider the likely social impact of the case, and attempt many mediations, and take much longer than a case dealt with by a judge who simply hears the case and then applies the law in an adjudicative process.

Consumer mediation in general has been characterised by Duggan as a 'cost-avoidance mechanism'. It is applied in the processes of small claims tribunals, dispute resolution by consumer agencies, and industry-specific dispute resolution schemes, and often attempts to make business defendants more realistic and less defensive about the nature of consumer grievances.[26] In China, the Shenzhen analysis offered in this book suggests there is perhaps too much emphasis on the cost-avoidance mechanism approach, and too little attention given to cost-spreading mechanisms, including meaningful legal aid, contingency fees and class actions, in consumers' access to justice. The public interest litigation system is by no means a mature system that consumers can easily access. The legal aid threshold is rather strict and legal aid is mostly confined to certain kinds of case, that for the most part do not include consumer disputes.[27] Such problems limit consumers' access to court justice. Partly as a result of this, local courts spend most of their time dealing with consumer cases brought by professionals – who are experienced repeat players in the processes of consumer dispute resolution and complaint reporting. Nevertheless, as this book has also shown, these limitations do not mean that many consumers with grievances fail to secure the consumer justice that they seek, for the Shenzhen Consumer Council mediation and other dispute resolving processes do manage, despite these issues, to deliver an outcome with which aggrieved consumers are at least reasonably satisfied.

Secondly, the distinctive feature of consumers' access to justice in a socialist society is the strong involvement of public organisations rather than civil society. As discussed above, the two main bodies that handle consumer disputes, the Consumer Associations in China as well as the SAIC throughout China, are both publicly funded. As the division between

[25] L Nader, 'Controlling Process of the Rule of Law: Hierarchy and Pacification in the Movement to Re-Form Dispute Ideology' (1993) 9 *Ohio State Journal on Dispute Resolution* 1.

[26] AJ Duggan, 'Consumer Access to Justice in Common Law Countries: A Survey of the Issues from a Law and Economics Perspective' in C Rickett and T Telfer (eds), *International Perspectives on Consumers' Access to Justice* (Cambridge, Cambridge University Press, 2003) 50.

[27] Art 10 of the Regulations on Legal Aid listed six situations when the plaintiff may apply for legal aid in civil cases: requesting for state compensation; requesting for social insurance treatment or minimum life alimony treatment; requesting for survivor's pensions or relief funds; requesting for the payment for supporting parents or grandparents, and children; requesting for the payment of labour remunerations; or claiming civil rights and interests arising from the brave act of righteousness.

public and private is blurred in the Chinese legal context, the government in effect handles many private law matters. Many other public channels are also available to consumers, such as making complaints to the government through government hotline or letters and visits, to relevant bureaux that regulate the businesses, to radio and local TV programmes, and even to the CCP's Commission for Discipline Inspection if a matter involves misconduct of a party official. Given the unclear division between the public and the private in the Chinese legal system, the government in effect handles many private law matters. Hence, as I have also emphasised, there is little likelihood of a meaningful consumer ombudsmen system emerging in China.

Thirdly, while the national legal framework protecting consumer rights and interests is important, the ways in which consumer problems are handled at the local level are also significant – highly so in a society such as contemporary China where administrative power remains strong and there is a political and cultural emphasis on 'harmonious' resolution of disputes. I discovered in the field that most of the rules for consumer dispute handling practices are relatively informal and opaque, and in any event consumers cannot easily access them. Instead, most of the information is handed down from leaders to staff, or is only permitted to circulate within the dispute resolution bodies' network. Also, the experience of the more persistent aggrieved consumers who attempt to use multi-channels of redress and who bring complaints repeatedly, as noted in chapter four, reveals a common problem in the Chinese context – although citizens are offered various complaint channels with which to pursue their grievance, none of these channels really possess final binding authority. Consumers may press their grievance in all the possible administrative even political complaint channels before they obtain (or not, as the case may be) a favourable outcome. The relevant administrative bodies at the local level do have a tendency to pass the buck when handling such 'stubborn' consumers, with the complaint going back and forth between different agencies, thereby leaving consumers both distressed and exhausted.

Fourthly, this book confirms the role of intermediaries through an investigation into the consumer complaint system in the local Consumer Council, the regulator and the local courts. My book shows that where the China experience differs from Ramsay's perspective is that Chinese lawyers do not involve themselves much in consumer dispute processes, and are far from being 'important political actors in any proposed reforms of consumer rights' in China. As discussed in chapter three, most of the consumer cases (complaints) are indeed handled by the public bodies (such as the Consumer Council and the regulator, the MSA). The staff or officials working in these bodies seem to be the more important intermediaries in consumer dispute processes, by offering solutions to consumers, as well as collecting consumer issues and reporting consumer concerns to leaders at the higher levels in the bureaucratic hierarchy in the system. On the other hand, the role of lawyers in consumer dispute resolution is limited. Factors limiting lawyers' involvement in consumer redress include the development of collective redress mechanisms, especially the public interest litigation (PIL) processes in China. As addressed in chapter seven, PIL suits were not feasible until a revision of the Consumer Protection Law in 2013, when for the first time a specific body is identified in the legislation as enjoying standing so as to represent consumers in the people's courts. Still, no practical mechanism has been developed for consumers to act collectively in private litigation. Up till now, the few successful consumer PIL cases are all attempted for non-compensation claims, and it is unclear whether there will be any PIL suits claiming compensation in the near future. The lack of development in this area means that lawyers do not have the standing for consumers in the court for bringing collective suits, nor are they able to secure financial returns from compensation awards made to consumers. At this stage, the consumer collective actions are largely brought under the direction of the public bodies, such as the Consumer Council and the People's Procuracy, and in the name of 'public interest'. Lawyers, where they are involved, are hired and work for the public bodies in bringing PIL consumer cases.

Another group of important figures that serve as effective intermediaries, I argue, are the 'professionals' in the consumer dispute processes in China. They are the consumer complainants who are often non-lawyers but ones who possess a professional knowledge of consumer issues, laws and regulations, and are skilled negotiators and frequent users of the consumer complaint mechanism and the courts. This group of 'professionals' has come to form a bottom up pressure group for consumer reforms, albeit the officials and the public have criticised them in many ways. Recent judgments and news reports have shown considerable support from the public and some officials for the activities of the professional, a point also made in chapter one. It may well be the case that the activities of this group of actors, who play an important role in the current consumer redress system, will in turn strengthen the role of the court and the use of court procedures in better protecting consumer rights and interests. At present, consumers' rights are far less vindicated in Chinese courts than they are in many other jurisdictions. The mediation system in China operates in the shadow of the administrative bodies, and this encourages acceptance of evaluative mediation, but the professionals, with incentives to vindicate rights and seek redress from the court, are in effect challenging this emphasis.

B. Consumer Citizen

As noted in chapter one, a very important issue in comparative studies of access to consumer justice is the role of the 'consumer citizen'. The literature on this important figure includes a range of ideas such as consumer rights as a matter not only of private interest but also of public concern, and a willingness of consumers to exercise their civil rights to pursue their grievances and secure their consumer rights and interests. As Livingstone and Lunt suggest, consumer interest focuses on 'wants, individual, private benefits, language of choice' while citizen interest focuses on 'needs, society, public benefits, language of right'.[28] As this book has observed, this notion has emerged and is beginning to take hold in China, albeit very slowly. It is doing so in a changing context in which new approaches to resolving consumer disputes are emerging and consumer disputes are becoming more complex. Describing the general public as 'comrades' in the planned economy who have been transformed into 'consumers' in the early stages of China's evolving market economy, is not sufficient to characterise the current situation. Looking at the activities of the professionals, it is obvious that a group of 'consumers' have started to act rather like 'consumer-citizens', with potential to create change in Chinese society.

[28] S Livingstone and P Lunt, 'Representing Citizens and Consumers in Media and Communications Regulation' (2007) 611 *The Politics of Consumption* 51 at 56.

In chapter four, I separated the consumer complainants into three types by reference to the goals they pursue in their claims: compensation orientated complainants, public-interest orientated complainants and anger-venting complainants. The first type of consumer complainant, as I have suggested, is the most common type in consumer dispute resolution. This type of consumer comes to the Consumer Council to get compensation, which, in terms of the 'consumer-citizen' rhetoric, is the 'individual interest' that they pursue, rather than their 'rights'. Similarly, consumer complainants, who are the anger-venting type, do not proceed with their disputes for rights assertion either. In most cases, they use the 'free service' provided by the public body to vent, hoping that they will have some chance, however slim, of being heard and only then perhaps even compensated. Because their losses are usually quite small, other than making a phone call to the Consumer Council, they will do little or nothing. These two types of consumer complainant, however, are representative of what the ordinary members of the public will normally do for their consumer grievances. I do not sense much of a 'rights-pursuit' spirit in their claims, and indeed their efforts invariably stop when the business makes a good compromise offer of compensation to them. Some consumer complainants even suggest that in the negotiations with the business party to their disputes, the latter have given them an individually tailored 'special treatment' – ignoring the claims of others, and giving the best possible monetary compensation only to themselves. This seems the very opposite of pursuing a claim for the prime purpose of creating some kind of publicly-available precedent that will then benefit the claims of others who experience a similar type of consumer rights' infringement. Only the public-interest orientated complainants are the consumers who take the time to assert their rights as a matter of law and justice. Mr Yang Jianchang, as mentioned in chapter four, is a typical public-interest orientated grassroots fighter for consumer rights. Mr Yang indeed in due course became a political figure who was elected as a people's representative (*renmin daibiao*) in the Shenzhen local people's congress.

As Hooper suggests, the consumer citizenship rhetoric often takes the form of a 'right awareness' enhancement of consumers.[29] I agree with him on this point in general, but would add that there is more to the story than this in China. There is indeed something of a growing rights' awareness among Chinese consumers, and some individuals have shown a particular concern with the public interest, such as Mr Yang, but such rights' awareness has not evolved into a robust 'consumer movement' as it has done in some societies elsewhere in the world. Instead, this book has found a group of individuals, who I have characterised as the 'professionals', who use various strategies to pursue not only 'interests' but also 'rights' in their practices. In this book, I have concluded that these individuals, albeit with mixed motives, are a Chinese approximate version of the 'consumer citizen'. As we noted in chapter five, those at the top of the 'hierarchy' of this 'profession' are more concerned about unfair rules and actively promote the public interest; while those at the bottom are mainly interest-driven and less concerned about the public good. The motives of those at the bottom are not all justified in terms of general enhancement of social justice, but they do speak about rights and are keen to use various political and social methods to pursue their interests.

[29] B Hooper, 'The Consumer Citizen in Contemporary China' (2005) *Working Paper No.12, Centre for East and South-East Asian Studies, Lund University* 3. More discussion on Hooper can be found in ch 2.

The reasons for identifying the professional as China's version of the consumer citizen are as follows: first, the professionals are often keenly aware of their political and social rights when they pursue their consumer interests. Secondly, they do have a sense of citizenship when they use the reporting system, acting in effect as a citizen supervisor for businesses' conduct. Thirdly, their actions may bring changes to the consumer rules and some of the professionals consciously try to improve consumer standards in the market. In the authoritarian political culture of China, the extent to which a civil society can exist is a matter under the careful control of the party and administrative departments, and there is little room for even moderately independent consumer groups. Despite China's unfavourable environment for the emergence of a robust civil society, these professionals have managed to develop a shared identity and an enclosed and self-reinforcing culture of professionalism in which there are frequent exchanges of negotiation skills and also knowledge about laws and other relevant information. They have largely filled a gap in consumer protection and have become a bottom-up force for better standards of consumer protection in authoritarian China.

It is not hard to see that the Consumer Protection Law as revised in 2013 tries to encourage consumers to pursue their rights and interests. For example, Article 55 has enhanced the possible amount of punitive damages to three times the costs, as compared to one time in the non-revised law for consumers in fraud cases. However, in practice, ordinarily consumer complainants will only push to secure compensation of the full refund of the original price, without asking for punitive damages. This punitive damages provision has in any event not been used by the ordinary consumer, but is often relied on by the professionals when they argue their cases in the court. Similarly, the provision allowing ten-fold punitive damages for defect food products is frequently drawn on by the professionals, particularly in their reports on problematic labels, packaging and misleading production information for food products. As mentioned above, it is encouraging to note that despite occasional criticisms of the 'lower-end' professionals (who are inclined to use threatening conduct as a way to secure compensation), some of the latest court judgments and relevant judicial observations do not ban the activities of the new consumer citizen, and even encourage the professionals to be co-regulators (alongside the government) of consumer sector business behaviour.

III. Delegalisation and Justice

In his important paper, 'China's Turn against Law', Minzner points out that one important feature of Chinese legal development is that 'in the early twenty-first century, Chinese authorities turned against law', which stands in contrast with the authorities' efforts in many legal reforms during the 1980s and especially the 1990s.[30] My fieldwork findings are consistent with Minzner's view that there is a continuing 'turn against law'. As Minzner points out, this turn does not mean that the processes of law making in China have stopped. Rather, it means that Chinese dispute resolution has, by large, reverted to mediation and other forms of 'alternative dispute resolution'. In this, there is some similarity between China and many

[30] C Minzner, 'China's Turn against Law' (2011) 59 *The American Journal of Comparative Law* 935, 936.

other jurisdictions, such as the US, which have been busily 'reviving' traditional dispute resolution processes such as mediation and other forms of 'alternative dispute resolution'. However, as Minzner also points out, the shift against law in China is somewhat different from, say, that in the US, where the search for alternatives has often been bottom-up and driven by legal and other professionals. In China, the shift is 'not led by lawyers or parties who are opting out of the court system in search of alternatives to litigation', and 'China's turn against law is a top-down authoritarian political reaction to growing levels of social protest and conflict in the Chinese system'.[31]

As noted above, staff of the Consumer Council are concerned to prevent small problems escalate into bigger issues while handling consumer disputes. This is indeed the practice of what Minzner describes as the party's reforms for 'preventing legal conflicts and citizen petitions from rising towards central officials'.[32] The fact that there are no consumer-specific NGOs existing in the Chinese consumer legal system indirectly confirms Minzner's view that the Chinese party-state leadership remains unwilling to allow the gradual emergence of independent legal institutions capable of dealing with civil conflicts between citizens, and between citizens and the state. As I pointed out earlier, this 'delegalisation of China' (or, at the very least, failure to continue with the legalisation process that was so important in the 1990s) also makes it impossible for an effective consumer ombudsman system to be transplanted into the Chinese context, where mediation is still the dominant form of dispute resolution, and one that functions as a mechanism for containing social unrest. However, the 'delegalisation' of consumer dispute resolution is somewhat different from the move away from law in civil disputes in other areas. It is the continuing emphasis on the administrative bodies and the governmental duty to resolving disputes in a reasonably fair and equitable manner, rather than the rule of law, that remains as the key context for consumer dispute processes.

The delegalisation of China may not in all cases be seen in negative terms. Establishing consumer ADR schemes is, after all, something of a global trend in consumer protection. Minzner suggests that in China's shift against law generally, the resurgence of mediation is not led or opted for by the parties. But in consumer protection in Shenzhen, the usage of mediation and other 'non-legal' processes is in part a reflection of consumers' choice. As my fieldwork shows, in most situations, ordinary consumers (except for the professionals) willingly opt to have their dispute resolved through extra-judicial dispute resolution schemes. These include various mediation services, the report system provided by administrative bodies, media exposure and online dispute processes. Because of the small value of consumer disputes, most consumers benefit from using the free consumer complaint and redress services provided by the state. For larger cases such as food safety issues, they are more likely to be dealt with directly by the administrative bodies through an investigation. Cases may appear at the local level as complaints, and then catch the upper authorities' attention and are handled collectively by the administrative bodies. The consumer dispute processes rely much on administrative processes, while lawyers, on the other hand, do not play an important role.

[31] ibid at 937–38.
[32] ibid at 938.

The delegalisation process may also mean that the state is taking care of consumers' welfare. The authoritarian state through its active role in consumer protection tries to offer a benevolent face, as in some other social laws, so as to take responsibility for the vulnerable person whose interests are threatened or harmed during the period of rapid economic development. The idea of protecting the consumer is part of a general paternalistic feeling for the government to protect more marginal people, such as women, children, elders, the disabled – and the consumer. In China, this is especially important because of the distinctive structure of the Chinese economy. The very imperfect privatisation that has occurred in the name of building a 'socialist market economy;' means that many apparently privatised companies are still in fact state-owned – they are listed on the stock exchange, but still with a strong sharing holding interest by the state. The benevolence shown by the state, by taking the responsibility to look after the ordinary citizen and disadvantaged persons, can also be seen as a strategy to generate general support from, and legitimacy in the eyes of, society. The state's paternalistic benevolence is not the result of a democratic process in which the people decide their own fate but, rather, it is a way for the state to show its care for citizens. Consumers continue to believe in the state and trust the state in protecting their rights and interests. Mediators, as a result, are often sympathetic to consumers and are considered to have something of a duty to speak for the consumers, though in many cases the mediators may feel that a consumer's grievance is not entirely right in terms of the law. So, from the point of many aggrieved consumers, the delegalisation of China does not mean that they are not able to effectively secure adequate justice for the infringement of their consumer rights.

IV. Consumers' Access to Justice in China: Final Reflections

While it is clear that the China consumer case has a number of distinctive features, the findings of the present work still have relevance for other societies and areas of study. The approach adopted throughout this book has been to use empirical fieldwork, especially participant observation, to understand better the manner in which consumer disputes are dealt with in China's socialist market economy. Although such fieldwork is far from straightforward in an authoritarian system, the findings of this book do show the importance of fieldwork-based understandings of how the law actually works (or does not work). Analysis of decided cases is insufficient for revealing the operation of the law in a society in which settlement and mediation have such an important role to play in dispute resolution. It seems likely that the findings of this book will have some relevance for other authoritarian socialist systems in East Asia, most notably Vietnam,[33] undergoing market reform. Some of the findings may also be also relevant to other communist party dominated societies for which a similar concurrence of influences on aspects of consumer protection and dispute resolution within an authoritarian setting can be demonstrated.

[33] See eg C Nguyen, *The Drafting of Vietnam's Consumer Protection Law: An Analysis from Legal Transplantation Theories* (Dissertation) (2011) University of Victoria; D Nguyen and E O'Shea, 'Consumer Rights Protection Law in Vietnam' in *Legal Update: Consumer Litigation & Class Actions* (Vietnam, Mayer-Brown JSM, 2012) www.mayerbrown.com/files/Publication/f01d2aa1-4cd1-4c46-963a-8027d3165ea6/Presentation/PublicationAttachment/1b8e4608-cc50-433e-acbe-8114022b785d/Consumer_Rights_Protection_Law_Vietnam.pdf.

In addition to this empirical contribution, and the new light the present work has thrown on issues in Chinese legal development, this book also contributes to understanding consumer law and dispute resolution. Consumer law in China's post-Mao society has been shaped not just by the socialist element of that society but also by its distinctive course of development and its embrace of the notion of a socialist market economy, by its legal culture and history and by the administrative domination of the system, in which little room is allowed for civil society. While it is clear that China's legal and political systems continue to be strongly authoritarian in nature, with limited appreciation of the value of human rights and civil society, an important finding in this book is that at the local level there has emerged a distinctive but very viable system for providing access to consumer justice. In the local system, the quasi-officials, who serve as mediators in what is essentially a form of administrative mediation, are concerned to handle complaints fairly and efficiently, and willing to adjust their style of third-party intervention so as to favour (to some extent at least) the weaker party (the consumer) even where the defending party is a large state-owned business.

While many government officials and judges may have doubts about the morality of the professionals making a living by means of making consumer complaints and reports, and by bringing consumer cases to the civil and administrative chambers of the people's courts, the fact remains that these professionals continue to be successful in their 'consumer litigation work'. The professionals are often able to secure settlement on favourable terms in their negotiations with business defendants in the shadow of either the regulatory body (ie, the Market Supervision Administration bureau), or the basic-level people's courts. It is true that some of the more prominent Shenzhen professional consumers have been subjected to police harassment, but this has been only from 'time to time' rather than regular, and has not prevented the professional consumers from forming an informal but active community which provides mutual support for its participants. One area of weakness that I have noted is the failure of the local system to deal adequately with complaints brought by online shoppers against e-commerce sellers, and while e-commerce law might be something of a controversial issue, it is at least a national-level attempt to introduce some reforms to deal with the problems.

GLOSSARY OF CHINESE TERMS

Romanisation (Hanyu Pinyin)	Chinese Characters	English Translation
baoliao	爆料	spill anything to the media
baoma	宝马	BMW
bian taoren	扁桃仁	Badanmu nuts
buheli	不合理	unreasonable
buyao lian	不要脸	shameless
buzuowei	不作为	act of omission
che	扯	to argue
chepi	扯皮	to argue about what has happened
dajiaren	打假人	the anti-counterfeit professional
danwei	单位	work unit
danzi da	胆子大	gutsy
dataiji	打太极	play Tai Chi
dazhong	大众	crowd
dazhong pingshenyuan	大众评审员	crowd or public adjudicators
Diyi Xianchang	第一现场	First Hand Report
dui zhe gan	对着干	go against
gao	搞	give somebody a bad time
gao ni	搞你	give you a bad time
Gong-shang Ju	工商局	State Administration of Industry and Commerce
gongdan	工单	work sheet of registered complaint
gong guan	公关	to network and communicate with
gongtong susong	共同诉讼	collective actions
guakao danwei	挂靠单位	attached institution
Guangdonghua	广东话	Cantonese
guanxi	关系	relationship
haoping	好评	good comments
hejie	和解	conciliation/facilitative mediation
hejie shifan qiye	和解示范企业	demonstration business for amicable settlement

Romanisation (Hanyu Pinyin)	**Chinese Characters**	**English Translation**
hen zhengmian	很正面	very positive
hou lianpi	厚脸皮	thick-skinned
huibi	回避	recuse oneself from a case
jiaozhen	较真	too serious
jiachang	家常	domestic trivia
jilü jiancha weiyuanhui	纪律监察委员会	The Commission for Discipline Inspection
jingji fa	经济法	economic laws
jingshen sunhai	精神损害	mental damages
jituan susong	集团诉讼	collective actions
jizhong shensuren	集中申诉人	concentrated complainants
jubao	举报	report
jubao ren	举报人	reports initiators
Jutousu	聚投诉	concentrated complaints
kaifangxing hezuo	开放性合作	open cooperation
Kejiahua	客家话	Hakka dialect
kentan	恳谈	earnest talk
laoban	老板	boss
Liang Jian	亮剑	Brave Sword
lingdao	领导	the leader
liyi	利益	interests
LuLu Tong	路路通	City No.1
meiguo da xinren	美国大杏仁	American Big Almond
mianzi	面子	face
mian zi guo bu qu	面子过不去	lost their face
minsheng	民生	people's livelihood
Minshi Caiding Shu	民事裁定书	Civil Ruling in Writing
minzhu quan	民主圈	democratic circle
Pinghu	平湖	Pinghu (Shopping Mall)
Putonghua	普通话	Mandarin
qian guize	潜规则	hidden rules
qianxian	前线	frontline
quanli liyi	权利利益	rights and interests
quanyi	权益	rights and interests
redian tousu ren	热点投诉人	hotspot complainant
renzhi	人治	rule of man

Romanisation (Hanyu Pinyin)	Chinese Characters	English Translation
ren fa	认罚	to take the punishment
Ren Ren Le	人人乐	Ren Ren Le retail store
renmin daibiao	人民代表	people's representative
renmin tiaojie	人民调解	people's mediation
rexin gongmin	热心公民	warm-hearted citizen
sanxiao tixi	三消体系	Three Consumer System
shangpin jingji	商品经济	commodity economy
shehui jiandu	社会监督	social supervision
shehui tuanti	社会团体	social entity
shehui zuzhi	社会组织	social organisation
shenpan weiyuanhui	审判委员会	Adjudication Committee
shensu	申诉	complaint (to a public body)
shewai	涉外	involving a foreign element
shichang jingji	市场经济	market economy
shiye bianzhi	事业编制	work unit personnel establishment
shoushi wo	收拾我	take care of me
shuli weiyan	树立威严	to establish an authority
sifa jieshi	司法解释	judicial interpretations
sifa xingzheng zhuangbeichu	司法行政装备处	an office which manages permanent assets, court vehicles, court police facilities and so on
sifa zhidu	司法制度	judicial system
si ma dang huo ma yi	死马当活马医	clutching at the final straw when in desperation
sucai chengxu	速裁程序	fast-track procedures
Taobao Panding Zhongxin	淘宝判定中心	Taobao Determination Centre
Taobao Xiao'er	淘宝小二	Taobao Assistant
taijiquan	太极拳	Tai Chi
tiaojie	调解	mediation
tiaojieshu	调解书	written mediation agreement
tizhi nei	体制内	within the system
tousu	投诉	complaints
tousu dahu	投诉大户	large complaint receivers
tui	推	pass the buck
wanhui	晚会	gala
weibo	微博	micro-blog
weifa xingwei	违法行为	illegal conduct

Romanisation (Hanyu Pinyin)	**Chinese Characters**	**English Translation**
weigui	违规	violation of administrative regulations
Xiaofei Guangchang	消费广场	Consumer Square
Xiaofei Tousu Tong	消费投诉通	a mobile telephone application for making consumer complaints
xiaofeizhe	消费者	consumer
xiaofei zhengyi hejie tongdao	消费争议和解通道	amicable settlement channel for consumer disputes
xiaofeizhe yundong	消费者运动	consumer activism
xiahu wo	吓唬我	scare me
xiao'e susong	小额诉讼	small claims litigation
xiaoxie	消协	consumer association
xigua da de shi	西瓜大的事	a matter as big as a water-melon
xingzheng fuyi	行政复议	administrative review
xingzheng susong	行政诉讼	administrative lawsuit
xingren	杏仁	(Chinese) almond
xingren niunai	杏仁牛奶	almond milk
xingzheng tiaojie	行政调解	administrative mediation
xinhen shoula	心狠手辣	ruthless
ya wo	压我	pressure me
yifa chufa	依法处罚	punishment in accordance with the law
yifa zhiguo	依法治国	rule of law
ying dui	应对	dealing with
yuan	元	the unit of Chinese currency
zaixian tiaojieshi	在线调解室	online mediation room
Zhengfa	政法	Politics and Law
zhengfu xinxi gongkai	政府信息公开	disclosure of government information
Zhengfu Xinxi Gongkai Tiaoli	政府信息公开条例	Regulations on the Disclosure of Government Information
zheng qian	挣钱	money making
zhengju tuxi	证据突袭	surprise evidence
Zhong Ying Jie	中英街	shopping street on the border between Hong Kong and Shenzhen
zhima da de shi	芝麻大的事	a matter as small as a sesame seed
Zhifubao	支付宝	Alipay
zhiye dajiaren	职业打假人	anti-counterfeit professionals
zhiye tousu ren	职业投诉人	professional complainant
zou jie jing	走捷径	short-cut

BIBLIOGRAPHY

Anderson, E, *Value in Ethics and Economics* (Cambridge, MA, Harvard University Press, 1993).

An, N, 'The Tainted Milk Powder Incident – Hope in the Midst of Despair' (*Human Rights in China*, 11 January 2011).

BBC 'Timeline: China Milk Scandal' (*BBC News*, 25 January 2010).

Benöhr, I and Micklitz, HW, 'Consumer Protection and Human Rights' in G Howells et al (eds), *Handbook of Research on International Consumer Law* (Cheltenham, Edward Elgar Publishing, 2010) 18–46.

Burke, J, 'The Social Credit System in China Is Another Way to Control Its Citizens' (*Vision Times*, 23 December 2015).

Cappelletti, M, 'Vindicating the Public Interest through the Courts: A Comparativist's Contribution' (1975–76) 25 *Buffalo Law Review* 643.

Cappelletti, M and Garth, B (eds), *Access to Justice: A World Survey* (Alphenaan den Rijn, Sijthoff and Noordhoff, 1978).

Chen, AHY, 'Through Pathways of Western Liberal Constitutional Development in Asia: A Comparative Study of Five Major Nations' (2010) 8 *International Journal of Constitutional Law* 849.

Chen, X and Huang, P, 'Xiaofei Zhuyi Wenhua yu Zhongguo Shehui' [Consumer Culture and Chinese Society] (2000) 12 *Shanghai Wenxue* [*Shanghai Literature*] 59.

Chen, Y, 'Nanjing: Nanzi ba Shangpin Cang Chaoshi Huojia, Guoqi Hou Goumai Yaoqiu Suopei' ['Nanjing: Man Hid Products behind the Shelf, Waited until It Expired and Bought it'] (*Yangtsz Evening Post*, 01 July 2015).

China Daily, 'Wang Hai, A Consumer Advocate in China' (*China Daily*, 26 July 2007).

China News, 'Dajia Mingren jie Hangye Luanxiang: Shipin Cang Huojiading deng Guoqi Suopei' ['Scandals Exposed by Famous Anti-Counterfeit Professionals: Expired Food Hidden on the Shelf for Claiming Compensation'] (*China News*, 22 October 2015).

Choukroune, L, 'Justiciability of Economic, Social and Cultural Rights: The UN Committee on Economic, Social and Cultural Rights: Review of China's First Periodic Report on the Implementation of the International Covenant on Economic, Social and Cultural Rights' (2005) 19 *Columbia Journal of Asian Legal Studies* 30.

Creutzfeldt, N et al, 'Consumer Protection in Turkey: Law, Informality and the Role of the Media' Melbourne, Australia (2016) *Department of Business Law and Taxation, Monash University: Working Paper* 21.

Croll, E, *Desires and Destinies: Consumption and the Spirit of Confucianism* (School of Oriental and African Studies, University of London 1997).

Croll, E, *China's New Consumers: Social Developments and Domestic Demand* (Abingdon and New York, Routledge, 2006).

Deng, J, 'Xiaofei Gongyi Susong de Qingqiu Leixing Wenti Yanjiu' ['Research on Types of Claim of Public Interest Litigation for Consumers'] (2017) 4 *Tan Qiu* [*Academic Search for Truth and Reality*] 59.

Duggan, AJ, 'Consumer Access to Justice in Common Law Countries: A Survey of the Issues from a Law and Economics Perspective' in Rickett, C and Telfer, T (eds), *International Perspectives on Consumers' Access to Justice* (Cambridge, Cambridge University Press, 2003).

Europe China Research and Advice Network, 'The EU and China, The EU-China Social Relationship'.

Felstiner, W, Abel, R and Sarat, A, 'The Emergence and Transformation of Disputes: Naming, Blaming, Claiming …' (1980) 15 *Law and Society Review* 631.

Friedman, M, *Capitalism and Freedom* (Chicago, University of Chicago Press 1962).

Fu, H and Cullen, R, 'From Mediatory to Adjudicatory Justice: The Limits of Civil Justice Reform in China' in M Woo and M Gallagher (eds), *Chinese Justice: Civil Dispute Resolution in Contemporary China* (Cambridge, Cambridge University Press, 2011) 25–57.

Galanter, M, 'Worlds of Deals: Using Negotiation to Teach about Legal Process' (1984) 34 *Journal of Legal Education* 268.

Galanter, M, 'Why the "Haves" Come Out Ahead: Speculations on the Limits of Legal Change' (1994) 9 *Law and Society Review* 95.

Galbraith, J, *The Affluent Society* (London, Penguin Books, 1999).

Gao, H, 'Jingji Quanli yu Jingji Fa' ['Economic Rights and Economic Laws'] (2012) 5 *Fazhi yu Shehui* [*Legal System and Society*] 69.

Gao, T, 'Chinese Consumer Protection Philosophy' (1992) 14 *Journal of Consumer Policy* 337.

Gao, M, '7 ge Gongzuori Weihuifu Jubao, Shenzhen Shijianju Huoyou jin Qiandan Baisu' ['Failed to Reply within 7 Days: Shenzhen MSA May Lose Near A Thousand Cases'] (*21CN Jutousu*, 31 October 2014).

Goldring, J et al, *Consumer Protection Law* (Leichhardt, NSW, The Federation Press 1998).

Gong, X and Cortese, C, 'A Socialist Market Economy with Chinese Characteristics: The Accounting Annual Report of China Mobile' (2017) 41 *Accounting Forum* 206.

Goodman, D and Zhang, X, 'The New Rich in China: Future Rulers, Present Lives' in Goodman, D (ed), *The New Rich in China: The Dimensions of Social Change* (London, Routledge 2008) 1–20.

Gulliver, P, *Disputes and Negotiations: A Cross-Cultural Perspective* (New York, Academic Press 1979).

Guo, SP and Shi, JC, 'Xiaofeizhe Yundong de Chansheng yu Fazhan' ['The Emergence and Development of Consumer Activism'] (1987) 3 *Beijing Shangxueyuan Xuebao* [*Journal of Beijing Business School*] 45.

Guo, BG, *China's Quest for Political Legitimacy: The New Equity-Enhancing Politics* (Lanham, Lexington Books, 2010).

Hai, H, 'Zhiding Xiaofeizhe Baohufa de Biyaoxing he Lifa Yuanze' ['The Necessity of Establishing the Consumer Protection Law and the Legislative Basis'] (1986) 02 *Faxue* [*Law Science*] 35.

He, X, 'China and its Adjudication Committees,' *East Asia Forum*, 3 December 2011.

Hodges, C, 'Consumer ADR in Europe' (2012) 15 *Zeitschrift für Konfliktmanagement* 195–197.

Hodges, C, 'New Modes of Redress for Consumers and Competition Law' (2012) 11/12 *Revista de Concorrência e Regulação* 227–50.

Hodges, C, Benöhr, I and Creutzfeldt-Banda, N, *Consumer ADR in Europe* (Oxford, Hart Publishing, 2012).

Hodges, C and Stadler, A (eds), *Resolving Mass Disputes. ADR and Settlement of Mass Claims* (Cheltenham, Edward Elgar Publishing, 2013).

Hodges, C, 'Consumer ADR and Appeals' in A Uzelac and CH van Rhee (eds), *Nobody's Perfect. Essays on Appeals and Other Methods of Recourse against Judicial Decisions in Civil Matters* (Cambridge, Intersentia, 2014) 339–52.

Hodges, C, 'Consumer Redress: Ideology and Empiricism' in K Purnhagen and P Rott (eds), *Varieties of European Economic Law and Regulation Festschrift for Hans Micklitz* (New York, Springer, 2014) 793–821.

Hodges, C, 'Unlocking Justice and Markets: The Promise of Consumer ADR' in J Zekoll, M Bälz and I Amelung (eds), *Dispute Resolution: Alternatives to Formalization – Formalization of Alternatives?* (Leiden, Brill 2014) 336–68.

Hodges, C, Creutzfeldt, N and Macleod, S, *Reforming the EU Consumer ADR Landscape: Implementation and its Issues* (Report of the Third Oxford Consumer ADR Conference, Oxford, October 2014).

Hodges, C, 'Consumer Ombudsmen: Better Regulation and Dispute Resolution' (2014) 15 *ERA-Forum* 593.

Hodges, C, 'Consumer Redress: Implementing the Vision' in P Cortés (ed), *The New Regulatory Framework for Consumer Dispute Resolution* (Oxford, Oxford University Press, 2016) 351–69.

Hodges, C, 'The Consumer as Regulator' in D Leczykiewicz and S Weatherill (eds), *The Images of the Consumer in EU Law: Legislation, Free Movement and Competition Law* (Oxford, Hart Publishing, 2016) 245–56.

Hooper, B, 'Consumer Voices: Asserting Rights in Post-Mao China' (2000) 16 *China Information* 92.

Hooper, B, 'The Consumer Citizen in Contemporary China' (2005) *Working Paper No.12, Centre for East and South-East Asian Studies, Lund University* 1.

Howells, G, Ramsay, I and Wilhelmsson, T, 'Consumer Law in its International Dimension' in G Howells et at (eds), *Handbook of Research on International Consumer Law* (Cheltenham, Edward Elgar Publishing, 2010) 1–17.

Hsü, I, *The Rise of Modern China*, 6th edn (Oxford, Oxford University Press, 2000).

Jérôme, L and Sun, JJ (eds), Buidling Food Safety Governance in China (Project financed by the Partnership Instrument of the European Union, 2018).

Keith, R and Lin, ZQ, *Law and Justice in China's New Marketplace* (London, Palgrave, 2001).

King, DB and Gao, T, *Consumer Protection in China: Translations, Developments, and Recommendations* (Littleton, Fred B. Rothman & Co, 1991).

Lardy, N, 'Markets Over Mao: The Rise of Private Business in China' (2014) *Critical Issues Confronting China Seminar Series*, 8 October 2014.

Lewinsohn-Zamir, D, 'Consumer Preferences, Citizen Preferences and the Provision of Public Goods' (1998–1999) 108 *Yale Law Journal* 377.

Li, CL and Xu, MY, *Xiaofeizhe Baohu Fa* [*The Law on Consumer Protection*] (Beijing, Law Press China, 1997).

Li, L, '"Zanghua" Shangsuzhuang Beihou de Zhengzheng Zhujiao' ['The Real Antagonist behind the Rude Words Petition for Appeal'] (*Legal Daily*, 21 May 2009).

Li, MY and Wang, ZC, 'Tan Weihu Xiaofeizhe Quanyi' ['A Discussion on the Protection of Consumer Rights and Interests'] (1987) 3 *Beijing Shangxueyuan Xuebao* [*Journal of Beijing Business School*] 47.

Li, XC, 'Hexie Shehui Shiyu zhong de Woguo Xiaofeizhe Quanyi Baohu Wenti Yanjiu: Guowai Xiaofeizhe Quanyi Baohu zhi Kaocha ji Jiajian' ['Analysis on Chinese Consumer Protection in the Perspective of Harmonious Society: Study and Lessons Learned from the Consumer Protection in Foreign Countries'] (2010) 11 *Faxue Yanjiu* [*Chinese Journal of Law*] 75.

Li, YS, 'Shilun Woguo Xiaofeizhe Suopeiquan de Xianzhuang he Wanshan' ['On Current Situations and Perfection of Consumers' Right to Claim in China'] (2012) 28 *Sichuan Jiaoyu Xueyuan Xuebao* [*Journal of Sichuan College of Education*] 45.

Liang, HX, 'Zhongguo Xiaofeizhe Zhengce he Xiaofeizhe Lifa' ['China's Consumer Policy and Consumer Legislation'] (2000) 5 *Faxue* [*Law Science*] 20.

Lin, Y, 'Xinzhongguo Falü Linian de Xiandaihua Jincheng Huimou' ['A Look Back at the Modernisation Process of the Legal Concept in New China'] (1999) 12 *Fujian Luntan (Jingji Shehui Ban)* [*Fujian Tribune (Economics and Sociology Monthly)*] 68.

Link, P, 'China: The Anaconda in the Chandelier' (*New York Review of Books*, 11 April 2002).

Liu, YG, 'Qiche shu Shechi Xiaofei Pin? Mai Siche "Xiaofeizhe Quanyi Baohu Fa" Guan Ma' ['Are Automobiles Luxury Goods? Is Buying Private Cars within the Scope of the Law on Protection Consumers' Rights and Interests'] (*Xinhua News*, 13 December 2006).

Liu, RX, *The Media, the Public and the Courts under Chinese Governmentality: Case Study of a Highly Publicized Trial in a Transitional Society* (Master of Arts thesis, University of Iowa, 2015).

Liu, ZD, 'Danwei yeying Shiyong "Xiaofeizhe Quanyi Baohu Fa"' ['"The Law on the Protection of Consumer Rights and Interests" Should Also Apply to State Enterprises and Institutions'] (2005) 3 *Guojia Faguan Xueyuan Xuebao* [*National Judges College Law Journal*] 95.

Livingstone, S and Lunt, P, 'Representing Citizens and Consumers in Media and Communications Regulation' (2007) 611 *The Politics of Consumption* 51.

Margolis, H, 'A New Model of Rational Choice' (1981) 91 *Ethics* 265.

Mengjie, 'Li Keqiang: China's Economic Structure Has Been Steadily Upgraded' (*Xinhua News*, 12 September 2017).

Mnookin, RH and Kornhauser, L, 'Bargaining in the Shadow of the Law: The Case of Divorce' (1979) 88 *The Yale Law Journal* 950.

Mo, YC and Lin, HC, '"Zhengfu Xinxi Gongkai Tiaoli" Shishi Zhunbei Diaoyan Baogao' ['A Research Report on the Enforcement Preparation of the "Government Information Disclosure Regulation"'] (2008) 6 *Faxue* [*Law Science*] 113.

Minzner, C 'China's Turn against Law' (2011) 59 *The American Journal of Comparative Law* 935.

Murphy, T, 'Durkheim in China' in M Freeman (ed), *Law and Sociology: Current Legal Issues*, vol.8 (Oxford, Oxford University Press, 2006) 107–18.

Nader, L, 'Controlling Process of the Rule of Law: Hierarchy and Pacification in the Movement to Re-Form Dispute Ideology' (1993) 9 *Ohio State Journal on Dispute Resolution* 1.

Ng, KH and He, X, 'Internal Contradictions of Judicial Mediation in China' (2014) 39.2 *Law and Social Inquiry* 285–312.

Nguyen, C, *The Drafting of Vietnam's Consumer Protection Law: An Analysis from Legal Transplantation Theories* (Dissertation) (University of Victoria 2011).

Nguyen, D and O'Shea, E, 'Consumer Rights Protection Law in Vietnam' in Legal Update: Consumer Litigation and Class Actions (Mayer-Brown JSM 2012).

Olesen, A, '"Lean Meat Powder Banned in China"' (*Washington Times*, 27 January 2011).

Olson, M, *The Logic of Collective Action: Public Goods and the Theory of Groups* (Harvard University Press 1971).

Overby, AB, 'Consumer Protection in China after Accession to the WTO' (2005–06) 33 *Syracuse Journal of International Law and Commerce* 347.

Palmer, M, 'The Emergence of Consumer Rights: Consumer Protection Law in the People's Republic of China,' in S Thompson, K Latham and J Klein (eds), *Consuming China: Approaches to Cultural Change in Contemporary China* (Abingdon and New York, Routledge 2006) 56–81.

Palmer, M, 'Mediation in China' in DS Clark (ed), *Encyclopaedia of Law and Society: American and Global Perspectives* (New York, Sage Publications, 2007) 1010–13.

Palmer, M and Xi, C, 'China' (2009) 662 *The Annuals of the American Academy of Political and Social Science* 270.

Parker, G, 'The Role of Consumer-Citizen in Environmental Protest in the 1990s' (2007) 3 *Space and Polity* 69–72.

Peerenboom, R, 'Rights, Interests, and the Interest in Rights in China' (1995) 31 *Stanford Journal of International Law* 359 at 367–68.

Pu, F, 'Zhiye Dajiaren Wanghai: Jukuan Mai Jiahuo 1nian Zuan 400wan' ['Anti-Counterfeit Professional Wang Hai: Spent Huge Money on Buying Counterfeit Products and Earned 4 Million One Year'] (*The Beijing News*, 23 March 2015).

Peerenboom, R, 'Judicial Independence in China: Common Myths and Unfounded Assumptions' (2008) *La Trobe Law School Legal Studies Research Paper No. 2008/11.*

Pound, R, 'Law in Books and Law in Action' (1910) 44 *American Law Review* 12.

Prévost, D, 'Food Safety in China: Implications of Accession to the WTO' (2012) 89 *China Perpspectives* 39.

Ramsay, I, *Rationales for Intervention in the Consumer Marketplace* (London, Office of Fair Trading, 1984).

Ramsay, I, 'Consumer Redress and Access to Justice' in C Rickett and T Telfer (eds), *International Perspectives on Consumers' Access to Justice* (Cambridge, Cambridge University Press 2003) 17–45.

Ramsay, I, *Consumer Law and Policy: Text and Materials on Regulating Consumer Markets*, 2nd edn (Oxford, Hart Publishing, 2007).

Ramsay, I *Consumer Law and Policy*, 3rd edn (Oxford, Hart Publishing, 2012).

Ran, J, 'Constitute Financial Ombudsman Institution Suitable for Our National Situation' ['Goujian Shehe Woguo Guoqing de Jinrong Shensu Zhuanyuan Zhidu'] (2016) 6 *Jinrong Jiaoyu Yanjiu* [*Research of Finance and Education*] 21.

Rawls, J, *A Theory of Justice* (Cambridge, MA, Belknap Press of Harvard University Press, 1971).

Reuters Staff, 'China to Ramp up Crack-Down on "Gutter Oil"' (*Reuters*, 24 may 2017).

Rickett, C and Telfer, T (eds), *International Perspectives on Consumers' Access to Justice* (Cambridge, Cambridge University Press, 2003).

Riskin, L, 'Understanding Mediator's Orientations, Strategies and Technique: A Grid for the Perplexed' (1996) 1 *Harvard Negotiation Law Review* 7.

Riskin, L, 'Decision Making in Mediation: The New Old Grid and the New New Grid System' (2003) 79 *Notre Dame Law Review* 1.

Ruo, F, 'Liu Dianlin: Dang "Dajia" Chengwei Yizhong Zhiye' ['Liu Dianlin: When "Anti-Counterfeit" Activity Becomes a Profession,] (*Guang Ming Daily*, Section 04, 15 March 2014).

Scott, C, and Black, J, *Cranston's Consumers and the Law*, 3rd edn (Cambridge, Cambridge University Press, 2000).

Shapiro, M, *Courts: A Comparative and Political Analysis* (Chicago, University of Chicago Press, 1981).

Shapiro, M, 'Appeal' (1980) 14 *Law and Society Review* 629.

Shen, S, 'Cong Wang Hai Xianxiang kan Woguo "Xiaofeizhe Quanyi Baohu Fa"'['Analysis on the Problems of "The Law on the Protection of Consumer Rights and Interests" from the Wang Hai Phenomenon'] (2005) 24 *Changchun Shifan Daxue Xuebao* [*Journal of Chang Chun Normal University*] 45.

Shenzhen Commercial Daily, 'Shenzhen 12315/12358 Shensu Jübao Zhongxin Qiyong' ['The Openning of Shenzhen 12315/12358 Centre for Complaints and Reports'] (*Shenzhen Commercial Daily*, 11 January 2005).

Shi, SS, 'Renmin Weihe Buzai Xinren 3.15' ['Why People No longer Trust 3.15'] (2010) 6 *Zhejiang Jingji* [*Zhejiang Economy*] 39.

Sohu News, 'Yang Jianchang, the Shenzhen Figure: Consumers Called him "Justice Yang"' ['Shenzhen Renwu zhi Yang Jianchang: Xiaofeizhe Chengta "Yang Qingtian"'] (*Sohu News*, 6 September 2010).

Sun, C, 'Singles Day Sale Beats Spectre of 2014 by Delivering Record US$10bn for Alibaba, After Arch Bachelor James Bond Launches event: Online Shopping Promotion Delivers for Jack Ma's Alibaba' (*South China Morning Post*, 11th November 2015).

Sun, TQ, 'Jinrong Xiaofeizhe Baohu: Xingwei Jingji Xue de Lilun Jiexi yu Zhengce Jianyi' ['Financial Consumer Protection: Theoretical Analysis and Policy Implications Based on Behavioral Economics'] (2014) 28 *Jinrong Jianguan Yanjiu* [*Financial Regulation Research*] 32.

Sunstein, CR, 'Social Norms and Social Roles' (1996) 96 *Columbia Law Review* 903.

Tian, CM, 'Wo Guo Xiaofeizhe Quanyi Baohu Xianzhuang jiqi Wanshan' ['Our Country Consumer Rights and Interests Protection Present Situation and Its Consummation'] (2008) 24 *Gansu Lianhe Daxue Xuebao (Shehui Kexue Ban)* [*Journal of Gansu Lianhe University (Social Science Edition)*] 44.

Tian, K and Dong, L, 'Consumer-Citizens of China: The Role of Foreign Brands in the Imagined Future China' (Abingdon and New York, Routledge, 2011).

Tiffert, G, 'Peering Down the Memory Hole: History, Censorship and the Digital Turn' (*Washington Post*, 21 August 2017) 1.

Thomas, K, 'Analysing the Notion of "Consumer" in China's Consumer Protection Law' (2018) 6 *The Chinese Journal of Comparative Law* 294.

Trebilcock, M, 'Winners and Losers in the Modern Regulatory System: Must the Consumer Always Lose?' (1975) 13 *Osgoode Hall Law Journal* 620.

Veblen, T, *The Theory of the Leisure Class: An Economic Study in the Evolution of Institutions* (Oxford, Oxford University Press 2009).

Veblen, T, *The Theory of the Leisure Class: An Economic Study of Institutions* (New York, Macmillan, 1902).

Waldmeir, P, 'Chinese Car Buyers Show Off with a "Baoma"' (*Financial Times*, 15 August 2011).

Wang, JY, *Xiaofeizhe de Falü Baohu Wenti* [*The Problems of Consumers' Legal Protection*] (Beijing, Law Press China 1990).

Wang, LP, 'Shiyi Xiaofeizhe Gainian de Falü Jieding' ['Discussion on the Legal Definition of the Concept of Consumer'] (2006) 4 *Jing Ji Shi* [*Economist*] 81.

Wang, QX and Guan, B, 'Jingji Fa Shiye xia de Xiaofeizhe Dingwei' [Positioning the Consumer in Law from the Perspective of Economic Law] (2002) 9 *Fali yu Shiwu* [*Jurisprudence and Vocational Work*] 12.

Wang, XM, 'Woguo Xiaofeizhe Quanyi Baohu Fa zhong Xiaofeizhe Gainian de Jieding' [The Concept of Consumer in Chinese Consumer Protection Law]' (2010) 8 *Beijing Lianhe Daxue Xuebao (Shehui Kexue Ban)* [*Journal of Beijing Union University (Humanities and Social Sciences)*] 76.

Waye, V and Xiong, P, 'The Relationship between Mediation and Judicial Proceedings in China' (2011) 6 *Asian Journal of Comparative Law* 1.

Williams, M, 'Foreign Business and Consumer Rights: A Survey of Consumer Protection Law in China' (2000) 18 *UCLA Pacific Basin Law Journal* 252.

Woo, MYK and Gallagher, ME (eds), *Chinese Justice: Civil Dispute Resolution in Contemporary China* (Cambridge, University of Cambridge Press, 2011).

Wu, Y, 'People's Mediation Enters the 21st Century' (2015) 10 *Journal of Comparative Law* 25.

Wu, ZL, 'The Procuracy Filed Public Interest Litigation, Fake-Salt Manufacturer Was Ordered to Pay 1,120,000RMB' ['*Jianchayuan Tiqi Gongyi Susong, Jiayan Zhishouzhe Panpei 112wan yuan*'] (*Southern Metropolis Daily*, 16 March 2018) GA01.

Xiao, FS, *Gonggongxing Shijiao xia de Dazhong Chuanmei yu Gonggong Zhengce Yanjiu* [*Study on Mass Media and Public Policy from the Angle of the Public*] (Beijing, China Social Sciences Press, 2013).

Xie, QQ, 'Jiehe "Wanghai Dajia An" Jianyi Falü Jieshi Buquedingxing de Yuanyin' ['Discussion on Reasons Causing Uncertainty of Legal Interpretation on Cases in Relation to "Wang Hai Phenomenon"'] (2010) 5 *Huainan Shifan Xueyuan Xuebao* [*Journal of Huainan Normal University*] 58.

Xinhua News, 'Quality Watchdog Cancels Inspection Exemptions for Food Producers' (*Xinhua News*, 18 September 2008).

Xinhua Net, 'Xinhua Insight: E-Courts Promise Online Justice for Chinese Shoppers' (*Xinhua Net*, 11 December 2015).

Yau, O, *Consumer Behaviour in China: Customer Satisfaction and Cultural Values* (New York, Routledge, 1994).

Yang, D, 'Research on the Categorization of the Financial Ombudsman Mechanisms' ['Jinrong Shensu Zhuanyuan Zhidu zhi Leixinghua Yanjiu'] (2013) 4 *Faxue Pinglun* [*Law Review*] 77.

Yang, D, 'Consumer Protection and Reform of China's Financial Law' (2014) 44 *Hong Kong Law Journal* 303.

Yangcheng Evening Post, 'Shenzhen shi Xiaoweihui Huo Shiye Danwei "Mingfen" Xietiao Xiaofeizhe Gengyou Diqi' ['Shenzhen Consumer Council has Obtained the Title of a "Work Unit" Making it Stronger in Negotiations for Consumers'] (*Yangcheng Evening Post*, 8 August 2014).

Yu, HQ, 'Cong Xiaofeizhe Quanyi Beisunhai de Xianzhuang Tan Xiaofeizhe Quanyi Baohu Wenti' [A Discussion on the Protection of Consumer Rights and Interests from the Perspective of the Current Situations of Consumer Rights and Interests Infringement] (1994) 4 *Guizhou Shangxueyuan Xuebao* [*Journal of Guizhou University of Commerce*] 33.

Yu, XZ, 'State Legalism and the Public/Private Divide in Chinese Legal Development' (2014) 15 *Theoretical Inquiries in Law* 27.

Zhang, LH, 'Taobao Jiaoyi Yinru Dazong Pingshenyuan Jizhi' ['Taobao Introduced Crow Adjudicator System to its Transations'] (*Hangzhou Daily*, 31 December 2013) B10.

Zhang, XC, 'Rethinking the Mediation Campaign' (2016) 10 *Journal of Comparative Law* 44.

Zhao, YH, 'Mediation of Environmental Disputes' (2015) 10 *Journal of Comparative Law* 237.

Zhou, L, 'The Independent Director System and its Legal Transplant into China' (2012) 6 *Journal of Comparative Law* 262.

INDEX